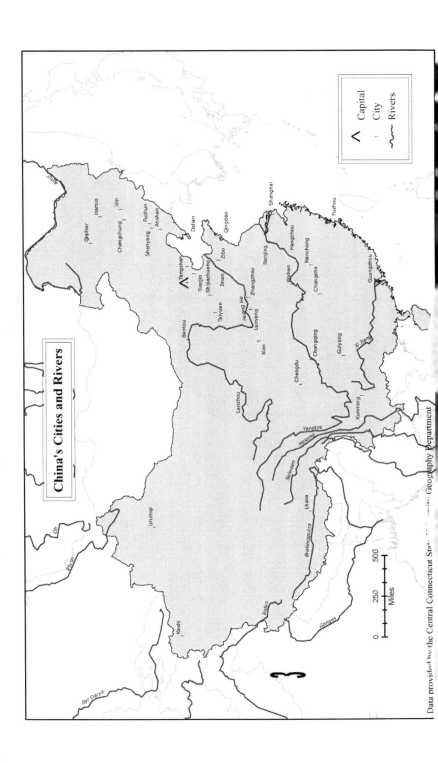

China's Cities and Rivers

Data provided by the Central Connecticut State University Geography Department

Capital

City

Rivers

Miles
0   250   500

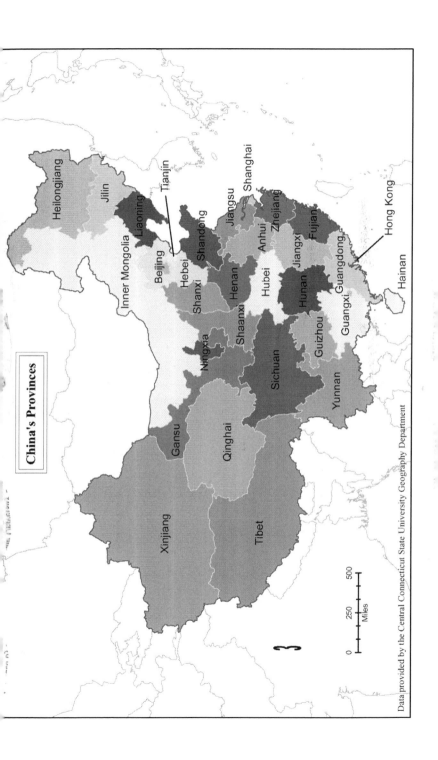

China's Provinces

Heilongjiang

Jilin

Inner Mongolia

Liaoning

Beijing

Tianjin

Hebei

Shandong

Shanxi

Shaanxi

Henan

Jiangsu

Shanghai

Anhui

Zhejiang

Hubei

Ningxia

Jiangxi

Fujian

Hunan

Sichuan

Guizhou

Guangdong

Hong Kong

Gansu

Qinghai

Guangxi

Yunnan

Hainan

Xinjiang

Tibet

0   250   500

Miles

Data provided by the Central Connecticut State University Geography Department

China and Globalization

"There are few books on China that are this coherent."—**Hong Zhang, East Asian Studies, Colby College**

". . . an exceptional accomplishment that will set the standard for works on China for years to come."—**Lisa Keister, Sociology, Ohio State University**

"*China and Globalization* provides a lot of information in a theoretically-informed way. The writing style is conversational and argumentative, so it is very good to spur discussion."—**Thomas Gold, Sociology, University of California, Berkeley**

In its quarter-century-long shift from communism to capitalism, China has transformed itself from a desperately poor nation into a country with one of the fastest-growing and largest economies in the world. Doug Guthrie examines the reforms driving the economic genesis in this compact and highly readable introduction to contemporary China. He highlights the social, cultural and political factors fostering this revolutionary change and interweaves a broad structural analysis with a consideration of social changes at the micro and macro levels.

In this new, revised edition author Guthrie updates his story on modern China and provides the latest authoritative data and examples from current events to chart where this dynamically changing society is headed and what the likely consequences for the rest of the world will be.

Doug Guthrie is Professor of Sociology and Management at New York University's Stern School of Business and Professor of Sociology in NYU's Faculty of Arts and Science.

Global Realities
A Routledge Series
Edited by **Charles C. Lemert**, *Wesleyan University*

The Series **Global Realities** offers concise accounts of how the nations and regions of the world are experiencing the effects of globalization. Richly descriptive yet theoretically informed, each volume shows how individual places are navigating the tension between age-old traditions and the new forces generated by globalization.

Books in the Series

Available

Australia by Anthony Moran
Global Ireland by Tom Inglis
Global Hong Kong by Cindy Wong and Gary McDonogh
The Koreas by Charles K. Armstrong
The Netherlands by Frank J. Lechner
The Globalization of Israel by Uri Ram
Morocco by Shana Cohen and Larabi Jaidi
On Argentina and the Southern Cone by Alejandro Grimson and Gabriel Kessler
The Philippines by James Tyner
China and Globalization, Revised Edition by Doug Guthrie

Forthcoming

Iberian Worlds by Gary McDonogh
Military Legacies by James Tyner
Urbanizing A New Global South by AbdouMaliq Simone
Turkey by Alev Cinar
South Africa and the Long History of Globalization by Kevin R. Cox

China and Globalization

The Social, Economic and Political Transformation of Chinese Society

Revised Edition

DOUG GUTHRIE

Routledge
Taylor & Francis Group

NEW YORK AND LONDON

This edition first published 2009
by Routledge
270 Madison Avenue, New York,
NY 10016

Simultaneously published in the UK
by Routledge
2 Park Square, Milton Park, Abingdon, Oxon
OX14 4RN

Routledge is an imprint of the Taylor & Francis Group, an informa business

Transferred to Digital Printing 2009

Typeset in 11/14pt Joanna by Swales & Willis Ltd, Exeter, Devon

Maps appear courtesy of Michael Fazio

Library of Congress Cataloging-in-Publication Data
Guthrie, Doug, 1969–
   China and globalization / by Doug Guthrie. – Rev. ed.
      p. cm.
   Includes bibliographical references and index.
   1. China—Economic conditions—2000–   2. China—Economic conditions—1976–2000.
3. China—Social conditions—2000–   4. China—Social conditions—1976–2000.   5. China—Politics
and government—2002–   6. China—Politics and government—1976–2002.   I. Title.
   HC427.95.G87   2008
   337.51 – dc22
                                                                2008012998

ISBN10: 0–415–99039–4 (hbk)
ISBN10: 0–415–99040–8 (pbk)
ISBN10: 0–203–89406–5 (ebk)

ISBN13: 978–0–415–99039–4 (hbk)
ISBN13: 978–0–415–99040–0 (pbk)
ISBN13: 978–0–203–89406–4 (ebk)

Contents

Figures

Tables

Series Foreword

Charles Lemert

In the earlier years of a millennium that can no longer be called new, the peoples of the planet are well aware that something that cannot be measured calendrically is happening. The word that comes to mind is "globalization." But this mushy, indefinite term explains little beyond what people in China today experience in the daily grind—sleeping in hotbeds warmed by workers from another province trying, like you, to make a new life at such a high cost; children of a greater privilege surfing the airwaves for bits torrenting from LA by way of Beijing through copyright-free havens in Central Asia; mothers without diapers to comfort the bleeding bottoms of their starving babies.

Globalization—some of it good for some of the people; some of it bad for many of the people; most of it good *and* bad in irregular measures poured mindlessly into the daily mix. It is far better, for the time being, to use "globalization" as shorthand for what we experience and know, but cannot yet explain. This is why Doug Guthrie's already famous *China and Globalization* appears in a series now called "Global Realities." It is not that "realities" is all that more precise a term, but at least it has the merit of opening the mind to the realities as they are vividly but differentially experienced across the world.

Books in this series are meant, as this one does so brilliantly, to give account of places where human experience is cut deep with global experiences. It is hard to say what it means to experience global realities because when they press down on us we find ourselves early in the day weary from too little rest, walking too far for the daily bread, wishing the local merchants had not been closed down, the reality of it all comes to us through a fog.

China and Globalization gives the facts and tells the larger stories of how China has became as much a brand name as a nation-state. Things Chinese are known for having issued from a system of production and distribution unlike any the world has seen until now. It is not that the things produced are cheaply, rapidly, and unevenly assembled but that they generate an unmanageable wealth that we can no longer measure by state-bound rulers like gross *domestic* products. The U.S.A. remains the world's largest economy by volume but its capital is tied to strange currencies and distant bankers. As China, along with other of the world's economic hotspots, has invented a new set of global realities for people around the world, so have the rest been sucked into the whirlwind. China causes us to consider a long-ignored truth—that once history breaks the ties that bind people to places, everything else on the globe comes loose. Global realities are like that. Doug Guthrie's learning and experience help us understand, in the most lucid of details, just what we are and are not in relation to China, and what she is or is not to us.

Prologue

This book is about the economic reforms that have been sweeping across China over the last three decades. As we view these changes through the filter of media representations, political rhetoric, and the many other distortions that have shaped perceptions of the reform effort in China, the picture is murky at best. In the chapters that follow, I examine the changes that have actually occurred in China and the forces that have brought about this process of change. The book is organized around three central points. First, the changes in China have been more dramatic than most people (especially in the United States) realize. The lack of a sudden shift in political structure and economic policy has often led observers to underestimate the significance of the social and political reforms that have occurred in China. The reality is that changes in China have been radical and deep, and the view that significant social *and* political reforms have not been pushed forward in China is simply mistaken. Second, reforms have been successful in China precisely *because* of state involvement. Contrary to the economic assumptions that have guided many reform prescriptions—that rapid privatization is a necessary ingredient of successful reform—I argue here that gradualism not only works, but is a superior policy. Third, democracy in China is inevitable. Despite the Chinese leadership's apparent goal of holding political reforms at bay, the process of economic reforms have fundamentally altered the structure of the political system. Reforming the economic realm has radically shaken the foundations of the one-party system. However, the thesis I advance here is not that there is an inevitable link between capitalism and democracy. Rather, it is through the purposive transformation of certain institutions that a gradual process of democratization has been set in motion in China, and although they do not advertise it, many key leaders of the economic reforms have been transforming China politically from within.

Finally, the economic reforms in China have been political, cultural, and above all, global processes. Understanding these processes of economic reform tells us much about the role of governments, culture, and globalization in the transition from socialism to capitalism, a transition that many countries across the globe are undergoing in one way or another. It also tells us a great deal about China's future role in the international community of nations. The social consequences of the transition to a market economy in China have been dramatic for the citizens of the most populous nation on earth, and these changes have implications for how we think about capitalism and the trade-offs between socialism and a market-based economic system.

This book has two points of departure. First, years ago, as I was finishing *Dragon in a Three-Piece Suit* (Guthrie 1999), I was determined to write something that was more accessible to a wider audience. Like many academic books, *Dragon* dealt in a technical way with specific theoretical debates that are central to a field of scholarship—in this case, the field of scholars studying economic reform in China and economic transitions more generally. It seemed to me at the time that, while there are many highly readable firsthand accounts of life in China—Nicholas Kristof and Sheryl Wudun's books, for example, are excellent windows onto the issues individual face in this rapidly transforming society—we still lacked an account that brought that firsthand experience together with a readable version of the staid academic debates. The field of scholars studying economic and social change in China still lacks a corpus of work that translates the scholarship in this field in the way that Jonathan Spence has made Chinese history readable for a wider audience.

Around the time that I was finishing *Dragon*, I was also developing a course at New York University on the economic reforms in China. That course would eventually draw nearly four hundred students per semester—testament, I think, not to my skills as a teacher but to the fervent interest of today's young students in the emergence of China as a global economic superpower. Once again, over years of teaching this course, I was struck with the fact that while the academic literature on Chinese society has dealt in rigorous detail with many of the ideas presented in this book, we lacked a comprehensive overview that rendered the key ideas portrayed in the scholarship on China's economic reforms understandable for a non-specialist audience. My goal in this book is to draw on the academic research, including my own, as well as my own experiences in China, to give a clear and accessible sense of the forces that have reshaped Chinese society over the last twenty-five years.

Parts of this manuscript have emerged from work that has been published previously in various venues, and I would like to acknowledge those publications for the use copyrighted material. Parts of Chapters 2, 4, and 6 originally appeared in various forms in the following publications: "Information Technology and State Capacity in China," in *Digital Formations: Cooperation and Conflict in a Connected World*, edited by Robert Latham and Saskia Sassen (© Princeton University Press,

2005); "The Quiet Revolution: The Emergence of Capitalism in China," *Harvard International Review* 25, no. 2 (2003): 48–53 (© Harvard University Press, 2003); "Organizational Learning and Productivity: State Structure and Foreign Investment in the Rise of the Chinese Corporation," *Management and Organization Review* 1, no. 2 (2005): 165–95 (© Plenum, 2005); "The Transformation of Labor Relations in China's Emerging Market Economy," *Research in Social Stratification and Mobility* 19 (2002): 137–68 (© Plenum, 2002); and "Entrepreneurial Action in the State Sector: The Economic Decisions of Chinese Managers," in *The New Entrepreneurs of Europe and Asia: Patterns of Business Development in Russia, Eastern Europe and China*, edited by Vicki Bonnell and Thomas Gold (© M. E. Sharpe, 2002).

Finally, for help in completing this project, a number of friends and colleagues read portions of the manuscript, and offered helpful advice along the way. I would especially like to thank Mira Edmonds, Niobe Way, and Gerald Frug for comments on the completed manuscript at a time when I most needed outside perspectives. My editors at Routledge, David McBride and Steve Rutter, were also very helpful in shaping the project. Indeed, this book probably would never have been finished without their patience and encouragement. The revised edition also benefitted from reviews from a number of educators like Thomas Gold, Zouhair Ghazzal, Jiping Zuo, and several anonymous reviewers. Finally, and most important, I would like to thank the roughly two thousand undergraduate students at NYU who have served as the sounding board for the ideas presented in these pages and the hundreds of Chinese executives who shaped the ideas presented here.

Doug Guthrie
New York City, 2008

Globalization and the Economics of Radical
Change in China
One

A PLACE OF RADICAL CHANGE

Shanghai, 2008—Standing on Shanghai's Bund, overlooking the Huangpu River, one cannot help but see how dramatic the changes have been in China in the last decade and a half. Especially in the evening. Neon signs light up the night sky; strobe lights dance across the river, as if to announce the arrival of the new city. Nouveau riche couples dining at the swanky restaurants overlooking this panorama enjoy a nightlife scene that might place them in London, New York City, or Paris. Across the river, an entirely new skyline has emerged from virtually nothing: In the early 1990s, when I started doing research on China, Pudong (the area east of the Huangpu River) was an area of fields and old housing projects; today it is a high-tech urban landscape with immaculate and gaudy buildings that touch the sky, including one of the tallest buildings in the world. The scene is eerily reminiscent of a futuristic science fiction movie.

Other places in China also show the signs of extreme change. The Beijing skyline lacks the panache of the development in Shanghai, but the changes occurring there are no less dramatic. In Beijing, cranes dot the skyline of the city's sprawling urban landscape; fast food restaurants and Starbuck's buttress up against the borders of the Forbidden City and Tiananmen Square; skyscrapers have been built upon the wreckage of Beijing's old urban neighborhood blocks. In western Chinese cities like Chengdu and Chongqing, China's most populous city, signs of urban development are everywhere as well. And in smaller towns in rural areas, new buildings run up against small houses made of straw-and-mud bricks.

The scenes are breathtaking, even to those unfamiliar with urban development and architectural planning. They are also clearly—even to the untrained eye—tied to foreign investment, economic reform, and the complex processes of globalization. Across the Shanghai skyline, for every neon sign advertising a Chinese company, you will also see the logo of a foreign multinational. The Motorola name is as well known as that of the famous Chinese handset and switching manufacturer, Huawei; DuPont is among the most well-known names for chemical manufacturers; Alcatel is the name associated with the most sophisticated telecommunications-switching technology; most cabs are made by a joint-venture corporation backed by Volkswagen; brands like Coca-Cola, McDonald's, and Kentucky Fried Chicken are ubiquitous; Shanghai-GM is one of the luxury cars of choice these days. At the same time, powerful Chinese domestic multinationals such as Geely (Jili) Automotive Corporation, Haier, Lenovo, PetroChina and SinoPec are shaking the world with their own economic power.

All of these facts and images are, by now, well known. Indeed, the headlines announcing "China's Century," "The China Challenge," "The China Syndrome," and many others, have thundered across the covers of such magazines as *BusinessWeek*, the *Economist*, *Forbes*, *Newsweek*, *U.S. News and World Report*, and many other major publications. However, if the fact of China's emergence as an economic and political superpower today is widely recognized, the *processes* by which we have arrived at this moment in time are somewhat less clear. What global and local processes lie beneath the dramatic transformation we have witnessed over the last quarter century in China? What are the political, economic, and social forces that have shaped the Shanghai, Beijing, and Chongqing skylines? And what impact do competing foreign and Chinese national interests have on the citizens of China and on the rest of the world? The story that lies beneath is one of deep-seated national interests of the world's most populous nation as it edges its way down the path of economic reform toward the hallowed land of capitalism, and of foreign investors that seek to find access to the world's largest single-nation marketplace. It is a story of the forces of globalization, played out locally; a story of the complex political situation that saw a dying communist regime transform itself, in part, by allowing foreign multinationals to set up shop in China for the first time since the Communist Revolution. Uncovering these forces and trends is the purpose of this book.

THE EMERGENCE OF CHINA AS A WORLD ECONOMIC POWER

There are many reasons why we should develop an informed understanding of the state of affairs in Chinese society. Not only is China the most populous nation on earth, but it has also, in recent years, stormed onto the world political and economic stages. The country has accomplished in twenty-five years what many developing nations have taken half a century or more to achieve. For the better part of the last two-and-a-half decades, China has had the fastest growing economy in the world, sustaining double-digit growth figures for much of the 1980s and 1990s and high single-digit growth for the 2000s. Throughout the 1980s, China's real gross domestic product (GDP) grew at an average annual rate of 10.2 percent, a level that was only equaled by the growth rate in Botswana. From 1990 to 1996, the average annual rate of growth for real GDP was 12.3 percent, the highest rate of any country in the world for that period. It has also had the highest industrial growth rate (an amazing 17.3 percent average annual growth from 1990 to 1996) and the second-highest growth in services (9.6 percent per annum, 1990–1996) in the world.[1] It is an understatement to say that China's economic reforms have been a remarkable and dramatic success. Table 1.1 shows how China compares with the countries that are generally considered to be the top ten economies in the world, according to various economic indicators. Where China was a third-world developing economy two short decades ago, today it has the fourth largest economy in the world overall in terms of gross domestic product (GDP), and it is second only to the United States when GDP is adjusted for purchasing power within the country.[2] To the extent that economic and political power are intimately intertwined, China's sizable role as a political force on the world stage is all but guaranteed. It is no longer a question of whether China is going to play a major role in world economic and political arenas; it is only a question of what role China will play.

The emergence of China as a world economic and political power has serious consequences for the structure of relations in Asia and for the global economy in general. If the twenty-first century will be Asia's century, as many scholars and pundits have predicted, then China is certain to be the major player in a region that is sure to play a definitive role in the current century. And this lumbering giant has only begun to flex its political and economic muscle. However, because of its size, China's role in the coming years is almost certain to have greater gravity than would be suggested by simply acknowledging its position as a leader in a pivotal region. Take, for example, food: because of the loss of crop land that comes with rapid industrialization and a still-growing population in China (despite austere family-planning measures), some

Table 1.1 Largest economies in the world according to various economic indicators

	GDP, $bn (rank)	GDP PPP, $bn (rank)	Largest industrial output, $bn (rank)	Largest services output, $bn (rank)	Largest market capitalization, $mm (rank)	Population, mm (rank)
United States	12,417 (1)	12,417 (1)	2,732 (1)	9,561 (1)	19,426 (1)	298 (3)
Japan	4,534 (2)	3,995 (3)	1,360 (2)	3,083 (2)	4,726 (2)	128 (10)
Germany	7,795 (3)	2,430 (5)	838 (4)	1,928 (3)	1,638 (8)	83 (14)
China	2,234 (6)	8,815 (2)	1,072 (3)	894 (7)	2,426 (5)	1,315 (1)
UK	2,199 (4)	2,002 (6)	572 (5)	1,605 (5)	3,794 (3)	60 (21)
France[a]	2,127 (5)	1,850 (7)	447 (7)	1,638 (4)	2,429 (4)	61 (20)
Italy	1,763 (7)	1,672 (8)	476 (6)	1,251 (6)	1,027 (6)	58 (22)
Spain	1,125 (9)	1,179 (11)	337 (9)	754 (8)	1,323 (9)	43 (29)
Canada	1,114 (8)	1,078 (13)	398 (8)	283 (9)	1,701 (7)	32 (36)
India	806 (10)	3,779 (4)	218 (12)	110 (13)	819 (15)	1,103 (2)

Source: Pocket World in Figures, 2008.

Note: [a] Includes overseas departments.

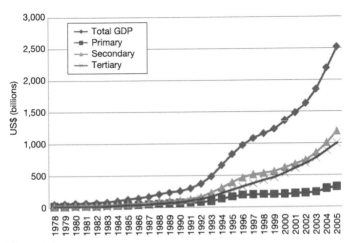

Figure 1.1
GDP growth in China, 1978–2005.

Source: *Statistical Yearbook of China* 2006.

estimates suggest that China currently cannot produce enough food to feed its citizens. These same estimates suggest that, at current rates of growth, all the excess in the world's grain markets will not meet China's needs by the year 2030.[3] So here we have a country that rose in two-and-a-half decades to be the fourth-largest economy in the world—a country that could very well cripple international grain markets and have a large starving population before the middle of the twenty-first century. As another example, consider information technology: based on the size of China's population and current rates of development in the country's telecommunications sector, industry experts expect that China will be the single largest market for Internet and telecommunications use in the entire world. Here again, we have the strange paradox of development in China: as the country struggles with the basic developmental tasks of laying phone lines and building roads, it threatens to be the crucial market in driving the evolution of one of the most important industries in the global economy. Then there is the issue of oil: China's rapid economic development has led to an insatiable thirst for energy and, more specifically, fossil fuels. With its consumption more than doubling over the last five years, China sits behind only the United States as the second-largest consumer of oil in the world.[4] The high demand for oil has contributed to rising rates of oil prices, which have hit record highs in cost-per-barrel terms over the last year, a fact that affects American consumers with higher gas prices. Another important, though less understood, issue involves China's influence over the U.S. bond market. China is now the second largest foreign holder of U.S. Treasury bonds. People frequently point to the oft-decried trade deficit between the United States and China, but China's rapid purchase of U.S. Treasury bonds in recent years is a much more significant factor in U.S.–China economic interdependence. If the People's Bank of China decided to begin dumping U.S. Treasury bonds, the effects could have a devastating impact on the already weakening U.S. economy. Understanding China's role in the world economy and how this country has arrived at its current position is imperative to an understanding of global economic and political trends as well as the interrelated nature of political, economic, and social change in developing economies.

Yet, while China's rise in power over the last two-and-a-half decades has been meteoric—and we are only beginning to feel the impact of that rise in power—our understanding of the changes that have occurred there lags far behind the reality. Many current views of China fail to grasp the depth and magnitude of the reforms, and we have even less understanding of the forces and processes that have wrought these changes. To some observers, China has succeeded in spite of the state's continuing presence as an authoritarian government. Indeed, some observers view China's current situation as quite tenuous precisely because of the partial and political nature of the reforms. In one example, Gordon Chang's famous screed, *The Coming Collapse of China*, warns that "beneath the surface . . . there is a weak China, one that is in long-term decline and even on the verge of collapse. The symptoms of decay are to be seen everywhere."[5]

However, China's dramatic success in economic reform has been precisely because of the state's participation in the process. Its emergence as an economic juggernaut has been the result of methodical and careful government policies that have gradually created a market economy in a stable fashion. An examination of China's reform effort gives rise to issues and questions that are fundamental to a full understanding of the global economic system: what is the current state of economic, political, and social reform in China, and to what extent are these realms inextricably intertwined in China's course of development? What are the forces that have given rise to the radical changes occurring in China? How are these changes related to the global economy? What does this process tell us about the transition from communism to capitalism, a process in which several countries in the world are currently engaged? How have the economic changes that have occurred in China over the last two-and-a-half decades influenced the lives of people there? And finally, what does a close examination of the process of change in China tell us about the prospects for the emergence of democratic institutions there?

In addressing these questions, I take two extreme positions in this book. First, the stunning success of China turns some key assumptions of economic theory on their head. The case of China gives clear evidence that privatization is not a necessary part of a transition to a market economy and, by extension, that private property is not a necessary cornerstone of a functioning market economy. There are many different ways to create the incentives that govern a healthy economy, and private property is but one of them. This is not only an issue of theoretical concern. Important institutions such as the World Bank and the International Monetary Fund (IMF) have long been guided by the arguments for rapid privatization and, in many cases, they have forced these policies on developing nations. Second, democracy is an inevitability in China. The basic argument here is that capitalism and democracy are systems that must be learned over time. Thus, where rapid transitions to either system often invite chaos, gradual transitions allow for the stable emergence of new institutions and systems. More to the point, China has been gradually developing the institutions of democracy. The ideological war between reformers and hard-liners has forced the former group to transform China's institutions without labeling them as a transition to democracy.

GLOBALIZATION AND THE TRANSITION TO CAPITALISM IN CHINA

This book is a general introduction to the process of economic change that has occurred in China since the country's economic reforms began in 1979. As many parts of society are shaped by, and intersect with, the economy, I explore different aspects of the ways that life has changed in China in the reform era. Before I dive into substance, however, it is useful to begin with a brief discussion of the theoretical edifice that will guide my analyses of economic and social change. There are a number of different ways to think about economic change. In this book, I begin with a political-cultural approach to understanding globalization, economic institutions, and social change. Economic institutions and practices are deeply embedded in political, cultural, and social systems, and it is impossible to analyze the economy without analyzing the ways that it is shaped by politics, culture, and the social world. This perspective is essential for understanding the complex process of economic and social reform in any transforming society, but it is especially critical for understanding China's reform path and trajectory. This position may seem obvious to some, but it is important to note that, for years, economists from the World Bank, the IMF, and various reaches of academia have operated from a different set of assumptions: they have assumed that a transition to markets is a simple and, basically, apolitical process. As Jeffrey Sachs, one of the world's most influential economists in the study of transforming economies in the 1980s and 1990s, and his coauthor, Wing Thye Woo, once quipped, "The long-run goals of institutional change are clear, and are found in the economic models of existing market-based economies." In other words, don't worry about the complexities of culture or preexisting social or political systems; if you put the right capitalist institutions in place (i.e., private property), transition to a market economy will be a simple process.[6] The perspective I present here is that the standard economic view of market transitions that defined a good deal of policy for the IMF and the World Bank in the late twentieth century could not be more simplistic or more wrong. In the sections that follow, I briefly discuss the ways that politics, culture, and the social world will play into the analysis of China's transition to a market economy presented throughout these chapters.

THE POLITICS OF MARKET REFORM

Beginning with Hungary in the 1960s, many communist countries have embarked on the path of transition from planned to market economic systems. Understanding the paths of transition from socialism to capitalism is a complex task, but it is also an important one, as this process opens up questions about the nature of markets, the nature of economic systems, and the extent to which markets and economic systems are embedded in political and social worlds. Research on transforming socialist economies has given rise to two basic views of economic change in these societies. On one side of the fence sit those who believe that markets operate primarily, if not solely, through private interests and individual incentives, and that market economies are built upon the foundation of private ownership and incentives. Given that communist-planned economies are basically organized around state ownership—an institutional arrangement that often leads to many distortions in terms of market relationships—those from the privatization school believe that rapid privatization is the only viable path of transition from planned to market economies. Rapid privatization, which can create an extreme "shock" to the society undergoing such a transition, has accordingly been given such labels as "shock therapy" and the "big bang approach" to economic reform. The approaches adopted in countries such as Bulgaria, the Czech Republic, and Russia fit this model of economic reform.

A second school of researchers—which includes scholars like Barry Naughton, Thomas Rawski, Andrew Walder, and Jean Oi—argues that markets are fundamentally political, social, and cultural systems, and a stable transition to a capitalist system must occur in a gradual fashion, with significant and constant support and guidance from the state. Market institutions and the economic practices that individuals and organizations adopt cannot be reduced to a simple equation of private interests and the individual pursuit of profits. The political, cultural, and social forces to which market institutions are subject are simply too powerful to ignore, so economic change must move forward in a slow, incremental fashion. The strategies of reform that arise from this view of economic systems see the state as a critical player in the transition to a market economic system. As practitioners, the architects of the Chinese reforms have embraced the gradualist view, and it has led to a gradual and stable path through the economic reforms. Furthermore, the dramatic success of the first two-and-a-half decades of reform in China (compared with the turmoil caused by rapid reform programs in countries like Russia) raises serious doubts about the shock therapy approach and the economic assumptions that undergird that view. In many ways, by spurning the views of Western economic advisors and then gradually piecing together the most successful reform process of any transforming planned economy, China has served as the strongest indictment of the simpleminded nature of the market-driven economic logic of the rapid privatization school.

At the center of the tension between these two schools of economic reform is a debate over the role of the state in the construction and maintenance of new markets and the extent to which economic processes are fundamentally political processes. China's reform process serves as a perfect example of the extent to which economic development and transitions to capitalism are, indeed, political processes. In the case of China, we see that strong guidance from the state has led to a high level of stability in a process that inevitably leads to social upheaval. In the two-and-a-half decades of economic reform in China, the state has consistently and methodically guided the reform process, maintaining control over the majority of the industrial economy and tightening fiscal constraints for the inefficient state sector at only a gradual rate. More than this, the state has experimented with, and gradually introduced, the policies and laws through which the new markets that increasingly govern economic processes in China have been constructed. Even beyond methodical involvement of the state in shaping China's transition path, the political nature of economic change runs even deeper, as the legacies of the former institutions of the state-run economy shape the country's development path in important ways.

The critical point here is that China's successful path through two-and-a-half decades of economic reform has been gradual, experimental, and fundamentally political. Politics and economics have been so closely intertwined that we cannot understand one part without the other. Advocates of the rapid privatization approach claim that China's reforms have been successful despite the state's close relationship with the economy. For example, Sachs and Woo (1994a, 1997) argue that the economic structure of China—a largely peasant-based agricultural economy with a large supply of surplus labor and a tight monetary policy—explains China's success relative to Eastern Europe. They argue that, even with the dramatic growth in China's economy over the last two-and-a-half decades, the reform effort there would have been much more successful if a program of rapid privatization were adopted. It is difficult to see, at this point, how one could argue that gradualism was not a dramatic success in the China case.[7] But these claims ring hollow, especially when one compares the undeniable success of economic reform in China with the serious problems experienced in countries such as the Czech Republic and Russia. As we examine China's successful path and trajectory through the economic reforms, the heavy hand of the state lurks everywhere, and we must understand this reform process through this lens. Other authors have argued that because of the state's role as a continuing agent in the economy, corruption is endemic (e.g., Kwong 1997; Gong 1994) and the collapse of this national economy is inevitable (e.g., Chang 2001). This position is also not credible, as it is simply not supported by the empirical reality of what is occurring in China. A third position on China's progress is that the authoritarian government has held onto power and not allowed a democratic transition to occur there. However, here again, the reality is very different: although China remains an authoritarian political system, over the last two-and-a-half decades of reform, the government has gone a great distance in gradually making the transition to democracy. Though many in the West—particularly among U.S. politicians—do not want to acknowledge it, China is gradually but steadily building the institutions of a democratic society.

CULTURE AND CAPITALISM

In the most general sense, culture refers to the norms, values, and systems that shape social action and behavior. It is that part of political, economic, and social systems that produces deeply ingrained understandings of the world. Many scholars have written on the nature of economic behavior in Asia and the ways that the economic decisions of Chinese people are shaped as much by culture as by the changing economic and political systems in which individuals are embedded (Hamilton 1996; Hamilton and Biggart 1988; Bian 1994a; Yang 1994). They have argued that there is something distinctive about Asian and, specifically, Chinese business practices. Despite the fact that some of these writings border on essentialism in their understandings of Chinese culture, it is important to take some of the notions depicted in these scholarly works seriously.[8] There are two ways that culture plays an important role in China's transforming economy. First, Chinese society is different in undeniable ways. Its institutional and cultural history is unique, and this history has an impact on the type of capitalism that is emerging in China. This becomes important as China enters the global market because, in the global marketplace, negotiations often hinge on common understandings, expectations, and norms of behavior, all of which can be heavily influenced and shaped by different cultural traditions.

Second, and perhaps more important, contrary to the economic assumptions that link capitalism and human nature, I argue here that capitalism itself is a system that requires deeply ingrained practices that must be learned over time. In this book, I am interested in the extent to which economic systems are shaped by political institutions and norms of behavior. The process of building a new global economic system in China is not only about a clash of cultures in the marketplace. It is also about the ways that economic systems are themselves cultural systems, where learned practices and behaviors become embedded in the norms and rules by which individuals operate over time. As Chinese managers make the transition from the old economic system to the new, they must unlearn the practices, norms, rules, and meanings through which the old system operated and learn the practices, norms, rules, and meanings of the new system.

Both of these elements of culture can be observed in the experiences of economic actors in China's emerging markets. With the passage of the Joint Venture Law in 1979, companies from around the world have flocked to China, enticed by the idea of a captive market of over a billion consumers, but many have been deeply troubled by the extent to which investment in China is a more complicated process than company executives anticipated. In one particular case, when the American corporation Dun and Bradstreet landed on the shores of China, company executives expected that the inchoate markets in China would be a perfect outlet for Dun and Bradstreet's product and trade—information.[9] Dun and Bradstreet's logic was not unreasonable: in new markets, when individuals are given the autonomy to make economic decisions as they like, they will seek the information upon which to make those decisions. What Dun and Bradstreet did not understand is that information has a very specific history in China—a history shaped by the preexisting institutions of China's economy and society. With the command economy, the system under which the managers of China's transforming economy learned economic decision making, information was a source of power hoarded by bureaucrats and managers alike. Under the command economy, managers learned to coax information from bureaucrats and peers by spending social capital and calling in favors. Similarly, they learned to closely guard the information they had. The idea that information was a commodity and that they could or should simply pay for information from an anonymous third-party organization like Dun and Bradstreet seemed strange, if not distasteful. Eventually, Dun and Bradstreet shifted to a marketing strategy that emphasized education as much as salesmanship. Chinese managers needed to be taught the norms and behaviors associated with a capitalist economy; they needed to learn why information was important in a market economy before they could be convinced to pay for it. It was through the adoption of a new marketing strategy—teaching what "appropriate" behavior in a market economy was—and a clear realization that China's culture and recent institutional history have shaped the ways that individuals there understand capitalism that Dun and Bradstreet's investment in China began to pay off. This narrative is not uncommon: many powerful firms, such as Goldman Sachs and McKinsey have spent significant resources educating potential clients and competitors and collaborating with the government on the building of new institutions and sectors of the economy.

THE SOCIAL CONSEQUENCES OF ECONOMIC REFORM

Markets allocate resources in ways that are fundamentally different from socialist command economies. This change in the allocation of resources has important consequences for individuals in Chinese society and around the world. One of my central concerns in this book, in addition to examining the economics and politics of the transition from a command to market economy in China, is to illuminate the impact this transition has on the lives of Chinese citizens. Changes in the economic system have consequences for the life chances of individuals in the society, and it is critical that we come to terms with the social consequences of the transition to a market economic system. These changes have fundamental implications for the stratification order of society.

Moreover, markets themselves are social systems. Rather than the abstract mechanistic structures that are often portrayed in theoretical economic models, markets are embedded in complex social worlds, and they are shaped by the social institutions, norms, and customs that define a given society. The social embeddedness of markets is a basic feature of capitalist systems, but it is particularly important for understanding the emergence of markets in China in two ways. First, the transition from a command to market economic system requires the destruction (or, in the Chinese case, the gradual erosion) of existing institutions and the construction of new institutions. In the period of transition between systems, institutional instability pervades, and the reliance on social networks and social institutions becomes exaggerated. This is exactly what occurred in Chinese society in the 1980s during the first decade of economic reform. However, that is a situation that has eroded as the new institutions of China's emerging market economy have become more stable. Second, in the case of Chinese society, there is a long tradition of emphasizing the importance of personal networks, and the cultural prominence of social networks in Chinese society has important implications for the emergence of markets there. This history makes an examination of the growing reliance on legal institutions all the more interesting. Throughout the chapters that follow, we will look extensively at both the extent to which markets are socially embedded in China and the ways the emergence of markets has shaped the lives of Chinese citizens.

THE OUTLINE OF THE BOOK

This book begins by examining the process of economic reform in China. It then examines a number of the social consequences the economic reforms in China have wrought and, finally, concludes with a consideration of China's place within the world economic system. Before outlining the content of the book, it is useful to provide a few notes on data and evidence. The evidence upon which this book is based comes from two sources. First, I rely heavily on my own firsthand experiences with research on the Chinese economy over the last fifteen years. Since 1994, I have conducted well over four hundred in-depth interviews with Chinese managers, Chinese officials, managers of Western multinationals investing in China, and American politicians.[10] In China, all interviews were conducted on-site, in Chinese, and they were unaccompanied (i.e., no state officials or other "chaperones" accompanied me). While these interviews and factory visits were conducted primarily in Shanghai, some were conducted in factories in the industrial cities of Beijing, Chongqing, Chengdu, Dalian, Hangzhou, Luoyang, and Shenyang. Over the course of these interviews, I also spent time in more than three hundred factories in China. The early portion of this research (1993–98) was the basis of my book *Dragon in a Three-Piece Suit*, with the other portion coming in shorter research trips over the years since 1998. Second, in this book I also rely on official statistics to give a general picture of the economic and social trends that have defined the reform period. While there is good cause to be concerned about the veracity of official statistics, the focus here is on general trends and the magnitude of change in a given area. Official statistics are a good baseline for giving us a sense of things like how large the economy is, how much the economy has grown, per capita income, urban/rural differences, and so forth, and it is for these types of measures that I employ those data here.

Chapter 2 lays out the logic of the prereform economy and the critical steps that were taken to dismantle this economy. In many ways, the reforms in China moved much more rapidly and went much deeper than the architects of the reform effort originally intended—despite the fact that China's transition to a market economy has been much more gradual than most—and it is important to begin with an understanding of exactly how the reforms unfolded in China. Command economies have a specific institutional logic, and an understanding of what has occurred in China must begin with a clear sense of the institutional structures and systems that preceded the current era of economic reform. In Chapter 2, I focus primarily on the transformation of the industrial command economy, but I also give significant attention to the transformation of the rural farm economy. The transformation of the rural farm economy parallels the transformation of the industrial economy in crucial ways, but the experience in rural China has also diverged from the industrial economy in important ways. In Chapter 3, I look at the social institutions that define Chinese society and the ways these social institutions are changing in China today. Family, social networks, and the social systems that have organized rural and urban life will be considered in this chapter. All of these social institutions are being remade in various ways in China's new market economy, but some are proving to be more resilient under the powerful forces of change than others. I also discuss the state, the party, and markets as social institutions that are transforming the political, economic, and social worlds that Chinese citizens face.

Chapter 4 presents an analysis of China's emergence as a global economy, with an examination of global business institutions, foreign investment, and the current state of economic development in China. From foreign investment to the Internet, business relations within newly emerging markets are having a dramatic impact on the structure of Chinese society. Business institutions and relations are critical to economic development and the transformation of Chinese society, as these forces are ushering China into the global economy. Technology transfer, foreign capital, and access to international markets are all important parts of this equation. But of equal or perhaps greater importance is the extent to which Chinese managers and entrepreneurs learn about the practices of capitalism and markets through the relationships they develop in China's emerging markets. Capitalism is a socially embedded system—just as the command economy was—and understanding the operation of a market economy requires a process of learning and observation. Thus, international business relations and newly emerging markets are having dramatic consequences for the type of economy that is emerging in China. But these relations are also shaped by the new institutions that are being set in place by the state, and the emergence of Western-style legal institutions in China constitutes a fundamental shift from the structure of the command economy.

In Chapter 5, I discuss the ways in which the new economy is transforming life chances for individuals in China. Stratification systems have changed in dramatic and fundamental ways in the era of economic reforms. This chapter looks at several of the critical factors that influence class, wealth, and poverty in the new economic system. Education, private enterprise, party membership, gender, inter-city migration, and the urban/rural divide all have implications for the changing life chances for individuals within China's new economy, and I discuss each in this chapter.

Chapters 6 and 7 engage a set of issues that has attracted a great deal of attention with respect to international relations with China: emergence of a rule-of-law society and the prospects for democracy in China. In Chapter 6, I look at the emergence of a rule-of-law society in China. The rule of law is a critical part of the emergence of a modern rational economy and society in China. However, the extent to which a rule-of-law society has been gradually under construction in China has not been widely understood. This chapter examines that process. In order to focus the analysis, I concentrate on the implications the rule of law has had for workers in China's economy. The reality is that although it is a part of a gradual process of reform, a rule-of-law society is emerging in China, and it has radical consequences for the rights of workers and citizens throughout the country.

In Chapter 7, I examine the prospects for democratic institutions in China. There is a certain teleological view of the future of democracy in transforming communist societies such as China's. The view here is not only that democracy is an inevitable outcome of progress, but that democracy must emerge if China is to be truly welcomed into the international community of nations. However, democracy is not an inevitable outcome. Indeed, many scholars, pundits, and popular writers believe China will remain a one-party authoritarian system. Nevertheless, democracy will emerge in China, but for reasons that are not well understood by Western politicians and pundits. While demands for democratic reform have come from both outside and within China, and while it is important to understand the role these demands have played, the structural transformation of China's political institutions has taken place on a much deeper level, set in motion by the architects of the economic reform. Yet, this is not a simple process, an inevitable outcome of the individual freedom that seems to come with a neoliberal economy. Rather, a very specific set of institutional changes set this process in motion at the beginning of the economic reforms. If we are to understand the prospects for democracy in China, we must understand the nature and causes of these institutional shifts.

I conclude the book with Chapter 8's discussion of China's place in the global economy. As this massive nation lumbers toward the position of being one of the largest and most powerful economies in the world, it is absolutely essential that we understand the process of economic, political, and social reform there. But it is also crucial that we understand its place within the global economic and political systems. While I discuss these issues in general terms, the primary substantive focus of the chapter is a political analysis of human rights, the implications of China's entry into the World Trade Organization (WTO), and other social issues such as the impact of China's development on the environment. With respect to human rights, this chapter continues this discussion with an exploration of the actual progress that has occurred in the realm of human rights in China, as well as a discussion of the trade-offs between communism and capitalism in the realm of human rights. On the one hand, China has made significant progress in the realm of human rights. As laws such as the Prison Law of 1994 and the National Compensation Law of 1995 transform social relations and spaces that marked the greatest abuses in human rights, a great deal of progress has been made in this area. On the other hand, the government seems determined to continue to take a hard line on such popular activities as membership in the Falun Gong movement. However, lest we think that the government's seemingly divergent approaches to these issues are simply authoritarian caprice, there are fundamental issues underneath the surface here, and they are shaped by the larger issues of the economic reforms. As a neoliberal ideology has spread across the globe and come to be associated with freedom and equality in markets, so too have we seen a convergence between the concepts of individual civil liberties and human rights. Individual civil liberties are certainly important aspects of human rights, and they happen to fit very well with the neoliberal idea of markets that is sweeping across the globe. However, there are trade-offs here as well, and some people—including many Chinese citizens—see these trade-offs as complications to the issue of human rights that Western nations like the United States tend to ignore. Access to health care, guaranteed jobs and wages—all part of the old system of China's command economy—are also believed by some to be part of the larger bundle of rights that fall under the rubric of human rights. This final chapter will explore some of these trade-offs and how they are emerging in the era of economic reform. As scores of workers are laid off from old state-owned factories with no guaranteed alternatives for employment, and as migrant workers (the so-called floating population) have no guarantee for education for their children, the trade-offs of the market economy become increasingly clear, and they are trade-offs that are experienced disproportionately, if not exclusively, by the poor. These trade-offs are important, because they lay bare the challenges and contradictions that circumscribe the transition to a market economy. Indeed, it is in this context that the government's crackdown on the Falun Gong movement must be understood: this movement, which has the largest organizational membership in China (larger, even, than the Communist Party)—a fact that surely strikes fear into the hearts of party leaders—is filled with constituents who are being left behind by the economic reforms. And when the movement leaders staged a sit-in in April 1999 in Tiananmen Square, this was, in part, a political statement about the nature and direction of the reforms. The state perceived this movement, then, as representing a direct threat; the ensuing crackdown was, in this context, as predictable as it was atrocious. A careful analysis of human rights abuses in China needs to carefully analyze the trade-offs among stability, economic growth and a rapid push toward democratization; it also must engage the question of how institutional change and democratization most effectively evolve. In addition to the general discussion of human rights and the rule of law in China, I will also address the specific issues of sovereignty with regard to the issues of Tibet and Taiwan.

With respect to China's entry into the WTO, when we stack up all of the evidence surrounding the political deals that have shaped this crucial issue of globalization, it is increasingly clear that this was not primarily a battle over human rights abuses in China. Rather, it was a battle between two geopolitical powerhouses; it was a battle over China's ascendancy as a world economic power and the desire on the part of the United States to restrict and contain what now seems like an inevitable process. Despite the rhetoric over concerns about extending economic relations with an authoritarian government, the U.S. has had economic relations with far too many authoritarian governments to make this claim credible. Further, if this were really the reason behind blocking China's entry into the WTO, our support of Taiwan during these years should have been suspect too, as Taiwan was run by an authoritarian government until 1996. Former North Carolina senator Jesse Helms, who for many years was a leader of the anti-China relations camp, likely cared much more about the impact on tobacco and textiles, two of the sectors that would be hit hardest with China's entry into the WTO—also, not coincidentally, two of the primary sectors fueling North Carolina's economy. Within China, agendas and behind-the-scenes strategizing were also in play: Zhu Rongji's play for China's entry into the WTO was, at its very core, about a political battle between hard-liners who still believe in an ideological communism and reformers who have used China's continued integration into the world economic system as a means to defeat the hard-liners. The reformers rightly believe that the best strategy for long-run radical reform in China is to gradually and continually integrate China into the inter-national community. As the norms that are widely associated with business practices and economic transactions of the international community—transparency of economic prac-tices, the rule of law, respect for individual civil liberties—become the norms by which China must operate, the changes within China will continue to be dramatic and deep.

As China grows in stature and power, it has also begun to play a major role in global geopolitical tensions around issues like international human rights and the environment. The quest for resources has led China into the Sudan, where the catastrophic bloodshed in Darfur has led to calls from various activist groups and individuals for China to use its influence to help stop the carnage. But the need for oil is a crucial element in China's economic development, and China's position in this crisis has certainly been influenced by that need. Add to this that the firm in question, PetroChina, is now one of the largest corporations in the world, worth, for a brief period, more than $1 trillion, and we have a complex intermingling of national interests, growing economic power, multilateral institutions (with resolutions by the Security Council in the mix), and human rights. These issues of energy consumption are not unrelated to environmental concerns, either. Currently, China is the largest consumer of coal in the world, and the sulfur dioxide produced by coal combustion as well as the carbon dioxide produced by the process will certainly contribute to environmental problems that extend far beyond China's borders.

China's role as a global economic superpower is intensified by its increasingly central role in geopolitical discussions in issues ranging from human rights to the environment. As that role continues to expand and grow, the intermingling of politics, economics, and social issues will continue to be a central part of that story.

Setting the Stage: A Primer to the Study of China's Economic Reforms

Two

When the communists proclaimed the founding of a "new China" on October 1, 1949, Mao Zedong and his fledgling government set in motion the creation of a new society. The emergence of communism under Mao fundamentally altered the social, political, and economic structure of Chinese life. While the chapters that follow are primarily about the ways in which Deng Xiaoping's economic reforms transformed life in communist China, it is useful to contrast those changes against a backdrop of the social, political, and economic order that preceded them. In this chapter, I will give a brief outline of the structure of society under Mao and then an outline of the changes that were set in motion by Deng. While the short descriptions here will not do these topics justice, it is important to give a basic outline of this background.[1] The basic theoretical points that guide the discussion of this chapter can be stated simply: (1) under Mao, the communists set in place a system that intimately wove together political ideology, economic production, and social control; (2) the task for Deng was to unravel this interdependent system; and (3) Deng's government undertook this task in a gradual fashion, experimenting widely with many policies that would gradually rationalize and cede governmental control over the economy and society.

To illuminate these processes of reform in China, throughout this text, we will need to focus on three levels of analysis—macro, organizational, and individual. By macro, I mean issues like national level policies such as the Joint Venture Law (1979), the Labor Law (1994), the Company Law (1994), and the Coastal Development Strategy. By organizational, I mean the firm- or factory-level changes that are redefining work-unit life in China. And by individual, I mean changes that affect people at the individual level, like labor markets, labor mobility, labor force changes, and changing life chances for mobility within the economy.

THE NEW SOCIETY UNDER MAO[2]

When the communists took power, they were largely a rural movement. The control of the cities was the crucial next step in taking control of the country. The strategy of the party, at this point, became the mobilization of the population through mass campaigns in which communist ideology would be spread, and people energized by the ideology and commitment to the party would emerge as urban cadres. In 1950, in a campaign called the Resist America and Aid Korea Campaign, the party ordered searches of all alleged spies—all foreigners—and investigated all public associations that were in any way connected with foreigners; many individual Chinese were also investigated for contact with foreigners. The party also moved against foreign businesses, freezing all assets in December 1950. Workers were encouraged to rise up against their exploitative employers. Companies were charged back taxes for all the business they had been doing in China up until the Communist Revolution. In no uncertain terms, foreigners were forced out of China.

The government followed this movement with a second mass campaign in 1951 directed at domestic "counter-revolutionaries." The targets of this mass campaign were officially the individuals who had served under or supported the Nationalist Party, but the target, more generally, was anyone who was suspected of not supporting the party. A large number of public executions took place: in Guangdong Province alone, 28,332 people were executed in 1951. Many of these were staged as public executions. An important development of this campaign was the setting up of neighborhood associations and committees to monitor members of society. Along with the work unit, these associations became one of the most important structures of social control in communist China. The "Three-Anti" and "Five-Anti" campaigns followed in 1951 and 1952, respectively. The first of these was directed at three sets of vices, which were associated with three groups: corruption, waste, and obstructionist bureaucracy, directed at Chinese Communist Party (CCP) officials, the wider spectrum of bureaucratic officials, and managers of factories. Ironically, though directed at corruption among officials and business leaders, this movement was also used to gain greater control over labor: government took over all labor unions and made them a part of the party infrastructure. The second campaign was designed to ferret out and vanquish the bourgeoisie class in China (similar to, and contemporaneous with, the campaign against capitalists and landlords in the countryside). The targets were those Chinese businessmen who represented the capitalist class. In addition to being arrested and forced to confess to crimes against the party, capitalists were also encouraged to denounce each other.

These campaigns not only asserted the communist control over the people ideologically, but it also allowed the communists to step in and take control of industrial organizations, ending the independent modes of operation and production in the Chinese economy. While these campaigns set the stage for a terror-driven ideological control, there was also an infrastructure for individual-level social control. The institutions for this individual-level social control were also integrally linked to the economy. In the urban industrial economy, these were the work unit and the neighborhood association system; in the rural economy, these were the collectives and communes. Thus, as they were creating a new order of discipline in society, the communists were also extending their reign over the economy. The new government adopted a number of measures that would allow them to control production in both agricultural and industrial arenas. The model adopted was that of the Soviet Union, where state-controlled industrial production in a sequence of five-year plans was believed to have been responsible for the nation's emergence as a world class power in the 1930s. There was close collaboration between the Soviet Union and China during this period, as Soviet technical advisers came to China to help with factory building, industrial planning, electric power, the railway system, and urban architecture.

The country was organized into a tightly nested hierarchy in which party planning was carried out through a central government (in Beijing), twenty-two provinces, five autonomous regions, and three municipalities.[3] Under these were approximately 2,200 county governments, which in turn supervised about one million branch offices of the CCP in towns, villages, army units, factories, and schools. In rural areas, in 1952 and 1953, the government put households together into groups of thirty to fifty households, and land and labor were pooled together into cooperative units. Originally, peasants held a private component in which they were allowed to keep private plots for their own use—to raise crops for their own consumption or to be sold. Balances after government quotas were met were divided based upon how much each family contributed originally. Thus, this was not a fully socialist system as richer peasants, who had contributed more land, did better in the end. Figure 2.1 shows the relationships among levels of government in this administrative system. One scholar has described this system in the following way: "This administrative structure forms the hierarchy in which national resources and incentives [were] allocated from the central command to the various levels of local governments."[4]

Different levels of government had direct control over factories—or "work units"—in this system. The ministry of a given sector had direct control and supervisory power over factories, as did provincial, municipal, and township levels of government. In general, the industrial work units at the upper levels of the administrative structure were large-scale, heavy industry, "state-owned" organizations of the industrial planned economy. "State ownership" is a bit of a misnomer here, as it has often directed scholars to focus on state property rights versus collective or private ownership. However, as one scholar has described this system, "In terms of the definition of property rights ... there is no fundamental distinction between state and collective enterprises. . . . The most important way in which government ownership rights in state and collective sectors do differ is in the extent to which they are regulated by higher levels of government. . . . What varies in this hierarchy is not the nature of government property rights but the composition and scale of industry and the degree to which government rights are attenuated by central regulations" (Walder 1995a, 271–273). Within this administrative system of the planned economy, resources flow up to the higher levels of government and are then redistributed based on need. However, work units had variable access to resources in the command economy: the higher a work unit was positioned in this "nested hierarchy," the greater the access to resources it had (Walder 1992a; Bian 1994a). Work units and cooperatives within this system were much more than units of production in the planned economy, however; they were also the sites of social welfare distribution and political and social control.

The first five-year plan seemed to pay off, as industrial production rose dramatically. Nevertheless, there were still significant problems with the economy that emerged in the 1950s. For example, by eliminating the private sector, the government had gained control over the economy, yet it had eliminated market competition. In establishing production quotas, the central government placed local officials (as opposed to business owners) in charge of production. These local officials were often ignorant of economic planning and were more concerned with meeting targets than they were with running efficient factories. This pressure to meet targets often led to false reporting. As well, the elimination of markets and the bureaucratic control of distribution channels often led to hoarding, bottlenecks, and, ultimately, shortages of production goods. The government job assignment system meant that factories could not control how large their workforces should be; factories simply had to accept the number of employees that were assigned by the government to the work unit. On top of this, the connection between the work-unit system and social welfare meant that work units were often burdened with large costs to support the livelihood of their employees.[5]

Mao's response to these problems, along with political challenges he was facing in the spring of 1956, was to "deepen" the revolution.[6] In 1957–58, Mao launched a disastrous movement called the Great Leap Forward. In rural areas, cooperatives were converted into people's communes such that, by the end of 1958, 740,000 cooperatives had been merged into 26,000 communes. These communes comprised

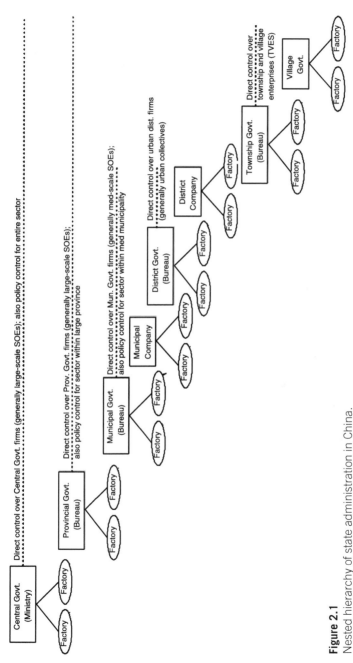

Figure 2.1

Nested hierarchy of state administration in China.

Note: Figure based on interviews with industrial managers and government officials. See also Walder (1992a, 1992b, 1995a) and Guthrie (1997, 1999) for further discussion of the "nested hierarchy" of state administration.

120 million rural households—99 percent of the rural population. One of the central problems in the rural economy was that grain was not being produced at a high enough rate. Grain was a necessary part of industrial growth, because it was the primary product China could export to the Soviet Union. As a result, in 1957, the CCP began organizing people into huge workforces for irrigation, construction projects, and the like. Mao also tailored his ideas about harnessing the peasantry for a truly communist revolution driven by the Chinese peasantry to the industrial economy, inducing the population in 1958 to create over one million backyard steel furnaces. These policies proved disastrous, as they led to a famine from 1959 to 1962 in which an estimated twenty million Chinese citizens died of starvation.

Following some of the devastating effects of these economic policies, Mao lost political power in significant ways. Deng Xiaoping and Liu Xiaoqi were gaining political credibility, and they were increasingly critical of Mao and his policies. But Mao was still the charismatic leader of China. He was the leader of a movement that, in retrospect, is appropriately referred to as the "cult of Mao." He was seen as the leader who gave self-reliance and self-respect back to the Chinese. Despite his failed economic policies, he was still the leader of the revolution. And he was the most powerful man in China in terms of his ability to mobilize political power.

THE CHAOS OF THE CULTURAL REVOLUTION

The mid-1960s saw the emergence of a group of intellectuals who were critical not just of Mao's policies but also of his isolation from the public. A well-respected Ming historian named Wu Han began to write extensively about Mao's poor judgment and policies. In September 1965, Mao attempted to begin a movement to criticize the "reactionary bourgeois ideology," but found little success because much of the state media were controlled by his political opponents. He left Beijing in November and disappeared from public view; it was later learned that he had gone to Shanghai, where he assembled a group of hard-line communist intellectuals to help him bring socialist order back to the country.

The leaders of the Cultural Revolution called for a comprehensive attack on the four "old" elements within Chinese society—old customs, old habits, old culture, and old thinking—but they left it to local Red Guards to direct this movement. As a result, the movement spun completely out of control. Eventually, everyone in power was in danger of being labeled a capitalist roader, a counterrevolutionary, and an enemy of the party. This led to clashes between the Red Guard radicals and the People's Liberation Army. By September 1967, all leaders, including those in the radical wing of the party, agreed that the chaos had reached an intolerable level. They began denouncing "ultra-left tendencies." It was not until the summer of 1968 that something resembling order was restored. A retrenchment movement followed, in which hundreds of thousands of Red Guard radicals were "sent down" to the countryside for "reeducation." Many of these youths spent a decade of their lives working in hard agricultural labor in the countryside. They were only able to return to their homes after Mao died in 1976.

Mao's death brought an end to the Cultural Revolution. But the chaos of the years since 1957 (when the Great Leap Forward began) had crippled the country economically. Under the terror that swept the country during the Cultural Revolution, a generation of students had lost the opportunity for high school and college education, as they were sent down to the countryside for ideological reeducation; industrial production declined precipitously during this era; and the country had become dramatically isolated from the rest of the world. For a brief time, it appeared that little would change in the wake of Mao's death, as Hua Guofeng, a conservative leader who sought to follow Mao's economic and social policies, emerged as Mao's successor. On October 6, 1976, the now infamous "Gang of Four"—Jiang Qing, Wang Hongwen, Yao Wenyuan, and Zhang Chunqiao, the radical leaders of the Cultural Revolution—were arrested on Hua Guofeng's orders. They were blamed for the excesses of the Cultural Revolution, even defying, it was alleged, the warnings of Mao himself. On October 7, Hua Guofeng was named to succeed Mao as chairman of the Central Committee of the CCP and chairman of the Military Affairs Commission. And in November, Hua formally laid the first foundation stone for Chairman Mao's mausoleum, which would be erected in the center of Tiananmen Square.

Deng Xiaoping sought refuge in Canton, where he was protected by a powerful military leader, Xu Shiyou, who despised Hua Guofeng, associating him with the Gang of Four. In 1977, Xu began pressuring the party to rehabilitate Deng, and in July of that year, Deng was reappointed to his position of vice premier. While Hua continued to champion the reforms of central planning and a more cautious version of the notions that Mao had articulated in pushing the Great Leap Forward, Deng had a different economic orientation. A pragmatist, Deng believed that economic reform was necessary and developed his political power through advocating reform. He saw central planning in industry and collectivization in agriculture as inflexible and unable to deal with the economic problems China was facing. Although the debacles of the Great Leap Forward and the Cultural Revolution were now past, several social problems now stood in their wakes. For one thing, there were the urban residents who had just returned from a decade in the countryside, with no guaranteed place in the planned economy and no plan for how the current system would absorb them. They were part of a new trend that saw unemployment rising to new highs within the system.[7] And by 1978, a ten-year economic plan—fashioned in 1976 to get the nation back on track after the Cultural Revolution—was already falling far below projected goals. In response to these challenges, in the late 1970s, Deng Xiaoping was positioning himself to lead China in a radically different direction economically and would introduce a set of controlled modifications into the structure of the socialist system. Deng advocated the implementation of a modernization plan that would incorporate foreign investment and technology and abandon state controls.

THE QUIET REVOLUTION: THE ERA OF ECONOMIC REFORM IN CHINA

When Deng Xiaoping unveiled his vision of economic reform to the Third Plenum of the Eleventh Central Committee of the Chinese Community Party in December 1978, the Chinese economy was faltering.[8] Reeling from a decade of stagnation during the Cultural Revolution and already appearing to fall short of the projections set forth in the ten-year plan of 1976, it would take much more than a new plan and the Soviet-style economic vision of Deng's political rival, Hua Guofeng. At the time, Deng's plan was to lead the country down a road of gradual and incremental economic reform, leaving the state apparatus in tact while slowly unleashing market forces.

Since that time, the most common image is of an unbending authoritarian regime that has engineered a remarkable period of rapid economic growth but has seen little real substantive change politically. There is often a sense that China remains an entrenched and decaying authoritarian government run by corrupt party officials (extreme accounts depict it as an economy on the verge of collapse). However, this vision simply does not square with reality on a number of levels. While it is true that China remains an authoritarian one-party system, it is also the most successful case of economic reform of any communist-planned economy of the twentieth century. Today, as the fourth largest economy in the world, it is fast emerging as one of the world's most dynamic market economies. Understanding how this change has come about requires an examination of three broad changes that have come together to shape China's transition to capitalism: (1) the gradual receding of the state from control over the economy, a process that brought about a shift in economic control without privatization; (2) the steady growth of foreign investment; and (3) the gradual emergence of a rational-legal system to support these economic changes.

During the 1980s and 1990s, economists and institutional advisors from the West advocated the rapid transition to market institutions as the necessary medicine for transforming communist societies. Scholars argued that private property provides the institutional foundation of a market economy, and, therefore, communist societies making the transition to a market economy must privatize industry and other public goods. The radical members of this school argued that rapid privatization—the so-called shock therapy or big bang approach to economic reforms—was the only way to avoid costly abuses in these transitional systems.[9] The Chinese path has been very different from the shock therapy approach. While countries like Russia have followed Western advice—constructing market institutions at a rapid pace, immediately removing the state from control over the economy, and rapidly privatizing property—China has taken its time in implementing institutional change. The state has gradually receded from control over the economy, taking the time to experiment with new institutions and to implement them slowly and incrementally within the context of existing institutional arrangements.

The success of gradual reform in China can be attributed to two factors. First, as Barry Naughton has argued, through gradual reform, the government retained its role as a stabilizing force in the midst of the turbulence that inevitably accompanies the transition from plan to market. Institutions such as the "dual-track" system kept large state-owned enterprises partially on the plan and, at the same time, gave them incentives to generate extra income through selling what they could produce above the plan in China's nascent markets. Over time, as market economic practice became more successful, the plan part of an enterprise's portfolio was reduced and the market part grew. Enterprises were thus given the stability of a continued but gradually diminishing planned economy system and the time to learn the practices of setting prices, competing for contracts, and producing efficiently (Naughton 1995; see also Rawski 1994, 1995, 1999). Second, the government has gradually pushed ownership-like control down the government administrative hierarchy to the localities. As a result, the central government was able to give economic control over to local administrators without privatization. But with economic control came accountability, and local administrators became very invested in the successful economic reform of the villages, townships, and municipalities under their jurisdictions. In a sense, as Andrew Walder has argued, pushing economic responsibilities onto local administrators created an incentive structure much like those experienced by managers of large industrial firms.[10]

Even as reform in China has proceeded at a gradual pace, the cumulative changes over two-and-a-half decades of economic reform have been nothing short of radical. These economic reforms have proceeded on four levels. First, the transformation of China's economy begins with institutional changes set in motion at the highest levels of government; second, they have been followed by firm-level institutions that reflect the rational-legal system emerging at the state level; third, these firm-level changes have been supported by a budding legal system that provides workers institutional support for grievance proceedings, a dynamic that is heavily influenced by relationships with foreign investors; and fourth, labor relations have been shaped by the emergence of new labor markets in China, which allow workers the freedom and mobility to find new employment when necessary. The result of these changes has been the emergence of a rational-legal regime of labor, where the economy increasingly rests upon an infrastructure of rational law, and workers hold the right to invoke these laws in the legal system when necessary.

The process began with a gradual introduction of economic autonomy to enterprise managers and local officials in industrial areas and decollectivization in the countryside. As of the early 1980s, individuals increasingly had the freedom to pursue their fortunes in the newly emerging markets of the Chinese economy, and many individuals chose to do so. Enterprise autonomy for managers and officials meant that the party and industrial bureaus were no longer leaning over the shoulders of economic actors in the industrial economy. Thus, the gradual reforms hit squarely at the heart of the central institutions around which communist China was organized. Once Deng wrested power from the conservative factions of the party, his tasks included:

- transforming incentives in the agricultural economy;
- forcing the central government to give local bureaucrats some measure of economic control over the localities they govern;

- creating a system that kept in place the planned economy while at the same time giving autonomy over the local enterprises;
- beginning a process that would address the economic burden that the social security system posed for Chinese enterprises;
- facilitating the development of a private economy;
- attracting foreign direct investment.

Several of these goals began to emerge explicitly onto the agenda at the Third Plenum of the Eleventh Central Committee of the Chinese Communist Party in December 1978. For example, on December 15, the party announced that it would establish full diplomatic relations with the United States on January 1, 1979. During this time, the party also laid the groundwork for the passage (in 1979) of the Law of the PRC on Chinese-Foreign Equity Joint Ventures, which would allow foreign firms to enter the Chinese economy for the first time since the founding of the PRC. It would also signal a reversal of Mao's "revolutionary" governance structure with the passage (again in 1979) of the Resolution of the Standing Committee of the National People's Congress Authorizing Provinces, Autonomous Regions, and Municipalities Directly under the Central Government to Change Revolutionary Committees to People's Governments.

Following his political breakthrough in 1978, Deng symbolically signaled these changes with a crucial visit to the United States in January 1979. During this trip, Deng officially normalized relations with the United States, which in turn officially ended formal U.S. diplomatic relations with Taiwan and explicitly conceded China's position on the "one-China" policy.[11] Many nations in the international community would follow by normalizing relations with China.[12] During that trip,

Deng also visited Atlanta, Houston, and Seattle to see the facilities of the first two companies with which agreements would be signed—Coca-Cola and Boeing.

DEVELOPING AN INDEPENDENT MINDSET IN THE RURAL ECONOMY

Initially, Deng's reform agenda aimed to loosen the central government's control over the economy, stimulating economic growth, controlling unemployment and inflation, and improving the Chinese citizens' living standards. It was not clear, in these early years of reform, that Deng had in mind the creation of a market economy; instead, he seemed to have in mind a one-step-at-a-time approach to creating a more robust economy in China. It was under these auspices that Deng became famous for the notion of "groping for stones to cross the river." In other words, "We don't know yet how we are crossing this river, but we will get there one step at a time."

One thing that was clear, even in the early years of the economic reforms, was that, if the central government was going to successfully break down the planned economy and allow the economy to be kick-started by the gradual emergence of markets, it would need to develop an economy of (semi-)independent market actors. One of the early keys to developing such an economy was to gradually allow individuals to harness individual-level incentives to participate in the market economy. With the breakup of the commune system and the establishment of the Household Responsibility System in the early 1980s, peasants in rural areas were allowed to lease land and produce agricultural goods on a household basis as if they were running a household business. They still had to deliver a minimum quota of grain to the government— usually to the collective from which the land was leased—but beyond that amount, they were free to sell the surplus in emerging rural markets. Rural markets were thus opened to a large portion of the Chinese populace (about 80 percent of the population at that time), the first step toward establishing a grassroots movement to a market economy. The "dual track" nature of this arrangement would also become a model for enterprise reform in the industrial economy.

This system had three immediate positive consequences. First, it allowed an infusion of cash to flow into individual households, which were still, by world standards, extremely poor. Annual per-capita net income in rural areas of China in 1978 was 133.6 yuan (about $16.25), or about $70 in total annual household income. Individuals were still reliant on the state for the provision of goods and services, so a low per-capita income overstated the poverty (because individuals had access to nonwage benefits), but the economy at this point was still extremely poor. As local governments began to withdraw the social support that was the hallmark of the "iron rice bowl," individuals would need new sources of income to cover those costs. The Household Responsibility System provided those sources of income. Second, although there were concerns that rural production of grain would suffer as a result of this semiprivatization effort, the system actually stimulated grain output significantly: from 1978 to 1984, grain production grew by over 100 million tons, from 305 to 407 million tons.[13] Third, by creating incentives for individuals to produce and then creating the autonomy for them to do so, Deng Xiaoping created a large constituency that supported the economic reforms from its early stages.

LOCAL GOVERNMENTAL AUTONOMY

One of the interesting differences between China's planned economy and that of the Soviet Union was that China's was much more decentralized. This fact has played a crucial role in the success of China's economic reforms, as a number of scholars have argued.[14] Nevertheless, despite the relative decentralization in China, giving autonomy over to localities was still a key factor that guided the economic reforms forward. Economic decentralization ushered in two forces that have been key to the economic reforms: (1) local officials, who were much closer to the economic strengths, opportunities, and necessities of their localities, would be given the autonomy to pursue various development strategies, and (2) this measure would introduce a level of competition among local officials vying for different economic opportunities. Deng Xiaoping clearly recognized the importance of these potential forces by passing the elaborately titled Resolution of the Standing Committee of the National People's Congress Authorizing the People's Congresses of Guangdong and Fujian Provinces and Their Standing Committees to Formulate Separate Economic Regulations for Their Respective Special Economic Zones.[15] This resolution, one of the early resolutions passed in the era of Deng's economic reforms, clearly recognized the importance of political decentralization in the reform project. National development has proceeded along these lines throughout the era of the economic reforms. Individual provinces and municipalities have had the autonomy to make economic decisions and innovations in developmental strategies to gain advantages over neighboring regions and provinces. It is also the case that individual regions, provinces, and municipalities were given the power to create small-scale special economic zones for the localities within their jurisdictions.

NEW AUTONOMY AND INCENTIVES FOR FACTORY MANAGERS

While creating a fledgling market economy mind-set among the peasantry and local officials was a crucial first step in the gradual creation of a market economy, tackling the industrial economy was an equally important, though exceptionally more complex, next step. Even before the Third Plenum, Sichuan Province had begun experimenting with giving autonomy to factory managers, a fact that would position Zhao Ziyang to emerge as one of Deng's early partners in the reform agenda. The basic strategy here was to turn autonomy over to economic organizations. There were a number of specific institutional reforms that pushed the development of enterprise reform in China forward. I will discuss a few of these reforms as examples here.

The Dual-Track System

One of the early enterprise reforms institutionalized by the Chinese government was the dual-track system, characterized by the coexistence of two coordination mechanisms (plan and market) within the state sector.[16] This economic policy maintained the elements of the planned economy while attempting, at the same time, to give state-owned organizations incentives to develop market-oriented strategies that would work above and beyond the plan. Continuing to govern each sector in the economy allowed the government to continue using direct controls over finance and investment and provided a degree of stability during the transition process. However, instituting the dual-track system also allowed the existence of a two-tiered pricing system for goods and allowed the state firms to sell the goods above plan quotas and keep extra profits. This two-tiered system greatly stimulated the incentives of the enterprises, as anything that firms produced above the plan could be sold within China's newly emerging markets at a market price. The system also provided valuable flexibility by allowing the state firms to transact and cooperate with non-state and foreign sectors. Economic growth was thus concentrated in the market "track," and, over time, the "plan" became proportionately less and less important in the transition process.

Allowing new firms into the marketplace was crucial, and reformers could not have anticipated how rapidly the non-state sector would grow. But even more important, they had little sense of the profound political and economic impacts the growth of this sector—combined with enterprise autonomy—would bring about.[17] As the market replaced the plan, the state fiscal system eroded, putting further pressure on reformers to experiment with new paths toward marketization; the pressure of the market and the fiscal crisis pushed bureaucrats to seek ways to help firms become more productive. Thus, the economy "gradually grew out of the plan" as the plan itself and the state sector became less important parts of the economy. Some of this may have been unintentional: as Barry Naughton (1995) describes it, China's reform effort is characterized by an interaction between early governmental policies and the "unforeseen consequences of economic change." While economic reformers adopted early strategies to make the initial move away from a purely command economy, it was only in the later stages of the reform period that the goal of a market-based system emerged. In other words, early policy decisions began the process of reform, but soon the consequences of this early reform effort caused the system to unravel, pushing the reforms far beyond leaders' original intentions. However, the gradual nature of this process allowed the state sector to remain, at least in the early years, the anchor of the economy that it had been in the prereform era, creating some degree of stability throughout the process.

Property Rights

In the realm of enterprise autonomy, it is also useful to examine the institutional transformation of property rights in China. On one end of the spectrum, the view of property rights in market transitions has been unequivocal: the rapid privatization of property is necessary in the successful transition to a market economy. This view is partly ideological, but it is also grounded in theory and experience. For decades, the planned economies of the Soviet Union and China were rife with the inefficiencies that accompany state ownership. State-owned factories operated on the principles of a redistributive system, whereby revenues were turned over to the government and input costs were drawn from state coffers and "redistributed" to the factories owned by the state. This system of "soft budget constraints," in which factories could draw endlessly from state coffers regardless of revenues, led to problems of rent seeking, a lack of connection between input and output costs, and the absence of pressure within factories to operate efficiently. Thus, the privatization of property, which places fiscal responsibilities squarely within the firm, came to be viewed by many Western economists as a necessary step in reforming the inefficiencies of the planned system.

The Chinese experience belies this view. As China has marched through two decades of double-digit economic growth, the rapid and complete privatization of property has not been part of this story. Property rights have played a complex role in reform-era China, in fact. In an insightful essay on this topic, Andrew Walder and Jean Oi begin by rejecting the notion that property can be adequately understood in the crude categories of private or state owned. Drawing on earlier work in this area (esp. Demsetz 1967; Furubotn and Pejovich 1974), Walder and Oi (1999) argue that property should be conceived of as a "bundle of rights," where questions of managerial control, the ability to extract revenue, and the ability to transfer ownership must all be addressed in a full understanding of this institution. The view of property rights as dependent upon shifting politics and relations has a long history in legal scholarship (Singer 1982, 1988), dating perhaps as far back as Hohfeld's (1913) re-conceptualization of rights nearly a century ago. Unfortunately, however, the field of economics has, until only recently, been blind to a more nuanced view of institutions such as property rights. The central point here is that while many firms in China are still officially state owned, individual parameters within these bundles of rights have been reformed to various degrees, so firms are often free to act independent of state control, despite the fact that they are still officially state owned. This perspective helps us resolve the puzzle of how it is that China has successfully reformed its planned economy—though this process is far from complete—without relying on the mandate of rapid privatization: the state has gradually allowed for the reform of some parts of these bundles of rights, while leaving others intact. To systematize this analysis, Walder and Oi (1999) also outline five ideal types of ownership arrangements that exist along a continuum, with state-owned enterprises occupying one end of this spectrum and fully private enterprises occupying the other. Between these ends of the continuum, we find firms that have incorporated innovative reforms including management incentive contracts, government-management partnerships, and leased public assets.

Local Governments as Industrial Firms

The central government kept control over policy making and shifted economic decision making down to local governments and to the management of the enterprises. One key effect of this policy is that it allowed local officials to aggressively pursue development strategies for the firms under their jurisdictions. The earliest sector of the Chinese economy to surge in growth and output in China's reform era was that of the township and village enterprises (TVEs). Indeed, the rapid growth of China's economy in the 1980s was largely due to the exceptional growth rates of the rural industrial economy, where the vast majority of TVEs are. As the primary segment contributing to China's high economic growth in the 1980s, the TVE sector expanded to 24,529 in 1993, almost fifteen times its size in 1978. By 1998, however, the number had dropped to 20,039 due to the informal privatization processes led by the local governments in the 1990s.[18] These organizations were essentially state owned. Though not controlled by the national or provincial governments, they were still controlled by the state, as township and village governments owned the property. Local governments were the residual claimants, and they controlled managerial decisions and the rights of transferring assets. However, after the economic reforms began, TVEs faced few of the institutional and organizational legacies of the planned economy that larger state-owned organizations controlled by higher levels of government faced.[19]

As the economic reforms progressed, managerial and ownership control were quickly decentralized to give local officials direct control over the firms under their jurisdictions. This strategy was partly borne out of necessity: as the central government sought to gradually dismantle the redistributive economy, firms in the rural economy were the first to be cut off from funds from state coffers. However, local officials were also given free reign to generate income as they could. Thus, local officials were given incentives to behave like managers and run their TVEs like local industrial firms (Walder 1995e). From this frame of reference, TVEs rapidly came to resemble business organizations in crucial ways, yet the property rights still resided in the hands of the local state. As a result, decentralization has greatly stimulated the rural industrialization driven by the development of TVEs. These sectors have been pushed to respond more to the market forces and less to the governmental plan. With harder budgets, the non-state sectors (which also include the private and foreign sectors) have become the most competitive firms and today contribute to over 70 percent of China's gross domestic product.

Organizational Structure: Dismantling the Old and Creating the New

Chinese industrial firms have been transformed in dramatic ways over the course of China's economic reforms. Perhaps the most important change set in place over the course of the economic reforms in China came when the state handed economic decision making over to industrial managers (Naughton 1995; Guthrie 1999). While some of the organizational changes occurring in industrial firms are in direct response to the hundreds of new directives and economic laws being promulgated by the state, many of the changes occurring in Chinese industrial firms come from decisions made by autonomous managers who are transforming their firms by force of creativity, will, and, in some cases, pure desperation. In the uncertain environment of China's newly emerging markets, managers have been impelled to innovate, create, strategize, and improvise their way through the economic reforms. For many of these managers, they learned the ways of markets, competition, and economic survival through experimenting with and implementing the new organizational strategies and structures their firms were adopting in this period.

Innovative managers within the organizations carried out these firm-level changes as organizational strategies. The transformation of Chinese industrial firms is just as much a reflection of managerial decision making, then, as it is some abstract notion of organizational strategies, because it is largely the general managers (along with the local bureaucrats in some administrative jurisdictions) who are running the show in

China today. These firm-level changes are very much about innovation, experimentation, and finding creative solutions to organizational problems; they are thus driven by entrepreneurial decisions of the general managers who run these firms. The first dramatic change that aggressive managers are implementing in their organizations is a clearing of the decks. Wiping out the old system has been an important step in aggressive enterprise reform in China, but it has not been an easy one. Inasmuch as industrial enterprises under the command economy served as the nation's social security system, dismantling this system of extensive benefit packages amounted to nothing less than a fundamental transformation of the labor relationship and the meaning of work in China. Although these changes are often not commonly acknowledged as such, they comprise a dramatic shift that is occurring in Chinese firms, leading to newly emerging organizational structures and forms. Since the late 1980s, we have witnessed the emergence of bureaucratic structures that look strikingly like the type of organizational structures we find in Western economies. The construction of these new "intra-organizational" structures in Chinese firms over the last decade has required innovation, experimentation, and imagination from industrial managers.

Today, the evidence of these new institutions and structures abound in the Chinese economy, yet industrial managers have embraced these changes at varying rates. Three key factors have driven this transformation forward. First, the background of the general managers has a significant impact on the extent to which they are actively reshaping the organizations they are running. Firms that are run by managers with backgrounds in business and economics are more likely to adopt the economic structures that are associated with the economic reforms. General managers with backgrounds in business and economics are also more prone to act in an entrepreneurial fashion with respect to organizational restructuring than their counterparts with training in other areas or no formal training at all. Second, the social world and the economic models present in that social world play a significant role in the aggressive adoption of new organizational forms in China. Firms that have joint ventures with foreign companies are significantly more likely to adopt the economic structures associated with the reforms. Third, the institutional structure in which a firm is embedded also plays a significant role in the adoption of new organizational structures and forms. Firms that are positioned under the jurisdiction of municipal companies tend to be aggressive adopters of the new organizational forms.[20]

The Company Law: Adopting New Corporate Forms

A second area of aggressive development can be seen as general managers lead their firms to take advantage of the institutional opportunities created by the state. As the state inundates society and the market with a horde of new laws and institutional rules, the really interesting question becomes which of these institutional changes have meaning for society. Which of these institutional reforms managers have adopted and which they have ignored is a key question in the reform era. In the end, the institutional reforms that really have meaning for the economic reforms are those that are aggressively adopted by actors in the economy. And it is often entrepreneurial managers taking advantage of—or, in some cases, avoiding—the institutional changes that breathe life into these reforms.

A fascinating case in point is that of the Chinese Company Law. Adopted by the National People's Congress on December 29, 1993, the Company Law provides the first legal basis in the history of the PRC for private, collective, and state enterprises to exist as autonomous legal entities. It is an institutional change that continues the process of separating—both legally and operationally—enterprises from the state redistributive system of the former command economy. Yet, while the law now exists in China, there is still considerable variation as to whether or not organizations have chosen to incorporate this change into their daily operations. Managers must actively choose to transform their firms into companies if they want to take advantage of the Company Law—they must apply to the Economic Commission to take on company status—and aggressive managers have seen this as an opportunity to become part of the "modern enterprise system." They must act as entrepreneurs with respect to this new institution, applying for this change in status, figuring out what it means for their organization, and adopting the changes that come with this economic transformation. As one general manager described this process,

> In 1986, business in our factory really started picking up. Before [that] we were a planned economy. But after the economic opening, our factory was one of the earliest to integrate a market economic approach. That year was actually the year that our profits really started picking up. Then last year we applied to have our factory changed from an enterprise to a company. So now we are under the Company Law, and our scope of business is much wider. It's really a much better situation for us in terms of development now.
>
> (Personal interview, 1995)

What types of managers and firms are transforming their organizations in this way? First, managers whose organizations are embedded in formal relationships with foreign companies are more likely to adopt the Company Law. Firms that are engaged in relationships with—and therefore under the influence of—foreign partners are more likely to pursue economic strategies that the state has defined as a "modern enterprise system." A general manager's decision to adopt the Company Law is not significantly related to the profit margins of the firm or the firm's overall organizational health—other variables that would presumably be proxies for economic success; in other words, this change itself has little to do with past economic success. I think the stronger interpretation of the joint-venture effect is that a foreign partner provides a Chinese firm with detailed examples of how foreign firms operate. The "modern enterprise system" is, in many ways, a rhetorical stand-in for Western-style management practices. Managers who are exposed to the concept of the "modern enterprise system" through contact with foreign companies and through setting up a joint-venture company are more likely to see the institutional advantages (real or perceived) of broadening the organization's scope of operation and becoming an independent legal entity. Entrepreneurial managers pursue this change as a way of helping to shepherd their firms into the modern economy.

Second, Chinese organizations that are at the highest level of the government administrative hierarchy are more likely than those under more local governmental offices to adopt the Company Law. Central- and provincial-level government offices, with jurisdiction over many enterprises, do not have the administrative resources to monitor and offer administrative advice or help to the firms in the large organizational fields under their jurisdictions (Guthrie 1997, 1998a). As a result, firms under these levels of government experience a greater sense of being set adrift in the economic transition. They are thus encouraged—or they feel the impetus—to pursue economic strategies on their own. Adopting the Company Law and thereby broadening the scope of action in China's growing markets is one such strategy that firms, especially those under bureaus, are taking. Firms under the jurisdiction of district companies, on the other hand, are much more closely monitored by their government organizations (relative to those under bureaus), and these firms are offered a significant amount of administrative help and attention in the economic reform. The result is that when the opportunity to apply to become a company and adopt the Company Law arose, managers under high-level governmental offices had the autonomy (and the impetus) to move their firms toward adopting this institutional change.

Price Setting: Flexibility and Competition in the Market

A crucial issue in the transition from a command to a market economy pertains to the setting of prices. Under the command economy, all price setting in large industrial organizations was controlled by the state. Reforming price-setting practices would prove to be a central issue of the economic transition. Price reform has followed the course of gradual reform that is indicative of China's reform process, laden with politics, experimentation, and piecemeal implementation. Government control of pricing began to change officially with general reforms in 1979 and then, more specifically, with the October 1984 Reform Declaration. Implementing a market pricing system may not have been a central part of the financial rationalizing system that was being promoted by Zhao Ziyang, but it was an important issue that was on the table for many years of the reform and often advocated by Zhao himself. The "price reformers" certainly saw the issue as crucial to the success of the reforms, and even if the "enterprise reformers" were antagonistic to the idea, the liberalization of prices was an issue that was central to the debates that raged between these two reform-minded groups. But if the debates over price control and liberalization were central to the reforms, progress on the issue was slow. By the end of 1984, factor prices were still unreformed, and product prices had still not yet been realigned.[21] Managers, for their part, have responded to the price reforms in China in a variety of ways—some have simply remained passive, following the market but pursuing few strategies in the negotiating that can often allow prices to shift in a market, while others have viewed price reform as an opportunity to aggressively negotiate with customers in the market (Guthrie 1999, ch. 5).

TRANSFORMING THE SOCIAL SECURITY SYSTEM: ENDING THE INSTITUTION OF LIFETIME EMPLOYMENT

Command economies were typically known for having small variation in wages while offering a range of living benefits that were tied to the workplace. In the prereform era, China sat on the extreme end of this spectrum, because wage differentials were extremely narrow, and virtually all social security was tied to the work unit. Further, in China, lifetime employment was the very essence of the labor relationship that existed between enterprises and workers.[22] Workers entered their work unit, and, from that moment on, the work unit was the social system that dispensed their salary, housing, medical insurance, and any other benefits the unit might offer. In different periods, especially in the late 1970s, a small fraction of the population was classified as "waiting for employment," but for the most part, the state still fulfilled its promise of finding employment for everyone. This relationship would extend through the worker's retirement. This system was colloquially referred to as the "iron rice bowl."

Although by 1980, state sector jobs had become more competitive than ever before (only 37 percent of workers were assigned jobs in state-owned enterprises), still 80 percent of workers were assigned jobs in either state enterprises or collectively owned enterprises in that year (Walder 1986a, 57, 68–74). Once jobs were assigned, the job assignment was for life, except in rare cases of disciplinary firing and even rarer cases of layoffs (which were often followed by reassignment to another enterprise). This is not to say that workers never changed jobs or resigned from a given enterprise, but once workers were assigned to a work unit, except in unusual circumstances, they had the option of staying at that organization for life. With tightening fiscal constraints in the reform era, the heavy burdens of social security coupled with lifetime employment have crippled enterprises, and redefining the social security commitments of enterprises has become a central issue for the industrial reformers. Even in the reform era, it is not uncommon to walk into a factory, department store, or bank and see far more employees than are necessary to accomplish the tasks of that workplace. Why? The reason is that, under the planned economy, workers are simply assigned to work within various work units, and these units are responsible for supplying social security benefits. In the reform era, these work units have been reluctant to simply fire workers or cut pensions for retired workers as a way to cut costs. As one manager explained,

> Many of these employees have been working for this factory for twenty or more years; they have spent most of their lives working for this factory, but they just haven't reached retirement age yet. To suddenly cut these people off would be cruel. Suddenly they would have no retirement security; that would be very unfair to them. . . . It's no way to treat people who have been working for you for so long.
>
> (Personal interview, 1995)

Another manager assessed the challenges that are associated with this mind-set:

> The biggest problem that our state-owned enterprises have is the retired workers. We are taking care of so many people in comparison to other private companies. We can't compete with them in terms of development. They take all of their profits and put them back into the company; we have to use all of our profits to take care of workers who are no longer working here. And many of these retired people are now working at other companies, but they still come here every month to get their pay.
>
> (Personal interview, 1995)

Nevertheless, many broad institutional changes have emerged to redefine the labor relationship, including the new pension system (which does not really function to cover the costs of retired workers), labor contracts, the Labor Law (PRC 1994), and the existence of Labor Arbitration Commissions, which give workers some recourse against the factories where they are employed (these issues will be dealt with in Chapter 6). The emergence of labor contracts in China marks an important turning point for the socialist system created under Mao, as it marks the effective end of lifetime employment in China. This fact relieves work units of a large future burden of lifetime commitment to the workers they employ while, at the same time, breaking the commitment of the iron rice bowl for individuals.

DEVELOPING A PRIVATE ECONOMY

While many scholars have argued that privatization is a necessary step in the transition from plan to market, the case of China belies this claim in important ways. However, an important distinction is necessary here: despite the fact that

China did not move quickly along the road of privatizing state-owned enterprises, the government did allow a private economy to emerge, and this private economy has played an important role in the reform era. As Barry Naughton (1995) has pointed out, the private economy in China played an important role in teaching the state sector how to compete. State-owned factories were not privatized, but they were subjected to market competition from below by the emerging private sector.

It is important to note here that the private sector in China actually consists of three components. First, there are the small-scale entrepreneurs of the household economy (the "household enterprises"), which occupy a legal category that demands that they do not grow beyond seven employees. These small-scale organizations were very important in the early years of the economic reforms, as they provided opportunities for the large numbers of individuals who were "waiting for employment," including those who had returned home to urban areas after being "sent down" to the countryside during the Cultural Revolution. Some scholars have also suggested that this sector of the population provided a much-needed outlet for innovation and political resistance in the early years of the reforms (Gold 1989a, 1989b, 1990, 1991; Wank 1999). Second, the private enterprises have also played a crucial role in the development of the private economy in China. Private enterprises are different from household enterprises because they are allowed to grow beyond seven employees. It is this group of enterprises that has grown to challenge the state sector across a number of sectors in the economy. Like their smaller-scale counterparts in the household economy, this sector of the economy has also been an important force in social change. Some scholars have argued, for example, that this sector played a crucial role in the evolution of the Tiananmen Movement of 1989, as they had the resources to help the students organize in significant ways (Guthrie 1995; Perry and Wasserstrom 1992). A third sector of the private economy has to do with the publicly listed companies on China's stock exchanges in Shanghai and Shenzhen. These companies are becoming "privatized" in some ways; as some 30 percent of shares enter the free-floating market, however, the ownership and control of these companies still largely rests in state hands, as it is typical for a firm listed on either of China's stock exchanges for the government to maintain control over 40–50 percent of the stock issued by the company.

ENTICING FOREIGN INVESTMENT

By the early 1990s, it was still premature for China to claim that its economic system was an established market economy, but it had already made important strides away from the planned economic system. The long-term debate on whether China should focus on a plan-track policy or a market-driven policy between "hard-liners" (e.g., Li Peng) and "pragmatists" (e.g., Hu Yaobang and Zhao Ziyang) among Chinese leadership ended in the spring of 1992, when Deng Xiaoping took his "southern tour" to Shenzhen and officially declared the Chinese economic system as a market economy with socialist characteristics. One of the most important forces that pushed toward the building and maturation of market institutions came from the influence of foreign capital, driven by the opening-up policy in late 1979. The establishment of Special Economic Zones in the 1980s in coastal areas greatly contributed to the inflow of foreign capital into China. China has taken a much more aggressive view toward FDI than any other developing country in recent years. Not only is the magnitude of foreign investment in China greater, but foreign-invested firms in China are playing a role in the growth of exports that has no parallel elsewhere in East Asia. The magnitude of foreign investment in China dwarfs that of Japan in comparable development periods.[23] China's foreign investment regime is also far more liberal than that of South Korea. At the same time, the state-led project of building a rational-legal system is helping the Chinese market system to get on track with the international community, deal better with its foreign partners, and introduce advanced technology (Guthrie 1999).[24]

It is still too soon to give a definite picture of, or evaluate, how open China's markets are today, but it is very clear that China's market for goods has developed significantly, driven by the export-oriented development strategy and the rise of consumption within China. Clearly, labor markets have developed in significant ways, which has resulted mainly from the restructuring of the state sector, the booming of the non-state sectors, and state-led law building. The openness of China's economy is also evidenced by its liberal legal provisions facilitating exports based on processing or assembly activity. In addition, over the last two decades, China has become one of the major trading nations of the world. Despite claims that markets in China have been closed to foreign producers, for the first decade of the reforms, China ran a trade deficit with the world, which meant that more goods were being sold in China than the country was able to sell to the rest of the world. However, today China does enjoy a trade surplus with respect to the United States. The ratio of U.S. imports from China relative to U.S. exports is somewhere around 3.5 to 1. Nevertheless, the main point here is that even at their early stages of development, domestic equities markets in China are significantly more open than those in Japan, South Korea, and Taiwan at comparable stages.

Beyond the openness of the export economy, which has been a crucial factor in attracting foreign capital, the Chinese economy has also attracted investors of another type—those interested in capturing the internal market in China. The lure of the billion-person marketplace has been a key factor in attracting the likes of Coca-Cola, DuPont, General Motors, Kodak, Motorola, and many other blue-chip foreign firms that have been positioning themselves for years to capture the internal marketplace in China. These investors have also played an important role in China's economic reforms, because they have something to offer in return for access to China's internal markets: technology transfer is a central point of negotiation in the joint venture and licensing agreements they negotiate.

TAXATION

Another significant change that has played a fundamental rule in the emergence of China's market economy lies in the area of taxation. One of the features that defined the redistributive economy was the fact that administrative offices collected the revenues and were therefore in a position to extract excess revenues from the factories under their jurisdictions; they would then redistribute these resources as they saw fit. In China today, however, this is largely a thing of the past. Three key changes have transformed this system. First, the extraction of revenues has been standardized in the taxation system (i.e., governing organizations are no longer permitted to simply extract all "excess" revenues), a change that officially came about with the Second Phase Profits Changed to Taxes Reform of 1985.[25] Second, today taxation is basically standardized— with value-added tax (17 percent of turnover) and income tax (33 percent of net income) as basic standards for firms and individuals. Third, most firms pay their taxes directly into the Government Tax Bureau, which has one bureau office for each district and each municipality, instead of to their governing organization.[26] Tax breaks and subsidized loan repayment make the concept of standardized taxation less meaningful, and it is often the case that implementing these internal policies is a problem (i.e., they exist on paper but not in practice). There are still ways for governing organizations to extract revenues from firms, such as negotiations over profits and "management" fees. But the main point here is that taxes are now being paid to a central office—rather than the administrative organization extracting revenues. Without the convenience of revenue extraction across a wide base of firms, the ability of governing organizations to skim or extract excess amounts of revenue is significantly reduced.

CONSTRUCTING A RATIONAL-LEGAL SYSTEM

Under Deng Xiaoping, Zhao Ziyang brought about radical change in China by pushing the country toward constitutionality and the emergence of the rule of law to create "rational" economic processes in China. This project would be carried on by Zhu Rongji after Zhao's ouster in 1989. These changes, which were set forth ideologically as a package of reforms that were necessary for economic development, fundamentally altered the role of politics and the role of the party in Chinese society. The early years of reform not only gave a great deal of autonomy to enterprise managers and small-scale entrepreneurs but also emphasized the legal reforms that would undergird this process of change. However, creating a body of civil and economic law, such as the Labor Law (1994), the Company Law (1994), and the National Compensation Law (1995), upon which the transforming economy would be based, meant that the party elites themselves would be held to the standards of these legal changes. Thus, in a number of ways, the rationalization of the economy led to a decline in the party's ability to rule over the working population.

In recent years, the next step in this process has come from global integration and the adoption of the norms of the international community. By championing global integration and the rule of law, Zhu Rongji also brought about broader political and social change in China, just as Zhao Ziyang did in the first decade of economic reform in China. Zhu's strategy has been to ignore questions of political reform and concentrate instead on the need for China to adopt economic and legal systems and norms that will allow the country to integrate smoothly with the rest of the global economy. From rhetoric on "linking up with the international community" (a very popular phrase among Chinese managers today) to laws like the Patent Law (2000) and institutions such as the State Intellectual Property Office and the Chinese International Economic Trade and Arbitration Commission, this phase of reform has been oriented toward creating the standards of the international investment community. Thus, Zhu's objective is to deepen all of the reforms that have been discussed above, but at the same time to begin to hold these changes up to the standards of the global economy.

After two decades of transition, the architects of the reforms have set in place about 400 new national laws, administrative laws, 10,000 local regulations, and over 30,000 administrative procedures; compare this to the decade of the Cultural Revolution (1966–76) when the government passed 9 new laws. These legal changes and many more regulations, along with experiments with new economic institutions, have driven forward the process of reform. A number of laws and policies in the 1980s laid the groundwork for a new set of policies that would redefine labor relations in fundamental ways. Take, for example, the policies that set in motion the emergence of labor contracts in China, which were officially introduced in 1986. The labor contract was further institutionalized by the Enterprise Law (PRC 1988, chapter 3, article 31), which codifies workers' rights for fair treatment and the right of due process in the event of unfair treatment. There are economic incentives behind the embracing of labor contracts by Chinese firms (the most important being the end of lifetime employment), but this institution, nevertheless, places the rationalization of the labor relationship, a guarantee of due process in the event of unfair treatment, and, ultimately, workers' rights at the center of the labor relationship. Other policies and laws also push this process forward (Guthrie 1998a). For example, the Labor Law (1994), Prison Reform Law (1994), and National Compensation Law (1995) are all examples of laws tied to labor that place the protection of individual civil liberties front and center. And the Company Law (1994), which has its roots in American and German corporate law, places much more emphasis on employee welfare than does the American version, to be sure. These laws and many others provide the legal infrastructure that allows workers to file grievances against managers, and individual citizens to file for compensation for past wrongs committed by the government. Laws such as these are a crucial part of the changes occurring in the conception of individual rights in China.

The obvious and most common response to these changes might be that they are symbolic rather than substantive in nature, that a changing legal and policy framework has little meaning when an authoritarian government still sits at the helm, but the scholarship that has looked extensively at the impact of these legal changes largely belies this view. For example, the rationalization of labor relations in the workplace is directly tied to institutional changes, such as the Labor Law, and other legal institutions that emphasize the individual civil liberties of workers (Guthrie 1999). Workers and managers take these new institutions seriously, and they have had a dramatic impact on the structure of authority relations and the conception of rights within the workplace. Research has also shown that legal and policy changes that place an emphasis on individual civil liberties matter in significant ways in other arenas as well. The most systematic and exhaustive study of the prison system to date shows that changes in the treatment of prisoners have indeed emerged in the wake of the Prison Reform Law (Seymour and Anderson 1998). And, although no scholarship has been done on the National Compensation Law, it is noteworthy that under this law, 97,569 suits were filed against the government in 1999, including such recent high-profile cases as a suit against the government for its hand in producing cigarettes and a suit against the government for the deaths in the Tiananmen Square massacre. These rational-legal institutions guarantee that, for the first time in the history of the PRC, individuals can now receive their day in court, and it is under this system that lawsuits against the government specifically have risen over 12,000 percent since the beginning of the economic reforms.[27]

The Labor Law (PRC 1994) and the Labor Arbitration Commission (of which there are branches in every urban district) work hand-in-hand in guaranteeing workers their individual rights as laborers. Chapter 10 of the Labor Law, entitled "Labor Disputes," is specifically devoted to articulating due process, which laborers are legally guaranteed should a dispute arise in the workplace. The law explains in an explicit fashion the rights of the worker to take disputes to outside arbitration (the district's Labor Arbitration Commission, or LAC) should the resolution in the workplace be unsatisfactory to the worker. Further, many state-owned enterprises have placed all of their workers on fixed-term labor contracts, which significantly rationalize the labor relationship beyond the personalized labor relations of the past. This bundle of changes has fundamentally altered the nature of the labor relationship and the mechanisms through which authority can be challenged (both within and outside the factory). For more than a decade now, it has been possible for workers to file grievances against superiors and have their grievances heard at the LACs, and, in 1999, out of 120,191 labor disputes that were settled by arbitration or mediation, 63,030 (52 percent) were decided wholly in favor of the workers filing the suits. These are official statistics, and we should be skeptical of their veracity. However, even if the magnitude is off, these numbers illuminate an important trend toward legal activity regarding workers' rights.

Many of these changes in labor practices were not originally adopted with workers' rights in mind, but the unintended consequence of these changes has been the construction of a regime of labor relations that emphasizes the rights of workers. For instance, extending upon the example of labor contracts, which were being experimented with as early as 1983, these were originally intended as a form of economic protection for ailing enterprises, allowing enterprises a formal way of ending lifetime employment. However, as the terms of employment were codified in these contracts, workers began using them as a vehicle for filing grievances when contractual agreements were not honored. With the emergence of the LACs in the late 1980s and the further codification of these institutions in the Labor Law of 1994, the changes that were afoot became formalized in a set of institutions that ultimately benefited workers in the realm of rights. In a similar way, workers' representative committees began as an institution formed in the state's interest, but once in place became an institution that workers claimed as their own. These institutions, which many managers I have spoken with refer to as "our own little democracy," were adopted early in the reforms as a compromise, a way of heading off the growing agitation for the creation of independent labor unions. These committees do not have the same power or status as independent labor unions in the West, but workers have nonetheless made them their own, and they are much more significant in factories today than they were originally intended to be.

HOMEGROWN MULTINATIONALS

China was never going to be on the path to becoming a dominant economic power in the world based on the size of its labor pool alone. It was always necessary that China make the transition from an economy built around supplying labor to the world's largest corporations, to one built around the development of great corporations of its own. Fortunately for China, and challenging for the rest of the world's corporations, China's domestic corporations have arrived. Only two of China's corporations have cracked the Global 50 in terms of revenues (Sinopec and CNPC at 23 and 39, respectively), but the tremors are being felt more widely than this statistic indicates. Companies around the world would readily admit to the competitive pressure they feel from Chinese companies: Lenovo's purchase of IBM's Thinkpad division; Haier's bid to buy Maytag; CNOOC's bid to take over Unocal; Huawei's tense competition with Cisco. And the recent listing of PetroChina, which led it to briefly become the largest company in the world in terms of market capitalization, and ICBC's record-setting IPO has certainly captured the world's attention.

China's arrival at this position has been the next step in the process of developing a first-rate economy. The process of securing technology transfer through joint venture agreements or, in some cases, the support of private companies through state-funded technology institutes (in the cases of Lenovo and Huawei), allowed these companies to develop into indigenous high-tech juggernauts. In other cases, the state's role in supporting the gradual growth of companies like PetroChina has been a central feature of these companies' emergence.

CONCLUSIONS: GRADUAL REFORM AND CHINA'S QUIET REVOLUTION

Much like the advocates of rapid economic reform, those demanding immediate political and social reform often take for granted the learning that must take place in the face of new institutions. The assumption most often seems to be that, given certain institutional arrangements, individuals will naturally know how to carry out the practices of capitalism. Yet, these assumptions reflect a neoclassical view of human nature in which rational humankind will thrive in a natural environment—free markets. Completely absent from this view are the roles of history, culture, and preexisting institutions, and it is a vision that is far too simplistic to comprehend the challenge of making rational economic and legal systems work in the absence of stable institutions and a history to which they can be tied. The transition from a command to a market economy can be a wrenching experience not only at the institutional level but also at the level of individual practice. Individuals must learn the rules of the market, and new institutions must be set in place long enough to gain stability and legitimacy; these are processes that occur slowly and over time. The government's methodical experimentation with different institutional forms and the party's gradual receding from control over the economy has brought about a "quiet revolution" in the Chinese economy. Yet this is a slow and gradual process and must be placed in the context of China's recent institutional history: when there is no immediate history of a rational-legal economic system, it is impossible to create it in one dramatic moment of institutional change. Thus, the architects of China's transition to capitalism have had success in reforming the economy. They have recognized that the transition to a radically different type of economic system must occur gradually, allowing for the maximum possible institutional stability as economic actors slowly learn the rules of capitalism. Capitalism has arrived in China, and it has done so under the guise of gradual institutional reform under the communist mantle.

Three

When I was doing my doctoral research in China in the early 1990s, like most graduate students, I did not have much money. Overall, China was still much cheaper than the United States, but Shanghai was fairly pricey, so the organization that sponsored my research, the Shanghai Academy of Social Sciences, helped me find a job teaching English to supplement my income. In the class I taught, I had one student, a middle-aged man named Mr. Zhang, who was extremely friendly and asked me often if he could take me out for an evening. It felt odd to me to accept the invitation, because the student had made clear that he wanted to treat me to a night out, and average people in China in the early 1990s had even less money than I did, but eventually I accepted. The evening began with dinner in a private room of an expensive Shanghai restaurant, where we were joined by another individual the student introduced to me as a friend of his, Mr. Li. When the bill came, I offered to pay, but Mr. Zhang insisted on treating. He leaned in close at one point and said cryptically, "Maybe you can help me in another way sometime." A few days later, I received a call from Mr. Li, the "friend" who had accompanied us at dinner. He said that he was interested in practicing his English and that Zhang had told him I would be willing to help him. I was a little confused, as I did not recall making such an agreement, but, remembering Zhang's comment about helping him in "another way," I decided to meet with Li and help him with his English. As the discussion unfolded over three or four meetings, I gradually came to understand that our transaction (me teaching Li English for free) was part of an extended series of social obligations and debts. In short, Zhang had treated me to an expensive dinner in order to manufacture some level of obligation with me, so that I could then be called upon to give Li English lessons. Li, it turned out, was the doctor of Zhang's ailing mother. And while Li did not have enough money to afford English lessons from a foreign teacher, he did control a very valuable asset—the allocation of beds in his overcrowded hospital. Zhang's mother was often sick enough that she required hospital care, and Zhang spent a lot of time worrying about whether she would receive the proper treatment when she was hospitalized. I came to understand that, in essence, my free English lessons to Li were helping to manufacture the debt that would ensure a hospital bed and quality hospital care for Zhang's mother. By the time I understood the web of social relationships I was entangled in, I was fascinated at the extended plans that lay behind what I initially thought was a simple invitation to dinner. It left me wondering about the rules of the gift economy in China. It also left me wondering what would happen to the gift economy as the economic reforms progressed.

This system of exchange—the gift economy—is a social system that is not uncommon in nonmarket economies, and it has played an extremely important role in Chinese society. It is but one of several key systems around which Chinese society was organized when the economic reforms began, one of the consequences of the institutional structure of Chinese society. Social scientific definitions of the word institution generally settle on three characteristics: institutions are organizations, structures, or systems that (1) involve two or more people; (2) involve rules—either formal or informal—that govern behavior; and (3) are stable over time.[2] If we are to understand the ways in which society is transforming as China becomes more integrated into the global economy, we must begin with an examination of the crucial social institutions that governed this society on the eve of the economic reforms. One scholar, Anthony Oberschall, made this point lucidly in an academic symposium on China's transition from plan to market, succinctly laying out the key institutions he observed when living in China in the early 1980s:

> [In the early 1980s] there were three institutions at the core of Chinese society: the family, the work unit in the city and the collective farm in rural China, and the communist party-state. Each Chinese citizen belonged to a family, and every family had been a permanent member of a work unit (*danwei*) or a collective farm. The party-state, accountable only to itself, penetrated and controlled every work unit and collective farm, and thus also every family and every individual. Chinese social organization was rigid and hierarchic. Work units were isolated from each other—even physically bounded by brick walls—with solidarity, loyalty, and collective identity encapsulating members against outsiders.
>
> (1996, 1028)

This set of institutional arrangements helped to create a type of dependence—a reliance by individuals on the party-state system—that Andrew Walder (1986a) has called "principled particularism," meaning that individuals were forced to develop personal relationships that would mitigate their reliance on the organizations and institutions that governed their lives. Individuals were engulfed by the institutions that governed their lives in communist China, as there was very little private space that was not shaped by these institutions in one way or another. As Oberschall put it, it was a "world of total institutions."[3]

In this chapter, I introduce some of the key institutions that govern life in China and discuss the ways in which they have changed as economic reforms have unfolded. I will look at the party-state, systems of allocation (such as work units), and the family. I will also introduce some of the consequences of these institutional arrangements, such as corruption and the gift economy. All of these are social institutions that are important in Chinese life, and all have undergone dramatic changes in the era of economic reform.

THE FAMILY AS A SOCIAL INSTITUTION

For more than two thousand years, the family has been the basic unit of Chinese society and one of the most important social institutions organizing individuals' lives. Yet the twentieth century has witnessed dramatic changes in the structure of the Chinese family. There were two major points of rupture at which the family was dramatically transformed, the first being the transition to the communist system after 1949, and the second being the changes that occurred in the era of economic reform. The traditional structure and values of the Chinese family were significantly weakened during the Communist Revolution and the early years of the communist regime and were further weakened in the era of economic reform. Today, some elements of traditional China have survived and have been interwoven with the new structures and values of the reform era; however, the family as a social institution in China has undergone dramatic changes in the last half century.

Family Structure Before 1949

Throughout the imperial period and before the fall of Qing Dynasty in 1911, the values of the Chinese family were stipulated by Confucian teachings. In very basic terms, Confucian thought can be characterized as a secular moral philosophy with a strong emphasis on social responsibility. Though often thought of as a religion, Confucianism is not built upon notions of heaven and hell, or sin and redemption, but, rather, on a simple sense of doing that which is ethical and right in the world (such as trustworthiness, propriety, altruism, filial piety, and having a sense of shame). Confucius was suspicious of law, believing that laws were for restraining and that a just moral society should emanate from individuals who acted morally and ethically within their family settings. Thus, he believed that morality stood in the realm of family, and family rules governed the lives of individuals (Mote 1989).

With the goal of building a peaceful and harmonious moral world, Confucius saw a family-centered system as the pillar of Chinese society, where an individual's primary duty was to the family, and then to the community or society, and finally to the state. These links among individuals and their families, and eventually the state, were realized through five fundamental relationships among individuals: (1) affection (qin) between parents (primarily fathers) and children (primarily sons); the rules regulating these relationships centered on the concepts of filial piety and respect for elders; (2) righteousness (yi) between ruler and subject (the notion of righteousness between ruler and subject parallels the relationships between fathers and sons, and the rules regulating it include loyalty and respect for the authority); (3) distinction (bie) between men (husbands) and women (wives), a rule that stipulates women's compliance to men; (4) the pecking order (xu) between old and young siblings; and (5) sincerity (xin) between friends. These basic concepts encapsulated social relationships within the Chinese family for more than two thousand years.

The family in the pre-communist era was a patriarchal institution in which fathers ruled with complete authority. When the state intervened in the realm of the family, fathers were heavily favored. For example, within the family structure, fathers committing a given crime against their sons were punished far more lightly than sons who committed the same crime against their fathers. The same was true of husbands harming their wives. Extended families became the social fabric of a society in which the state was significantly removed from the lives of individuals. Functioning as a social security system of sorts, several generations often lived under one roof, creating a self-sufficient institution that provided mutual support among family members, including the care of children and the elderly. A certain amount of wealth would be pooled in the form of lineage land, the income from which would pay for the upkeep of ancestral temples and graveyards, and for teachers who served as instructors of lineage schools.

Arranged marriage was common, with matchmakers arranging marriages for the mutual benefit of both families. Marriages between children of powerful lineages were carefully negotiated by the parents, and great care was taken to preserve lineages and bring together powerful clans. Marriage transfers in traditional China usually consisted of direct and indirect dowries—the groom's family made a contribution, which was returned with the bride as part of the dowry. Bride prices varied across classes, and marriage transfers were often built upon social prestige. While elites used dowries to maintain their wealth and enhance their status, poor families often "sold" their daughters to finance their sons' marriages. Elites in the imperial period organized their extended families around immense patriarchal power, smothering the younger generation's pursuit of individual freedom.

During the Imperial Period, the state was conspicuously

absent within the Chinese family before the building of the modern Chinese state in 1911. However, following the Nationalist Revolution, the established relationships and family structures prescribed by Confucian thought were disrupted by the rising militarization of Chinese society with the warlord period (1912–27), the period of Nationalist Party control (1927–49), and the occupation of China by the Japanese Army (1937–45), each of which established their own social controls. Despite more intervention by state power into Chinese families during this time period, the state still largely relied on family-run social control much more than state-based social control. As an "official" (guan) space with limited social control, the state was still removed from the "private" (si) realm of individuals and families, and also the "public" (gong) field where the clan systems prevailed.

The Post-1949 Family

Following the Communist Revolution, the Chinese family underwent considerable changes. The revolution and the mass movements under Mao Zedong's regime set out to break up traditional familial bonds and establish an ideologically based egalitarian social order. Confucian ideals were recast as the "Four Olds" (sijiu)—old ideas, old habits, old customs, and old culture—and were attacked, destroyed, and replaced by communist ideology. During this period, the communist state began to encroach upon all aspects of individuals' lives to a much greater extent than ever before.[4]

In the Maoist era, the attack on ancestor worship and lineage organization struck directly at the cultural and religious core of the extended family. Individuals and their families were subjugated to the greater goal of running a communist country. Collectivization of the economy and the elimination of private property destroyed much of the economic motivation that had previously shaped family loyalties. In urban areas, both men and women were organized by the work-unit systems that provided them with social welfare (income, housing, medical care, and the like) and also facilitated the Chinese Communist Party's centralized political control over individuals. In rural China, communes were set up and rural families were organized around collectives that functioned as the basic units of agricultural production until the late 1970s. Thus, the state destroyed the power and authority of patriarchs and the material basis for the clan-based system.

These institutions and organizational practices continued to break down family bonds throughout the communist period. The fates of individuals and their families were tightly tied to the state through party membership and party loyalty. This was most dramatically demonstrated during the Cultural Revolution (1966–76), when Chinese families were broken apart and family members were encouraged to favor state ideology over the shared family values inherited from Confucian ideals. The Red Guards, supported by Mao during the early period of the Cultural Revolution, were encouraged to challenge the older generation and their traditional authority. Many people had to separate themselves from "class enemies" within their families in order to show their loyalty to the party. After Mao betrayed his revolutionary followers and sent them to the countryside for "reeducation," many families fell farther apart, as family members spent years away from each other.[5]

Beyond tightening the ties between the individuals and the party-state, the communist state eliminated many family rituals and ceremonies, as well as the traditional social order that arose out of them. The most striking characteristic of the family in communist China was that women—at least in theory— were elevated to a position equal to men. Women were assigned to work in the urban work-unit system or the rural collectives. The Marriage Law of 1950 outlawed many harsh practices directed against women, including arranged marriages, concubinage, dowries, and child betrothals. Article 2 of the Marriage Law stipulates, for example, that a marriage must be "based on the free choice of partners . . . and on equality between man and woman. . . ." Article 3 declares, "Marriage upon arbitrary decision by any third party . . . shall be prohibited." And Articles 9 and 13 entitle women to the same status within their families as men, stipulating, "Husband and wife shall have equal status in the family," and, "The property acquired by the husband and the wife during the period in which they are under the contract of marriage shall be in their joint possession. . . ." Women were also granted the legal right to file for a divorce. Marriage transfers still existed, but they became less predictable. Marriage was commonly delayed until somewhat later in life, with the encouragement of the law. In addition, lavish dowries and wedding feasts were stigmatized as feudal extravagance in both urban and rural areas under Mao's rule. The land reform changed the ability of rural elites to transfer land as part of a dowry. Even though second-generation families in the Mao era began to revert to some of the old traditions surrounding marriage, most of the rituals and ceremonies fell out of practice in communist China.

Since the late 1970s, the economic reforms have brought about another revolutionary change to the Chinese family, with the party's control being gradually withdrawn from the lives of individuals. In urban China, most people have continued to receive housing and health care from their work units, but younger generations depend less on the state redistributive system, as increasing numbers find work in the private and foreign sectors. Economic liberalization, the resulting economic boom—especially in the coastal areas—and changes in the restrictions against migration have led rural

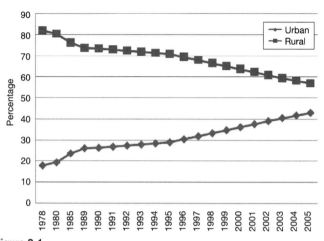

Figure 3.1

Percentage of urban and rural population.

Source: Statistical Yearbook of China, 2006.

men and women to migrate into cities (see Figure 3.1) to seek employment often far away from their homes. Young women form a big part of the labor force that is steadily migrating to urban and coastal areas—a fact that has fundamental consequences for the structure of the Chinese family in rural areas. The liberalization of state policies in the reform era has also led to the reemergence of many traditional practices that were eliminated by the communist regime. Wedding ceremonies and dowry practices, for example, have returned in rural regions as a way of reinforcing social status for new elites of the reform era. Marriages and deaths are marked by important rituals that display the importance of continuing the family lineage, especially in rural China.

State Control over the Family and Population

Despite the reduction of the state's direct control over family life during the reform era, state control over population growth has nevertheless continued to play a significant part in shaping the Chinese family and economy.[6] Since 1949, the Chinese population has more than doubled, from 565 million in 1953 to nearly 1.3 billion at the 2000 Census. The country has undergone five stages of population growth during this period. The first baby boom in China occurred between 1949 and 1957, when the birth rates were fairly high (32–38 per thousand). During this time period, death rates were remarkably reduced due to a more egalitarian distribution of food and universal (albeit rudimentary) medical care. Consequently, natural growth rates were high (16–25 percent). The first real push for population control began in 1953, with the passage of laws legalizing abortion. Following that, a series of propaganda campaigns—such as the formation of birth control study groups in 1954—made it very clear that the state would control all aspects of individuals' lives, including their family plans. In 1956, the government actively pushed for limitations on childbirth but to little real effect. Overall, this period saw the creation of a new institutional and moral environment for Chinese family planning.

The period 1958–61 witnessed high death rates caused by the catastrophic policies of the Great Leap Forward, along with decreasing birth rates and natural growth rates.[7] But as normal conditions were restored, the death rate fell to 10 per thousand in 1962 from 25.6 per thousand in 1960, and the postcrisis birthrate and natural growth rates were very high, causing the period to be known as the second baby boom. The birth rate in 1963 was 43.3 per thousand, and it remained high until 1970. The natural growth rate remained at about 25–33 per thousand. The Chinese government attempted a new family planning program in 1964, but it was disrupted by the Cultural Revolution, which began in 1966.

It was not until the 1970s that real attention was paid to the problems of population growth. The *wan xi shao* ("late" marriage, "long" birth intervals, and "fewer" children) campaign was enforced and led to rapid reductions in the birth rate (down to 18 per thousand during this period) and natural growth rate (down to 12 per thousand). Following this campaign, the fertility rate declined from 4.2 in 1974 to 3.2 in 1976 to 2.2 in 1980. The solution to the population problem, known as China's one-child policy, was launched by the government in the early 1980s. In 1982, a national census advised by the United Nations counted the Chinese population at over one billion; but even earlier than this, officials had a sense of the magnitude of the problem, which was that China's population would soon be too large for the country to feed itself. In September 1980, Hua Guofeng announced this policy, and austere measures were subsequently enforced. Over the next two years, in addition to a propaganda campaign, the State Planning Commission oversaw compulsory intrauterine device insertion and, in some cases, compulsory sterilization of 16.4 million women, as well as sterilization of 4 million men. In addition, the Chinese government created various disincentives through the work-unit system to enforce the one-child policy in urban areas, particularly in the 1980s. The couples that violated the one-child policy were subject to high taxes, loss of jobs, decrease in wages, loss of benefits from the work units, and loss of bonuses for the entire work group, in some cases. In rural areas, the household incentive system was set up to offer a premium on family-based labor for those families who would comply with this policy.

While China's one-child policy has decreased the population growth rates and arguably contributed to China's rapid economic growth in the past twenty-five years, it has remained a subject of considerable controversy both in academia and in the population policy field. There is little doubt that the

Table 3.1 Demographic changes in China

	1978	1989	1997	2001	2005
Family					
Total number of households	206,410,000	270,780,000	328,900,000	353,300,000	395,590,000
Average household size, urban areas	NA	3.55	3.19	3.1	2.96
Average household size, rural areas	NA	4.86	4.35	4.15	4.08
Marriages and divorces					
Registered number of marriages	5,978,000	9,372,000	9,141,000	8,050,000	8,231,000
Number of divorces	285,000	753,000	1,198,000	1,250,000	1,785,000
Housing					
Per capita living space, urban areas (sq. ft.)	72.11	145.31	191.6	269	280.94
Per capita living space, rural areas (sq. ft.)	87.11	185.14	242.19	300.32	319.69

Source: Statistical Yearbook China, 2006.

Table 3.2 Basic statistics on national population census

	1953	1964	1982	1990	2000
Total population	594,350,000	694,580,000	1,008,180,000	1,133,680,000	1,265,830,000
Male	307,990,000	356,520,000	519,440,000	584,950,000	653,550,000
Female	286,360,000	338,060,000	488,740,000	548,730,000	612,280,000
Sex ratio	107.56	105.46	106.3	106.6	106.74
Average family size	4.33	4.43	4.41	3.96	3.44
Population by age group (%)					
0–14	36.28	40.69	33.59	27.69	22.89
15–64	59.31	55.75	61.5	66.74	70.15
65 and over	4.41	3.56	4.91	5.57	6.96
Nationality population					
Han nationality	547,280,000	654,560,000	940,880,000	1,042,480,000	1,159,400,000
Percentage to total population	39.94	94.24	93.32	91.96	91.59
Minority nationalities	3532	4002	6730	9120	10643
Percentage to total population	6.06	5.76	6.68	8.04	8.41
Population by residence					
Urban population	77,260,000	127,100,000	210,820,000	299,710,000	458,440,000
Rural population	505,340,000	567,480,000	797,360,000	833,970,000	807,390,000

Source: *Statistical Yearbook of China*, 2003.

enforcement of the one-child policy in the reform era has brought about crucial social changes in family structure, as well as a series of social problems. Family size has decreased, and an entire generation of "only children" is expected to support a disproportionately old and retired population in the near future. With the gradual withdrawal of state support for the elderly, their care has grown to depend more on the family system, thereby exacerbating this demographic problem. Among the social implications is also a generation of "only children," who have been nurtured by their parents and four grandparents, leading to a phenomenon that some authors have referred to as the "little emperor syndrome."[8] Some demographers note that China also faces the prospect of an insufficient labor force in the decades to come.

The most serious and often noted social problem linked to the one-child policy is female infanticide and abandonment of female children. Historically and culturally, sons in Chinese families are responsible for taking care of the elderly, along with carrying the family name and inheriting the family property. As a result, male offspring are preferred in Chinese families, especially in rural areas, and female offspring suffer accordingly. Female infanticide has become relatively common—it has been estimated that 200,000 female babies have been killed each year since the 1980s. Abandonment of female children is also common, though no estimates on the numbers are available. Many of the girls' births go unregistered, causing them to lose access to many legal benefits, including educational opportunities and other forms of social welfare. In addition, the use of advanced technologies such as ultrasound has increased the numbers for female infanticide, thus leaving China with a significant gender gap. Official statistics placed the sex ratio at birth (male/female) in China at 116.86 in the 2000 Census, a figure outrageously high compared to the natural ratio of lower than 105.[9] This is up from 108.5 in 1982, 110.9 in 1987, and 111.3 in 1990.[10]

Entering into the new century, the Chinese government has not yet officially relaxed its one-child policy, but in 2002, the Population and Family Planning Law was passed to rationalize the state's control over family planning. According to the law, equal importance is attached to measures providing contraception services and promoting the one-child policy, beyond simply ensuring the control of the country's population. Those who have an extra child, according to the law, must pay for the extra burden they impose on society because they will use more public resources.

THE STATE AND STATE ALLOCATION SYSTEMS

The state is a crucial institution in Chinese society. In a state-dominated society like China, on the eve of the economic reforms, the state is forever present, setting the rules by which individuals live and finding more subtle ways to control behavior and command loyalty. From the fall of the Qing Dynasty through the building of the People's Republic of China following the Communist Revolution, the role of the state in Chinese society has changed in critical ways over the course of three periods: (1) in the precommunist era, the state was an instrument of symbolic and cultural power, with some limited elements of social control, but it was far removed from the private realm of individuals and families; (2) in the communist era, the state steadily penetrated down to the level of the individual; and (3) in the period of economic reform, the state's control over society has been steadily receding.

The Imperial Period

Before the establishment of Mao's communist regime, the imperial government ruled largely through a cultural power and family-centered social system that Confucian thought prescribed. After the fall of the Qing Dynasty, more direct systems of coercion were imposed upon the Chinese. For instance, in rural China, gentry families began to use access to government offices to build up networks of power, becoming "buffers" between the modern Chinese state and individual families in rural society (Fei 1946). Despite more intervention by the state into the life of the Chinese family during this period, the state still relied primarily on family-run social control. The *baojia* system was the key link between the state and family in late imperial China. Stemming from the Qing judicial system and strengthened by the Nationalist's rule, the *baojia* system was a locally autonomous institution that made the rural elite responsible for enforcing public order and collecting taxes for the state. Ten families (households) formed a *bao*, and ten *bao* formed a *jia*, which contained one hundred families. The heads of each *baojia* were responsible for social control within their *baojia*. Based on the family as the primary unit, the *baojia* system placed "the collective responsibilities for the proper and law-abiding conduct of all its members" (Yang 1959, 103).

The Communist Era: The Party and the Political System

Originally established in 1921, the Chinese Communist Party (CCP) is China's only ruling party, holding exclusive political and institutional power over the country. From 1949 until very recently—the mid-1990s—the party and the state overlapped in almost every aspect of governance, as the party exercised firm control over state bodies through interlocking organizations. In practice, all decisions of central government units had to be approved by the party, which meant that de facto political power rested in the hands of the party. All top positions are held by communist party members, further bolstering the party's power. In addition, Communist Party branches exist within all central and local government organizations. In the prereform era, these branches were the actual decision makers. In the early years of the economic reforms, they removed themselves from direct decision making, but they still kept a watchful eye over the decisions of virtually every governmental office. Today, the role of communist party offices is receding further and further from direct control over the governmental offices they used to run; however, all key officers of government organizations are Communist Party members. And, although recently the residents in more and more villages have begun to elect non-party members as chairs of the Village Automatic Administration Committees, all of the leadership positions from the township governments on up are still occupied by party members.[11]

Within the CCP, the Political Bureau and its Standing Committee are the real centers of political power of the People's Republic of China (PRC). Although the Politburo Standing Committee (PSC) has existed since the beginning of the PRC, the actual power wielded by the PSC has varied over time. During the Cultural Revolution, the PSC was essentially powerless, while real power was exercised by the Revolutionary Committees set up by Mao Zedong. Deng Xiaoping revived the PSC's political power after he took over and built the second generation of CCP leadership. Recently, the former president of China, Jiang Zemin, stepped down from this powerful committee to make way for a fourth generation of leadership led by Hu Jintao. Currently the PSC, elected by the CCP's Central Committee at the 2002 Sixteenth Party Congress, is composed of nine members: Hu Jintao, Huang Ju, Jia Qinglin, Li Changchun, Luo Gan, Wen Jiabao, Wu Bangguo, Wu Guanzheng, and Zeng Qinghong.[12] Among them, Hu Jintao is president of the People's Republic of China, general secretary of the Communist Party of China, and Chairman of the Central

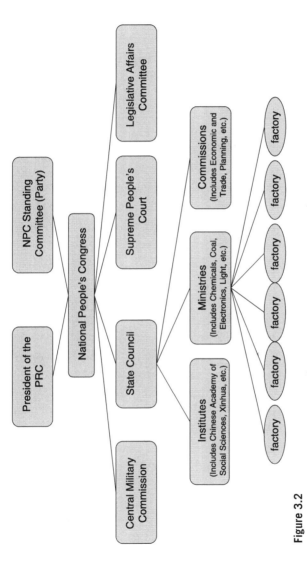

Figure 3.2
Structure of the PRC Government.

Military Commission, as of 2004; Wen Jiabao is premier of the State Council of the PRC; and Wu Bangguo is Chairman of the Standing Committee of the National People's Congress. Although Hu Jintao has begun to institute certain changes within the CCP, Jiang's influence may continue, given that six out of the nine new members of the PSC—Huang Ju, Jia Qinglin, Li Changchun, Wu Bangguo, Wu Guanzheng, and Zeng Qinghong—are Jiang protégés.

The Reform Era: From Revolutionary Party to Governing Party

In the past twenty-five years, there have been two major transitions within China's political institutions, both of which demonstrate the CCP's attempt to maintain its political legitimacy in the reform era through self-transformation. One is the changing relationships between the party and the government. Though he did not publicly express an intent to make radical changes within China's political system at the beginning of the economic reforms, Deng did move to rationalize the government by replacing Mao's dictum of "politics in command" (*zhengzhi weigang*) with "economics in command" (*jingji weigang*), essentially reversing Mao's creation of a "revolutionary government" in 1957. To ensure the success of the economic reform agenda, Deng effected the removal of the party from the daily management of the state system and economic enterprises (*dangzheng fenkai* and *dangqi fenkai*). Although the party remains the ultimate institutional authority and there are still conservative voices within the CCP leadership, reforms within China's political system have achieved critical changes.

The encouragement of grassroots democracy (discussed in greater detail in Chapter 7) is among the important reforms influencing China's political institutions today. Faced with serious local corruption in the late 1980s, the CCP realized it was losing legitimacy in rural areas. As a result, a law on village committee organization, stipulating that directors, deputy directors, and members of village committees would be chosen by direct democratic elections, was introduced in 1987 on a trial basis. In 1989, a similar law, defining neighborhood committees in cities as autonomous organizations, took effect. Since then, village leadership has changed five times through direct elections in most provinces, autonomous regions, and municipalities across China,[13] and urban community leaders have been directly elected in twenty Chinese cities. Apart from the heads of autonomous organizations, deputies to the People's Congresses at county and township levels are also chosen through direct elections, in accordance with the election laws for local organizations. The deputies at county and township levels, who serve for five years and three years, respectively, number about three million nationwide. According to the Ministry of Civil Affairs of China, to date, more than 700 million Chinese have been involved in voting for their community leaders and deputies to the People's Congress at county and township levels though direct elections.

The National People's Congress (NPC), China's legislature, has moved far from the "hand-raising machine" or "rubber-stamp" institutions that have historically operated in Leninist political systems. By turning party decrees into state laws, Leninist legislatures functioned to provide the party with "a veneer of legal-democratic legitimacy" (Tanner 1999, 100). Although China's NPC today is far from a liberalized legislature with genuine accountability, and it is still subject to the party's manipulation and intervention, the NPC's lawmaking and policy influence has been greatly transformed in the past two decades. Tanner (1999) cites a number of new phenomena revealed by NPC voting data that show the increasing institutional capacity and influence of the NPC. First of all, it is now rare for proposed laws to pass unanimously, as before.

Second, it is no longer the case that all laws pass. In addition, large dissenting-vote totals are becoming relatively common. As Murray Tanner notes, of the full NPC's twenty-three known votes on personnel appointment and other motions in the 1990s, six of them received dissenting vote totals of over one-fifth. The political power and leadership position of the NPC over the State Council only appeared on paper before, but today, the State Council has had little choice but to make changes in its legislative drafts in order to get approval by the NPC deputies and leadership.

In 2001, the CCP made another notable stride in the form of the "three representatives" theory proposed by Jiang Zemin—the former president and general secretary of the CCP. By permitting private entrepreneurs to be recruited into the party, the CCP announced that it not only represents the traditionally represented group of workers and peasants but also the interests of capitalists ("advanced social productive forces") and intellectuals ("advanced cultural forces"). Over 100,000 private entrepreneurs reportedly applied to join the party in the weeks immediately after Jiang's announcement (Dickson 2003). At the Sixteenth Party Congress in 2002, this theory was enshrined in the CCP's constitution. The moment indicated a remarkable change in CCP ideology, even if it seemed out of date with China's rapid change. Yet, this recognition also took the CCP one step further away from the revolutionary party it claimed to be. The CCP and its new generation of leadership can hardly claim them to represent a "revolutionary" party after twenty-five years of economic reforms and social change occurring in China.

The Communist State and the Work Unit System[14]

The Chinese state under Mao was often referred to as a totalitarian regime under which society was atomized to a large extent and the social ties between individuals and families were destroyed.[15] Political pressure from the state down to the individual, secret police surveillance, and the intensive mass campaigns (discussed in Chapter 2) initiated by Mao were the main tools by which the totalitarian regime functioned. While the party-state itself is a large-scale institution that has shaped life in communist China, it is impossible to fully understand the role of the communist state without understanding the fundamental institutions around which communist societies are organized.

In the Chinese setting, the work unit was the key institution of state allocation that organized Chinese urban society for over thirty years of communist party rule. In the prereform era, the work-unit system of China functioned as a unit of economic production, social welfare, and political control. Economically, when the communists came to power, one of the first things they did was eliminate private ownership of economic organizations and establish different levels of state-owned industries in urban areas. The work-unit system was developed to bring together a centrally planned economy with the redistribution of social welfare benefits. It was through their work units that urban citizens could obtain housing, medical care, and job opportunities. Moreover, the system allowed the party-state to directly monitor and supervise individuals within the work unit. Work units established security surveillance and secret dossiers (*danan*) on individuals, thus playing an important role in maintaining political stability in communist China. Martin Whyte and William Parish's classic book on the subject, *Urban Life in Contemporary China*, describes the ways in which work units and neighborhood committees shaped life in China from 1949 to the early 1980s. Through work units and neighborhood committees, Chinese communist bureaucracy permeated urban society, leaving few barriers between the individual and the state. The communist state had managed to largely eliminate urban poverty by restricting migration into the cities, maximizing urban employment, and maintaining a relatively egalitarian distribution system and a high degree of economic security. The system led to high stability in jobs and residence, involvement and familiarity with neighbors and coworkers, minimal differentiation of consumption patterns and life styles, and high female work participation. But it was also a system of intense monitoring and social control by the party-state. As Whyte and Parish put it, "Chinese urban residents [were] victims rather than masters of their own fate" (1984, 295)

Another classic book on this topic, Andrew Walder's *Communist Neo-Traditionalism: Work and Authority in Chinese Industry*, provides insightful analysis into the ways in which work units established the economic, political, and personal dependence of workers on their work units and their leaders, a set of relationships that formed the basis of authority relations and political stability. The creation of patron-client relations between managers and workers became the primary way that state power was exercised in communist China. Walder (1995b, 1995c, 1995e) has further explored the institutional mechanisms that served to maintain order within this system, including organized dependence (the dependence of subordinates on their superiors for the satisfaction of needs and career opportunities), monitoring capacity (the capacity of superiors to obtain information about the activities of subordinates), and sanctioning capacity (the ability to reward or punish the political behavior of subordinates). These relationships were central to the ways in which the communist state institutionalized control over society, maintaining stability of state power even during the chaos of the Cultural Revolution.

The Receding Role of the State in the Reform Era

It is the breakdown of these institutional bases of power that have led to the decline of the communist state's power in the reform era. Deng's reform program, initiated in 1978, made economic development a priority for modernizing China and aimed to build a market economy while leaving the party-state intact. Despite the focus on economic reform, the fact that the political, economic, and social systems were intertwined in the past meant that reforming the economy would lead to fundamental political and social changes as well. As I discussed in the previous chapter, as of the early 1980s, individuals, collectives, and local areas were empowered to make their own economic decisions. And with the reemergence of the private sector, individuals increasingly had the freedom to pursue their fortunes in the newly emerging markets of the Chinese economy. Through these two critical changes, the party-state removed itself as the key economic decision maker, and, with the emergence of the private sector, it broke the dependence of individuals on the state because it no longer held monopoly control over livelihoods. The party and government offices no longer stand over the shoulders of economic actors in the industrial economy. State officials still hold—and can use—their power to trade official favors for other benefits (e.g., housing) and pursue personal profits, but they have lost most of their control over the distribution of goods. In today's markets, individuals can access nearly all necessities in their everyday lives. Thus, the relations of authority based on the patron-client ties in the workplace have broken down, and the organizational dependency of individuals on their work units and superiors has been largely eliminated.

In rural areas, decollectivization in the late 1970s transferred production decisions from the commune to the family. The establishment of the "household responsibility system" afterward provided peasants with more economic resources, opportunities, and choices than could be obtained through the party in the prereform era. The collective industrial sector emerged especially in towns and villages in the 1980s, offering peasants new job opportunities in the emerging rural industrial sector. Once peasants began to farm land rented from the state on a household basis, establish their household enterprises, and make their own economic decisions, the bases of communist power and the grassroots mobility of the Communist Party in rural areas greatly eroded. These declining institutional mechanisms, which once organized communist urban and rural worlds in China, have triggered a "quiet revolution from within" (Walder 1995b, 1995c, 1995e) in China's reform era.

UNINTENDED SOCIAL CONSEQUENCES

The declining role of the state in economic activities in the reform era has had unintended consequences, confronting the party-state with a series of challenges from within and outside the political system. Official corruption is among the most serious crises with which the Chinese government has had to deal. Corruption comes in two primary forms—economic and noneconomic (Lu 2000). Within each of these two categories are three additional subtypes of corruption—graft (bribery), rent seeking (resource extraction), and prebendalism (perquisites and benefits connected to a public office). China was rated one of the most corrupt countries in the world by Transparency International in the 1990s. Though recently China has been removed from this blacklist,[16] the CCP in the reform era seems to have a greater problem with corruption than at any other time since its establishment. The massive scale of official corruption in the late 1980s was one of the catalysts of the 1989 Tiananmen student movement, and many commentators explain the initiation of village-level elections as a response to the widespread corruption among local officials in rural areas. In the past decade, the CCP has initiated a number of political campaigns to curb official corruption, and today the central government seems more determined than ever to eliminate the problem. However, among the challenges China faces in dealing with official corruption is the very nature of its political system. The CCP still holds enormous and exclusive political power in China, which provides many opportunities for officials to abuse their power and trade favors for profitable deals. There is strong evidence that China is well on the way to rationalizing its rule by law, but during the long-term transition toward that goal, there has been much room for abuse of the emergent system.

Xiaobo Lu's (2000) work in this area provides an insightful explanation of why a revolutionary party like the CCP has trouble institutionalizing a modern bureaucracy that should bring about impersonal, rational offices and functions. Lu argues that corruption among communist cadres is not a phenomenon of the post-Mao reform period, nor is it caused by purely economic incentives in the emerging marketplace. Rather, it is the result of a long process of what he calls "organizational involution," which began as the communist party-state embarked on the path of Maoist "continuous revolution." Lu argues that there is a fundamental contradiction inherent in the routinization of revolutionary movements. After a revolutionary party comes to power through a wave of change, and political offices are occupied by the same revolutionary personalities who brought about the change, these individuals are often more committed to the revolutionary goals and the process of change that brought them to power than they are with maintaining a strict organizational structure. Eventually, the prescribed organizational norms become unglued from the value system of the party members who brought about change in the first place. These members continue to act through personalistic, informal modes, and organizational deviance becomes inevitable.

In the CCP's case, after the Anti-Rightist Campaign of 1957, when many of the party's policies of the early years were questioned, Mao adopted an aggressive policy of revolutionary reform as a way of furthering his communist legacy. This period made it impossible for revolutionary goals to be routinized in organizational norms and practices. The 1966–76 Cultural Revolution that followed nearly eliminated China's bureaucratic system and made it very difficult to develop institutionalized routines. The CCP gradually lost its ability to sustain officialdom with either the Leninist-cadre or Weberian-bureaucratic modes of integration. Instead, the party unintentionally created a neotraditional ethos, mode of operation, and set of authority relations among its cadres that have fostered official corruption.

Apart from the internal crisis, the CCP has had to deal with challenges from the societal level, even under so-called totalitarian controls. In order to institutionalize political control, the CCP established the dual institutional structure of the state-society relationship in the communist era: strong organizational control over the society by the state (Whyte and Parish 1984), and the organizational dependency of the individuals on socialist economic institutions (Walder 1986a). By monopolizing the resources for organizing private interests, the communist state effectively denied the legitimacy of any organized interests outside its control. However, according to Zhou (1993a), such an institutional structure of state socialism actually facilitates collective action based on "unorganized interests" and systematically transforms individual behavior into "collective action." The structure of the system reduces barriers to collective action by producing "large numbers" of individuals at structurally similar positions vis-à-vis the state and with similar sets of experiences and interests.

Zhou's theory explains the puzzle of why, without any independent organization, large-scale social movements have repeatedly erupted in Chinese society during the period of communist party rule. On a number of occasions, massive numbers of individuals were able to spontaneously converge to express their common interests despite the tight control exercised by the communist state. For example, when Mao encouraged the intellectuals to speak out on the ideologies and policies of the CCP in the spring of 1957, the immediate groundswell of discontent was largely unanticipated by the CCP. Mao put an immediate stop to this "collective action" by labeling intellectuals as rightists and sending many of them to the countryside for "reeducation." Seemingly spontaneous moments of collective action also seemed to occur during the Cultural Revolution; upon the death of Zhou Enlai in 1976; during the Democracy Wall movement in 1978–79; and during the reform era, when a million students occupied Tiananmen Square for six weeks in 1989 in pursuit of political freedom. In all of these cases, individuals in structurally similar positions vis-à-vis the state came together with common interests and common grievances to rebel against the party-state system.

One final note on corruption: Despite the significant over-representation of reports of Chinese corruption in the popular media (Guthrie 1999, chapter 8), it is important to note that China today is not nearly as corrupt as it is generally reported to be. According to Transparency International's most recent Corruption Perceptions Index (2006), China scored exactly the same as several other countries at similar stages of institutional development (Brazil, India, Mexico) and significantly better than countries like Russia.

Social Networks (Guanxi) and the Gift Economy

It is nearly impossible to travel to China and avoid being confronted by the view (if not the reality) that *guanxi* is a central part of social life in China. There are two distinct concepts, both of which are important for discussing the role of *guanxi* in Chinese society. The first is that of social relations, or *guanxi* itself. This concept is often used to denote some type of friendship, kinship, or other type of social tie—as in, "I have a [good] relationship with him" [*wo gen ta you guanxi*]. A second concept, which is sometimes used interchangeably with *guanxi* but is more accurately referred to as *guanxi xue* (literally, "the study of *guanxi*"), is the gift economy. The gift economy is a concept that implies the use of social relations to "manufacture obligation and indebtedness" in order to accomplish some set of future tasks (Yang 1994, 6). The Chinese can hardly claim to have the only society where social networks (*guanxi*) or a gift economy (*guanxi xue*) play important roles in social life, but China scholars have, in general, not questioned the centrality of *guanxi* in Chinese society, culture, and everyday life. There are two major theoretical orientations toward understanding *guanxi* in Chinese society. One is the cultural perspective, which views *guanxi* and *guanxi xue* as products of deep-seated aspects of Chinese culture; the second is an institutional perspective, which maintains that *guanxi* and *guanxi xue* arise from specific types of institutional relationships and constraints.[17] Recent debate around these two approaches is based upon disagreement over the extent to which *guanxi* is something unique to China and Chinese culture or whether it is an outgrowth of the institutional arrangements that are common to command economies.

The cultural orientation is based on the concept of *guanxi* as a distinctly Chinese phenomenon, inextricably linked to Chinese culture and social structure (e.g., Yang 1994). The scholars adhering to this approach trace *guanxi* to its enduring significance in traditional Chinese philosophy, in particular its stress on the centrality of social interaction in the formation of the individual's identity. Among the Confucian-based discourse that placed social relationships at its center, Liang Shuming's relations-based (*guanxi benwei*) perspective (King 1985) and Fei Xiaotong's model of "different mode of association" (*chaxu geju*) (Fei 1992) are often cited to demonstrate the centrality of *guanxi* as a cultural element of being "Chinese" regardless of time or place. According to this view, Chinese culture creates a deep psychological tendency for individuals to actively cultivate and manipulate social relations for instrumental ends. In the context of China's economic reforms, the cultural approach stresses the increasing roles of *guanxi* and social networking in doing business and attributes the practices of *guanxi xue* in contemporary China to the cultural characteristics of Chinese society. The scholars holding this view contend that *guanxi* and *guanxi xue* will not decline over the course of China's economic transition, since they are something fundamentally Chinese, or alternately, that *guanxi* practice may decline in some social domains, but it may find new areas in which to flourish, such as business transactions, and may display new social forms and expressions (Yang 2002).

The institutional orientation considers *guanxi* to be a general phenomenon less related to Chineseness and more a response to specific institutional and historical conditions that happen to exist in China. It is the institutional structure of Chinese society at certain time periods that facilitates or encourages the reliance on networks to accomplish tasks in Chinese society. *guanxi* practice is thus no different from the gift economy in other societies that are at similar or analogous stages of development. Particularly during the communist era, a shortage economy combined with a weak legal infrastructure facilitated the reliance on networking and trust as fundamental parts of transactions in communist China. Andrew Walder's (1986a) institutional analysis of the work-unit system, as discussed above, illuminates the use of *guanxi* in the form of patron-client relations as a response to a situation in which powerful officials controlled access to scarce necessities and job opportunities during the communist era. It follows logically that as the institutions of these developing economies and societies change, so too should the reliance on social networks. Thus, from the institutional perspective, *guanxi* is an institutionally defined system—a system that depends on the institutional structure of society rather than on culture—that is changing alongside the institutional changes of the reform era (Guthrie 1998b, 2002a). In general, culture offers important perspectives in understanding the ways in which *guanxi* and *guanxi* practice function in Chinese society, and it would be inaccurate to claim that *guanxi* does not matter in China. However, the empirical reality of the industrial and commercial economies in China today suggests that practices and perceptions of *guanxi* are changing in important ways in the urban industrial economy, and these changes suggest a trend that does not fully fit with theories that emphasize the cultural importance of *guanxi* in Chinese society or that see an increasing role of *guanxi* and *guanxi* practice throughout China in the economic transition.

Guanxi *and* Guanxi *Practice in the Urban Industrial Economy*

In the urban industrial economy, there is a growing emphasis on the distinction between social relationships (*guanxi*) and the use of these social relationships in the gift economy (*guanxi* practice), and managers in the industrial and commercial economies are increasingly likely to distance themselves from the institution of *guanxi* practice in the economic transition. While managers often view social connections as important in business transactions, they view the importance of *guanxi* in market relationships as secondary to the market imperatives of price and quality. Increasingly today, managers will often say things like, "*Guanxi* only helps if you are competitive" (Guthrie 1999). In addition, managers do not view the use of personal connections in China as being any different from the ways in which business is conducted in economies throughout the world.

Currently, the Chinese government is engaged in the project of constructing a rational-legal system that will govern the decisions and practices of economic actors. This is especially true for large-scale organizations that are more closely monitored by the state administrative offices than are individuals or small-scale entrepreneurs. Through the construction of this rational-legal system, the state pushes actors—especially large-scale industrial firms—to approach economic activities in ways that are sanctioned by the rational-legal system. In addition, as the government continues to place economic responsibilities directly on the shoulders of firms, organizations are forced to consider many factors that make economic sense, many of which often lie in conflict with the use of social connections. Once again, the argument here is not that *guanxi* and *guanxi xue* are insignificant in Chinese society. Clearly these practices are important in many aspects of Chinese society. However, whether they are important for "all types of commercial transactions" and whether their importance has "increased at an accelerated rate" (Yang 1994, 167, 147) in the economic transition are empirical questions. To a large extent, the empirical data indicate that the "art" of *guanxi* (i.e., *guanxi* practice) may in fact occupy a diminishing role in

China's urban industrial and commercial economies as the economic transition progresses.

In China today, powerful economic actors often pay increasing attention to the laws, rules, and regulations that are part of the emerging rational-legal system. Many managers of large industrial organizations increasingly view *guanxi* practice as unnecessary and dangerous in light of new regulations and prohibitions against such approaches to official procedures. Understanding how the system of *guanxi* interacts with the rational-legal system at the state level and formal rational bureaucratic structures that are emerging at the firm level is important for understanding how this system is changing in the reform era, and it is important for understanding the reforms more generally. Changes surrounding *guanxi* in the reform era vary with a firm's position in the state administrative hierarchy (Guthrie 1998b, 1999, 2002a). The higher a firm is in China's administrative hierarchy, the less likely the general or vice general manager of the firm is to view *guanxi* practice—that is, using connections to get things done—as important in the economic transition. Conversely, the lower a firm is in the administrative hierarchy, the more likely the firm's general manager is to view *guanxi* practice as important to success in the economic transition. Attitudes toward *guanxi* practice also vary with a number of organizational factors, ranging from the background of the firm's general manager to whether or not the organization has a joint venture with a foreign company.

Of the two types of *guanxi* that shape action in China today (i.e., *guanxi* and *guanxi* practice), *guanxi* practice lies in conflict with the rational-legal system emerging at the state level (i.e., formal laws, policies, and rational procedures), while *guanxi*, more broadly conceived, is often viewed as a necessary part of the market reforms and business transactions in a market economy. The importance of this distinction is increasing in the urban industrial economy for two reasons. First, large industrial organizations are monitored by the state much more closely than individual actors in the economy are. Given that the official discourse surrounding *guanxi* practice is negative, it is not surprising that large-scale industrial organizations are more careful about the extent to which they engage in this institution. In addition to the fact that markets are becoming increasingly competitive, the very existence of markets changes the meaning and significance of *guanxi* in China's transitional economy. In China today, emerging markets and the transition from a command to a market economy allow actors the freedom to make economic choices in an open market. If one element of *guanxi* practice for industrial managers under the command economy was the necessity of gaining access to distribution channels (input and output) that were controlled by state officials under that system, in China's transitional economy, officials have no such control over the distribution of resources and products. In the economic reforms, in many sectors, an open market increasingly controls the flow of goods. This change has profound implications for the transition away from a focus on *guanxi* practice to a more general focus on *guanxi* as business relationships. Industrial managers no longer need to curry favor with state officials to overcome bottlenecks or gain access to resources, and, as a result, they do not view *guanxi* practice as an important part of decision making in China's industrial economy.

Guanxi *Practice and Hiring Decisions*

While managers often express views that imply a declining significance of *guanxi* practice in China's economic transition, we are still faced with the problem of rhetoric versus empirical reality in the analysis of qualitative evidence. Are these managers simply presenting normative statements—or an official party line—on the way the economic transactions in China should be, irrespective of how things really are, or do their words reflect the empirical reality of changes that are actually occurring in China's transforming economy? Evidence that might help adjudicate between these two possibilities would be whether these managers, despite their views of *guanxi* practice, still use connections to accomplish specific tasks in the transition economy. If managers espouse views that the significance of *guanxi* practice is declining while still using *guanxi* to accomplish specific tasks, we should approach their views skeptically; if, on the other hand, managers who present a picture of the declining significance of *guanxi* do not use *guanxi* in accomplishing specific tasks, this fact would lend credence to the picture these managers paint.

One specific task or practice that has been analyzed in depth with respect to *guanxi* practice is the use of connections in hiring decisions. While industrial managers in China often acknowledge that connections figure into hiring decisions to some extent, many managers describe a scenario that fits with the declining-significance-of-*guanxi*-practice theory (Guthrie 2002a). The positions taken by these managers square with those presented on the more general issue of *guanxi* practice presented above: in China's economic transition, some organizations have constructed formal rational bureaucracies that transform organizational practices in fundamental ways; other organizations are responding more directly to market constraints, hiring individuals who are most qualified for the job, irrespective of social connections. Both types of transformations suggest the declining significance of *guanxi* practice.

CONCLUSIONS

In this chapter, I have given a brief introduction to some of the key institutions around which Chinese society is organized. The family, the party-state, and the work-unit system are all important institutions in the structure of life under communism. However, key changes in each of these institutions have brought about fundamental changes in the lives of individuals. The economic reforms have transformed the family and its relationship to the state. Following the communist takeover in 1949, the state methodically broke down the boundaries that had isolated families from state control in the imperial period. Breaking up clans and extended families, and placing individual families in state-controlled organizations like neighborhood associations in urban areas and collectives (and later communes) in rural areas, institutionalized an unprecedented level of control over Chinese families. With the economic reforms, decollectivization, and the receding of the party-state from organizations like neighborhood associations, the party-state's control over family life has steadily diminished—it is no longer the force of ideological or social control that it was prior to the era of economic reform. However, state control over the family in the current era has taken a different form of control. Beginning with the austere measures of the one-child policy, the state's control over families took the form of official policy. Austere measures of forced sterilization and the threat of job loss have been replaced by more subtle policies, such as tax penalties, but the state control over family size remains a key issue in China today.

The economic reforms have also transformed the party-state itself. Official reforms, such as removing the party from economic control over organizations, creating democratic elections in villages, reforming the National People's Congress, and allowing private entrepreneurs into the party ranks, have all gradually transformed the party from within. Most important, perhaps, has been the transformation of the party-state's ability to control individuals by breaking its monopoly over the allocation of social services. As the party-state receded from direct control over the economic decisions of enterprise managers, it became less and less of an ideological force at the organizational level. And with the concurrent emergence of a private economy and the opening of labor markets, individuals no longer solely rely on the party-state for the allocation of jobs and social welfare benefits.

There have been many consequences of the changes in the institutions that govern communist society in China. In this chapter, I have named only a few. Corruption has been one immediate consequence of the party-state's receding from direct social control. Removing itself from direct control over local officials left open new opportunities for local officials to behave unchecked. New laws have been set in place to deal with these issues, but establishing control over the situation has been gradual, just as the economic reforms have been. Social networks and the gift economy have changed as well. Where the gift economy constituted one of the basic ways in which individuals dealt with the shortage economy, the reforms have opened up new channels for economic exchange for people living in China today. People no longer need to curry favor with officials or other individuals in their lives who control resource allocation.

Four

On a recent trip to Shanghai, I spent a day conducting interviews out in the Waigaichao industrial district of Pudong. The Waigaichao industrial district is an area northeast of Shanghai that offers foreign corporations special tax incentives for investing in the region. It also allows corporations which are importing parts easy access to the Huangpu River as well as access to a bonded zone, which is the initial stop for such imported parts. Many of the most modern factories in China, such as the General Motors factory, are positioned within or near this zone. On the drive back to the city center, as we crossed the southernmost bridge of the Huangpu River, my colleague glibly noted, as he gazed out the window up the river, "There it is, the busiest river in the world." And looking up the river from that vantage point, the sight is almost amusing. There were so many barges plodding their way up the river that it looked like a traffic jam of cargo. There was barge after barge, separated from each other by only a few feet, for as far as the eye could see.

In this chapter, I examine how it has come to be that China's transition to a market economy has produced remarkable growth rates and fundamental changes in the organization of economic action. Though lacking the basic institutional shifts that have defined many transforming socialist economies around the world, China's gradualist reforms have nevertheless been radical and deep. In order to understand the process of economic transformation in China, it is necessary to examine a few key areas of development. This list is by no means exhaustive, but it does comprise some of the key areas in which economic development has transformed China in fundamental ways. I look first at China's engagement in global markets. Second, I examine the varieties and types of organizations that have been successful in transforming themselves in China's market economy. Third, I look at the forces of change that have contributed to this success.

The basic thesis of this chapter is that economic development in China has been shaped by three key factors. First, the central government has driven reforms forward through several key policies that have allowed China to engage fully in the global economy. These policies of engagement have had both external and internal orientations. In terms of China's external focus, the most important policy has been the export-oriented coastal development strategy, which has played a key role in helping China to emerge as the third-largest trading economy in the world in 2004, with total trade of $1.16 trillion. In terms of internal focus, the government has adopted a surprisingly open stance vis-à-vis foreign direct investment (FDI), liberalizing internal markets to a degree greater than is commonly understood and certainly to a greater extent than in India and Japan, for example, at similar stages of development. The reasons for aggressively attracting FDI range from capturing advanced technology through technology transfer agreements and studying management practices from advanced market economies to attracting foreign capital. Second, the government decentralized decision making in significant ways. This point cannot be overemphasized: the decentralization of economic decision making is one of the key factors that has pushed China's reform effort forward. This economic decentralization had several key effects, including giving incentives for local development to local officials and creating competition among localities. Third, while the government has reformed industrial organizations without privatization, it has, at the same time, allowed a private economy to emerge from below. This is an important distinction: in the sector controlled by the Chinese state, state-owned enterprises (SOEs) (*guoying qiye*), urban collectives (*jiti qiye*), and township and village enterprises (TVEs) (*xiangzhen qiye*) have all remained state owned throughout much of the reform era. Though the incentives for such enterprises shifted downward and were placed in the hands of local officials, they remained state property. They have been transformed through a process of reform without rapid privatization, something many observers of transforming planned economies argued was not possible. However, the government did allow a private sector to emerge, and these private sector firms became an important factor in the creation of competition for state-owned firms and in the creation of new markets.

THE EARLY YEARS OF REFORM AND THE COASTAL DEVELOPMENT STRATEGY: CREATING AN EXPORT ECONOMY

A fundamental part of the economic reforms has been the move to recast China as being part of the global economy. At the same time that it was embarking on the domestic reforms that transformed the economy in the 1980s and 1990s, China was opening itself to the global economy. This transformation included:

- the construction of new institutions, both nationally and internationally;
- the development of new industrial strategies;
- the creation of special economic zones (e.g., Pudong, Shenzhen, Zhongguancun), which allowed firms (domestic

and foreign) to take advantage of specific tax incentives and other types of policy goals in targeting specific kinds of investment in China;
- the adoption of trade and aggressive export strategies;
- the adoption of development strategies that were regionally specific within China.

The 1979 Joint Venture Law was the first in a series of regulations allowing the flow of foreign capital into China. In 1980, China enforced its opening-up policies in a small part of the coastal region where four special economic zones (SEZs) in Fujian Province (Xiamen) and Guangdong Province (Shantou, Shenzhen, and Zhuhai) were established. After witnessing the rapid growth of these SEZs, in the mid-1980s, Zhao Ziyang implemented a coastal development strategy to accelerate the flow of FDI and expand foreign trade to a wider region, including eastern and southern provinces in coastal areas.[1]

Zhao Ziyang had good revolutionary credentials. Born in 1919 to a land-owning family, Zhao joined the Communist Youth League as a schoolboy in 1932. At the age of nineteen, he entered the Chinese Communist Party (CCP) and served the communists in a military capacity through the revolution. After the revolution, Zhao was transferred to Guangdong Province, where he steadily rose in power. In 1975, he was transferred to Sichuan and proved to be a strong, reform-minded voice in the party. Then, in 1978, when Deng Xiaoping began consolidating his own position of power by surrounding himself with reform-minded politicians, Zhao was among the first to whom Deng turned. By the early 1980s, it was clearly perceived that Zhao would play a major role in the economic reforms on a national level and that he could potentially be the successor to Deng. In December of 1987, Zhao was elected secretary general of the CCP. Economic policies have always intertwined with political power in communist China, and the situation for Zhao was no different. He was best known for the rationalization of enterprises and price reform, but he also championed and implemented the critical policy known as coastal development strategy.

As with all economic strategies in communist China, it is important to view the coastal development strategy in a political light. One of the primary reasons this strategy was launched was to give Zhao more power in defining the direction of China's reform and thus shift the balance of power away from the more conservative voices in the party. Conservatives were pushing for a slowing down of economic reforms. Zhao's main challenger here was the conservative Li Peng, and Zhao urgently needed new initiatives to prove that he was a worthy successor to Deng Xiaoping. In addition, money was needed in the reform process for Zhao to solidify his power base, and he also needed support from local officials as well as the intellectual community in China. The coastal development strategy would allow him to achieve all of these ends.

The goal was to allow coastal regions greater autonomy in the area of export trade. These regions included Beijing, Fujian, Guangdong, Guangxi, Hainan, Hebei, Jiangsu, Liaoning, Shandong, Shanghai, Tianjin, and Zhejiang. There was precedent for this development strategy in the region, as Japan, South Korea, and Taiwan had prospered through an export-oriented development strategy. The strategy provided an enticing solution to two of China's major problems: employment of the surplus labor from the rural areas and improvement in industrial competitiveness; it would also provide much-needed income for industrial enterprises. However, implementing the strategy meant further decentralization of China. The decentralization of development that China had adopted was not only tied to a lack of political control at the center (which led to corruption in the provinces) but also a lack of economic control over prices, raw materials, and the like. Trade decentralization contributed to inflation, which was already moving in a startling direction as a result of the price reform initiative of 1988.[2]

Nevertheless, by this time, China was deeply enmeshed in this process; for reasons of employment, growth in gross domestic product (GDP), and cash for foreign technology, even the conservative reformers could not hold back foreign trade for long. As a result, behind Zhao's leadership, China launched the coastal development strategy in early 1988. Since that time, China's exports have soared. By 2005, $761 billion worth of goods a year were being pumped into the global economy. This is compared to imports of about $660 billion, creating a trade imbalance with the rest of the world of $102 billion. As Table 4.1 shows, China's export economy grew at an average annual rate of nearly 27 percent over the period 1978–2005. The import of goods grew at a rate of nearly 26 percent over the same period. These goods have over-whelmingly been in the category of manufactured goods, as opposed to those classified as "primary" goods (agricultural products and raw materials).[3]

The coastal development strategy has transformed China's economy in dramatic ways. It has transformed what was an isolated country twenty-five years ago into the primary pro-ducer of goods across a number of different sectors. It has brought a huge infusion of cash into the economy. And it has led the way in an open-door policy that has had fundamental consequences for other aspects of internal growth across a number of sectors in the economy. Despite claims that markets in China are closed to foreign producers—an allegation that is often raised in the face of the growing trade deficit with the

Table 4.1 Total trade, 2002 (US$, billions)

	Total imports and exports	Total exports	Total imports	Balance
1978	20.64	9.75	10.89	−1.14
1980	38.14	18.12	20.02	−1.9
1985	69.6	27.35	42.25	−14.9
1989	111.68	52.54	59.14	−6.6
1990	115.44	62.09	53.35	8.74
1991	135.7	71.91	63.79	8.12
1992	165.53	84.94	80.59	4.35
1993	195.7	91.74	103.96	−12.22
1994	236.62	121.01	115.61	5.4
1995	280.86	148.78	132.08	16.7
1996	289.88	151.05	138.83	12.22
1997	325.16	182.79	142.37	40.42
1998	323.95	193.71	140.24	43.47
1999	360.63	194.93	165.7	29.23
2000	474.29	249.2	225.09	24.11
2001	509.65	266.1	243.55	22.55
2002	620.77	325.6	295.17	30.43
2003	850.99	438.23	412.76	25.47
2004	1,154.55	593.32	561.23	32.09
2005	1,421.91	761.95	659.95	102

Source: *Statistical Yearbook of China*, 2006.

United States and the rest of the world—it is important to think through the complexities of this claim. First, the magnitude of foreign investment in China dwarfs that of Japan in comparable development periods. China's foreign investment regime is far more liberal than that of Japan or South Korea (Lardy 1994). Second, as U.S. trade with China has grown, its trade with other East Asian economies has shrunk. This is not surprising, given that countries such as South Korea and Taiwan have moved production units to China to take advantage of cheaper labor there.[4] Under these circumstances, exports from China grow; however, this commodity-chain

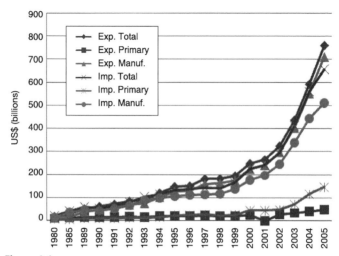

Figure 4.1

Imports and exports by category, primary and manufactured goods (US$, billions).

Source: Statistical Yearbook of China, 2006.

cooperation amounts to a reorganization of export flows across the region rather than a simple net growth of exports from China. In other words, in order to really think accurately about the trade imbalance with China, we need to also account for the fact that as production in Taiwan has declined, many of the Taiwanese businesses have moved their factories over the China's eastern seaboard. Third, of the top forty exporters from China, ten are U.S. companies.[5] Multinational corporations like Dell, Motorola, and Wal-Mart benefit tremendously from producing in China and exporting to the rest of the world—benefits that include healthy profits, which boost stock prices and, thus, market capitalization. These exports, however, count on China's side of the export ledger, because the goods are produced in China. The shift from gross national product (GNP) to gross domestic product (GDP) in 1991 had critical implications for this accounting.[6] By GNP accounting anything made by a U.S. corporation *anywhere* figures into the U.S. side of the trade balance; by GDP accounting, anything produced outside of the U.S. does not. Thus, although Wal-Mart is one of the largest importers to the United States from China, those imports count as Chinese exports in the balance of trade. Fourth, these trade imbalance figures do not account for recent changes in the flow of information around the globe. As reporter James Flanagan has noted,

> [In the garments industry] patterns and instructions are sent over the Internet to factories in China, where the garments are made. They are then shipped back through the ports of Los Angeles and Long Beach and on to stores. Although the patterns that go out over the Internet don't count as "exports," the garments that come back in through the ports count as "imports." . . . The pattern is the same in toys. Jordan Kort's Northridge-based What Kids Want Inc. designs toys under license from Walt Disney Co. and the Nickelodeon division of Viacom Inc. Princess dolls and other toys are manufactured in China, but the lion's share of the proceeds from making and selling the toys go to Kort's firm, the retailers and Disney and Viacom. Indeed economists estimate that the Chinese manufacturers earn only 20% of the value of the goods they make for export.[7]

The bottom line is that, while the trade deficit is clearly a problem for many U.S. policy makers, it is a complicated development that encapsulates many more commodity-chain relationships than the statistic itself reveals.

ENTERPRISE REFORMS AND THE RULE OF LAW

Over the course of the reforms, the central government has transformed its role as the country's economic decision maker into one of macroeconomic policy maker, passing a battery of key laws and regulations that changed the practices of organizations. For example, in 1979 the Chinese government passed the Joint Venture Law, allowing foreign firms to enter the Chinese economy for the first time since 1949. Decollectivization policies in rural areas and the creation of the categories of household business and private enterprise stimulated the emergence of the private enterprises. The entry of these start-up firms quickly gave rise to increasing market pressure on the state sector. In 1986, the State Council passed regulations that changed the nature of employment relationships, essentially marking a formal end to the institution of lifetime employment.[8] Also in 1986, the Chinese government passed the Enterprise Bankruptcy Law, which for the first time established that insolvent enterprises may apply for bankruptcy. Two years later, with the passage of the Enterprise Law, the state not only underscored the government's policies toward hardening budget constraints for SOEs but also stipulated the government's policies and legal guaranty for protecting the non-state sector, through regulations such as the Rules of Foreign Invested Enterprises and the Provisional Regulations of Private Enterprises.[9]

In 1992, coinciding with Deng's "southern tour," the State Council further specified that enterprises were entitled to up to fourteen rights: decision making in production and operation, price setting for products and labor, selling of products, material purchasing, import and export, investment decision making, disposition of retained bonuses, disposition of property, decision making on joint operation or mergers, labor employment, personnel management, distribution of wages and bonuses, internal structuring, and refusing apportioning. Since then, SOEs have been expected to independently operate in the market according to law and be responsible for their

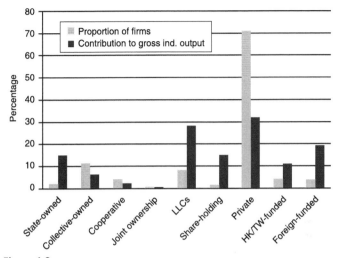

Figure 4.2

Various organizational types in China, 2004.

Source: Statistical Yearbook of China, 2006.

own profits and losses. Two years later, the Company Law was passed. As mentioned earlier, this law governed the process of converting enterprises into shareholding companies and stipulated that companies funded by investing bodies of different ownerships were all equal under the law. More important, the Company Law encouraged enterprises to build new corporate structures and standardize organizational bodies (mainly with regard to shareholder meetings, corporate boards, and managers) in order to further block political interventions in the decision making process. By the mid-1990s, the government would formally define its role in the economy as "creat[ing] the conditions for all sectors of the economy to participate in the market competition on an equal basis, and guarantee enterprises from all sectors to be treated indiscriminately."[10]

Coinciding with these legislative changes was the founding of the Shanghai and Shenzhen Stock Exchanges in the early

1990s. Since 1993, the number of listed companies rose from 10 to 1160 with a total market capitalization of US$525.6 billion (Gao 2002). Following the gradualist model, the Chinese government's construction of the institutions that govern public ownership has been spread across the period of economic reform. After a series of regulations, such as the Opinions on Standardizing the Joint Stock Limited Companies and the Provisional Regulations on the Administration of Issuing and Trading of Stocks, the Securities Law was passed in 1998, forming legal guaranty for the standardized operation of the listed companies. Yet, even in the area of public ownership of listed companies, we must acknowledge the complexities of enterprise-state relations in the Chinese model, as the government's receding from control over publicly listed state enterprises has, like every other institutional change in the Chinese economic reforms, been a gradual process. A typical ownership transformation for a state-owned enterprise would allow the state to retain between 40 and 50 percent of the company's shares; between 20 and 30 percent of the shares are designated for institutional shares; the remaining 30 percent are designated for public consumption (Guthrie *et al.* 2007).

Since 1979, the non-state sectors have also been increasingly entitled to the legal acknowledgment and protection from the capricious whims of the state. In 1997, at the Fifteenth National Congress, the government issued the significant formal statement that "the non-state sector is an important component part of this country's socialist market economy," and the statement was incorporated into the Constitution in 1999. At this point, the status of the non-state sector—especially the private sector—in China's economic system was officially legitimated. In 2004, the government further amended its constitution to protect private property rights for the first time since the People's Republic of China (PRC) was founded in

1949; under Hu Jintao, the National People's Congress further bolstered property rights in 2007. Over the course of China's market transition, the law-building process of the central government, especially since the 1990s, has gradually rationalized the institutions that govern autonomous business practice in China. These changes have brought about the rapid growth of the non-state sectors and intensified the transformation of the state sector in the reform era. They have also codified the autonomy of organizations operating as businesses in China. As a result, all types of China's business organizations have been more or less driven toward independent market behavior with diminishing reliance on the government system.

FISCAL REFORMS AND THE RISE OF LOCAL STATES

While it is certainly true that the state has gradually withdrawn from economic management and control of enterprises in the reform era, it is premature to conclude that the Chinese state has become insignificant in its relationships with business organizations. In particular, it is important to note that local governments have risen to play important roles in the development of local enterprises and the economic development of their regions more generally (Huang 1995a; Walder 1995e; Lee 1991), though this has occurred at varying rates depending on a given locality's relationship to the central government (Li 1997). Since the beginning of the reform era, policies of economic decentralization have transferred most economic decision-making power from the central government to localities by a series of tax and fiscal reforms. In 1980, the fiscal reforms started with the implementation of a fiscal responsibility system, under which the central government and provincial-level governments signed revenue-sharing contracts. According to this contract, taxes collected by local governments were to be divided into two parts: (1) central fixed revenues, which were to be remitted to the central government and (2) local revenues, which the central and local governments were to share in terms of various standards across regions. This revenue-sharing system provided local governments both strong incentives and institutional means to increase their revenue base by allowing them to retain more when they collected more revenues and guaranteeing the rights of localities to income from their assets. The direct outcome of these reforms was an explosion of local revenues in the 1980s, which lasted until 1994, when the central state was forced to enforce new fiscal reforms (Wang 1995; Wong 1997; Wong et al. 1995). In addition, economic decentralization policies have involved local governments in a number of responsibilities for carrying out national social policies and a variety of economic activities. For instance, the governments at the city level are responsible for 100 percent of expenditures for social security, unemployment insurance, and social welfare, and the governments at the county and township levels account for 70 percent of education expenditures and 55–60 percent of health expenditures.[11]

The increasing responsibilities in the reform era have made local governments actively involved in economic activities and business affairs in the localities. Lower levels of local governments have played significant roles in the development of TVEs, which became the most dynamic sector in China's transitional economy in the 1980s and early 1990s. By the early 1990s, the TVEs were contributing between 40 and 50 percent of tax revenues for local governments. As noted above, local governments, in many cases, actually came to behave like "industrial firms" themselves during the rural industrialization process, engineering the development of collective enterprises and forming the corporate structures to govern them.

The fiscal reforms of 1994 put more duties on the localities and requested the lower levels of local governments to be responsible for expenses and social welfare. At the same time, the early 1990s liberalization policy of foreign investment and foreign trade increased local government responsibility for managing the foreign sector in localities. These conditions created both fiscal pressure and incentives for local states to be more involved in the local-global business activities for capital accumulation. Aside from directly dealing with foreign capital, local governments were given the authority to relax the rules governing foreign exchange balances, power and water fees, land prices for factory buildings, restrictions on hiring nonlocal workers, and other policies related to foreign investors.

Local governments often interpret the Central Government's policies flexibly and have frequently implemented them strategically for their own good.[12] As a result, foreign investors have begun to realize that "favorable investment policies issued by Beijing" are not nearly as advantageous as the "special deals" that can be crafted with local officials. Rather than dealing with the central government, foreign investors often prefer to build up long-term alliances with local officials for more stable and favorable investment conditions and cheaper local resources. In addition to directly developing enterprises for more revenues and dealing with the foreign investors for more capital, local governments have formed various relationships with local business organizations, including those in non-state sectors. The result of these macro-level policies is that the state has established the conditions under which a variety of organizational types, including those that are still state owned, have the latitude to behave like business organizations in China today.

THE DEVELOPMENT OF MARKET-ORIENTED ORGANIZATIONS IN CHINA

We turn now to the internal focus of economic development in China. One of the key goals of China's economic reforms since 1979 has been to transform the relationships between enterprises and the state. Under the planned economy, almost all of China's enterprises were state owned and state run (here again, state-run enterprises include collectives and TVEs). Enterprises varied in terms of the level of government under which they resided (from central to local) and in terms of the resources they were able to extract from the government, but there was no question that the state was the residual claimant, exercised managerial control, and controlled the transfer of assets. There was a small number of collective enterprises, but their managerial system was not essentially different from that of state-owned enterprises. These organizations—state-owned and collectively owned enterprises alike—served as not only production units of the governmental system but also as redistribution units for the goods of social welfare. Enterprises before economic reform were essentially inseparable from the government and highly dependent on it.

As discussed briefly in Chapter 2, Deng's reforms transformed enterprises in two significant ways: (1) relieving them of the responsibility for social benefits and (2) turning economic autonomy over to both economic organizations and the managers who ran them. In the 1980s, the decentralization of economic responsibilities for TVEs and the local officials who governed them transformed the responsibilities and rights of both governments and the enterprises they governed. In similar ways, the "dual track" policy rebuilt the incentive structures of the SOEs and the responsibilities and rights of both the government and enterprises, though, as discussed earlier, this process occurred in a much more gradual fashion.

Thus, these enterprises obtained, in many cases, enough financial control and freedom from the burden of social welfare costs to transform their practices in the market economy. In addition, as the party and the administrative arm of the government—the administrative bureaus—receded from direct control over enterprise behavior, managers throughout the Chinese economy have become the key decision makers of TVEs and SOEs, along with their counterparts in the private and foreign-funded economy.

It is far too simplistic, then, to think of business organizations as only covering the private enterprises in the economy; this sector, while important, constitutes only one of the organizational types that are behaving like business organizations in China today.[13] SOEs, TVEs, private enterprises, and foreign-funded enterprises are all part of the group of Chinese organizations that have, to varying degrees, become oriented toward the market in China. In this section, I focus on the institutional changes that have shaped business organizations in China today, specifically looking at (1) the evolution of government-enterprise relationships, (2) the impact of foreign direct investment (FDI), (3) the transformation of social relationships in China's market economy, and (4) the emergence of business associations. Through each of these areas of change, I address the question of the forces that have transformed Chinese economic organizations.

By classical definitions of markets and firms, only private enterprises and some foreign-funded enterprises in China would fall under the category of business organizations. However, strict classifications of business organization do not capture the variety of organizations that behave like capitalist firms in China. An analysis of economic development in China must focus on what it means to operate like a capitalist firm rather than on official categories or types. The evolution of the study of property rights is illustrative here: Where classical studies of property rights defined the institutional arrangements into basic categories (private, public, or state owned), more recent work in this area has focused on the specific practices that define property rights as a "bundle" of rights, including (1) the right to residual income flows, (2) the right of managerial control, and (3) the right to transfer assets (Demsetz 1967; Furubotn and Pejovich 1974; Oi and Walder 1999). The property rights issue is especially important in this case, because many firms in China have long operated like private firms while still retaining a state-owned status (Walder 1995e; Oi and Walder 1999). In China, beyond private and foreign-funded enterprises, SOEs and TVEs have also evolved to behave like market firms in various ways. As of 2004, China had 25,339 state-owned and state-holding enterprises, occupying 2 percent of total enterprises; these organizations contributed 15 percent of the output value to the total gross industrial output of the country. The 141,772 collectively owned enterprises (11.1 percent of the total) contributed just over 8 percent of the output value to the total gross industrial output; limited liability corporations 102,392 (8.1 percent) contributed 28.4 percent to the total output; 902,647 private enterprises (71.1 percent) contributed nearly 32 percent to the total output; 17,427 shareholding corporations (1.4 percent) contributed 14.9 percent to the total output; 54,910 firms funded by Hong Kong and Taiwan money (4 percent) occupied 11 percent of the total output; and 51,255 firms funded by foreign sources (3.7 percent) contributed 19.2 percent to the gross industrial output.[14]

TVEs and SOEs as Market Firms

In Chapter 2, I introduced the concept of local governments and the TVEs they preside over as behaving like industrial firms. SOEs were slower to see true reform than their counterparts in the rural industrial economy. In the early stages of the economic reforms, the "dual track" policy provided a degree of stability for the early enterprise transitions when the state sector was still evidently dominant in China's economic system. According to this policy, SOEs were allowed to sell the goods above the "plan" quotas and keep extra profits, a system that significantly shifted the incentive structures for these organizations. Thus, even in the early period of the economic reforms, when SOEs still largely operated under the rubric of the planned economy, managers were given incentives to direct their enterprises to behave like business organizations in the emerging market economy.

In 1992, the Chinese government made clear its market-driven reform direction and shifted its policy making toward creating the rules, laws and institutions that govern a market economy, and from this point forward, the dual track system was phased out. Since then, substantial restructuring of state-owned industry has been central to the reform agenda. By the mid-1990s, SOEs were increasingly being pushed to restructure their operations in fundamental ways, causing them to be treated—and to increasingly behave—like business organizations in practice if not in legal form. Firms were placed on independent budgetary systems, many were cut off completely from the redistributive funds of central government coffers, and many were given full latitude to make decisions over how they would govern themselves in China's emerging markets. Laws like the Enterprise Bankruptcy Law (1986), the Enterprise Law (1988), the Company Law (1994), and the Labor Law (1995) established a framework for these changes. But the key point here is that although the transition away from the planned economy was a gradual process, managers in many of China's SOEs were increasingly being handed the key responsibilities that fit with the management of business organizations: although they did not possess the right to transfer assets, they increasingly had the rights to residual income flows and the power and responsibility of managerial control.[15]

In addition to the declining scale of the SOEs, their contributions to China's GDP and total industrial output have also significantly decreased. In 1978, the SOEs generated about 80 percent of China's GDP, while in 2004, the contribution of the SOEs dropped down to 15 percent and the collective, private, and joint-venture sectors generated over 70 percent. In 1978, the state sectors contributed over 75 percent of China's industrial output and collective sectors accounted for about 22 percent (Naughton 1995). In 1995, the state sectors' portion in industrial output had declined to 35 percent, while collective sectors contributed over 36 percent of industrial output values and private sector and other nonstate sectors produced the rest (*Statistical Year book of China* 1996). By 2004, the shares of gross industrial output being produced by the private firms, combined with foreign funded enterprises, rose to 52 percent, while the share of the SOEs was only 18 percent and the share of collective sectors was down to 10 percent (*Statistical Year book of China* 2006). It is very clear that through the reform era, the non-state firms have been growing at a strikingly faster rate than the state sector. However, even today, SOEs still remain a massive force in China's economy. They provide basic employment and social welfare for the majority of urban workers and the bulk of fiscal revenues for most levels of government. They still control more than half of China's industrial assets and dominate vital industries such as financial services, power, telecommunications, steel, and petrochemicals, among others. China cannot fully accomplish its market reforms without successfully restructuring and further reforming the state sector. It is also worth noting that state-owned firms officially only account for 2 percent of firms, it is also important to note that this is a conservative estimate of the state-owned firm category, as many of the firms in the "private" or "limited liability" or "shareholding" categories could just as easily be thought of as state-owned (many publicly trading shareholding corporations, which are officially categorized as shareholding corporations, are firms in which the state controls up to 70 percent of the shares). Finally, it is worth noting that strong contribution to industrial output by the relatively small proportion of firms funded by Hong Kong and Taiwanese money.

Private and Foreign-Funded Enterprises

In the era of economic reform, however, the entry and success of large numbers of collectives, private firms, joint ventures, and foreign firms have significantly driven China's market reforms and sharply overshadowed the status and roles of SOEs in the industrial sector and the national economy. The organizations that populate these categories of economic organization are the closest to the classic definitions of market firms. Private firms, for their part, are fairly clear cut: they are organized around relationships between principals (owners) and agents (managers and workers), and they are basically oriented toward the pursuit of profits in exchange for the production of goods and the provision of services. There are a couple of key distinctions among types of organizations within this sector—namely, that between household businesses and private enterprises: household businesses employ a maximum of seven employees, while private enterprises employ eight or more workers. In addition, private enterprises are subject to the Enterprise Law (or the Company Law, depending on whether the organization has made this transition), while household businesses are not. It is worth emphasizing again here that while the Chinese government has allowed private firms to emerge, this process is different from the process of privatization. SOEs, urban collectives, and TVEs have remained largely in state hands, but a private economy has also emerged to coexist with the state economy. This private (and foreign-funded) economy has competed with—and built markets in conjunction with—the state sector.

Foreign-funded organizations are a little more complicated than private organizations. In general, these organizations come in two primary forms. First, wholly owned foreign enterprises (WOFEs) are private organizations that are funded by a foreign parent or benefactor. However, these organizations are different from private business organizations in that they are largely extensions of the parent organizations that formed them. Thus, while these organizations may appear to be the most similar to private organizations in the Chinese economy in terms of property rights, they are most often closely tied subsidiary organizations. Further, especially for larger organizations in this category, their operation in the economy depends in part on their relationships with other organizations and with the local or national government (depending on their scale and scope). The second form that appears within this category is the joint-venture firm. Joint ventures are usually fully independent entities from the parent organizations that have contributed resources to their formation. However, these parent organizations may control their business decisions to varying degrees. In some cases, joint ventures operate as fully independent entities, exercising managerial control and control over residual income. In other cases, parent companies from both the foreign and Chinese partner sides can occupy significant managerial control over these entities.

In the 1990s, private and foreign-funded firms replaced TVEs as the most dynamic sectors of the economy. With respect to foreign-funded firms especially, these organizations have seen the highest levels of labor productivity, ratio of output to assets, and ratio of profits to cost (see Figure 4.3 and Table 4.2) (Guthrie 2005). In contrast with the decline of the SOEs, the non-state sectors have become the most dramatic driving forces of China's market-led reforms, the most competitive firms, and the most important force in supporting the high-speed growth of the national economy in the past twenty-five years.[16]

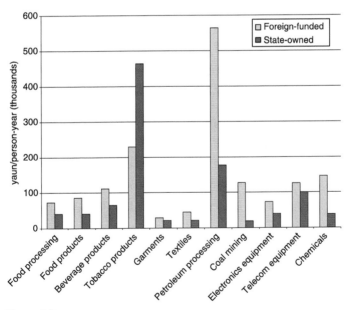

Figure 4.3

Labor productivity by selected sectors, 2001.

Source: Statistical Yearbook of China, 2002.

Table 4.2 Comparison of state-owned and foreign-funded firms

	Foreign-funded	SOEs w/no foreign funds
Ratio of output to assets (%)	9.83	8.17
Ratio of profits to cost (%)	5.85	5.75
Labor prod (yuan/person-year)	75,913	54,772

Note: "Foreign-funded" refers to those firms that are Sino-foreign joint ventures or Sino-foreign cooperative projects.

Source: *Statistical Yearbook of China*, 2003, pp. 446, 456.

FDI, GLOBAL BUSINESS, AND ORGANIZATIONAL CHANGE

Since the early 1990s, China has become a major recipient of foreign direct investment (FDI), which occupies the major part of total foreign capital (including foreign loans, FDI, and other investments) that China has received. Beginning in 1991, the amount of FDI in China rose precipitously. In 1993, China received more FDI than any other country and, since then, has been the second largest recipient in the world, behind only the United States (see Figure 4.4). By early 1999, FDI in joint ventures and wholly foreign-owned companies exceeded one-quarter of a trillion U.S. dollars, several times larger than cumulative FDI since World War II in Japan, Korea, and Taiwan combined (Lardy 2002). In 2002, China's total inflow of FDI reached near half a $US trillion, making it the world's largest recipient of FDI. According to Nicholas Lardy (1996), four factors contribute to such dramatic increases of FDI that China attracted in the early 1990s: (1) the increasing magnitude of aggregate FDI flowing to developing countries in the 1990s; (2) China's political stability in the post–Tiananmen Square era, combined with the explosive growth of domestic economy, rebuilt the confidence of foreign firms and investors; (3) after one decade of economic liberalization, and the practice of the coastal developmental strategies, China's foreign investment regime had been systematically liberalized, and more sectors had been opened to foreign investors; and (4) it is widely believed that Chinese firms disguised their money as "foreign investment" to take advantage of the special policies only provided to those enterprises that attracted foreign investment. (This final point likely accounts for the high rates of FDI flowing in from Hong Kong.)

With the country's rapid economic growth in GDP and its explosive growth in foreign trade, China's business organizations have experienced dramatic changes. The nation's economic architects aspired to force rational economic actions and organizational structures onto the development agenda of business organizations through initiating several waves of enterprise reforms at different time periods. From Zhao Ziyang in the 1980s to Zhu Rongji in the 1990s, Chinese leaders have clearly focused on the creation of rational accountability and the embracing of international standards. The enterprise

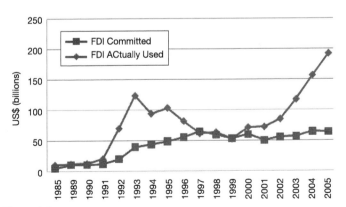

Figure 4.4
FDI in China (US$, billions).

Source: Statistical Yearbook of China, 2006.

Table 4.3 Utilization of foreign capital (US$, billions)

Total amount of foreign capital to be utilized through the signed agreements and contracts

	Total		Foreign Loans		Direct Foreign Investments		Other Foreign Investments
	Number of Projects	Value	Number of Projects	Value	Number of Projects	Value	Value
1979–1984	3,365	28.77	117	16.98	3,248	10.39	1.40
1985	3,145	9.87	72	3.53	3,073	5.93	0.40
1989	5,909	11.48	130	5.19	5,779	5.60	0.69
1990	7,371	12.09	98	5.10	7,273	6.60	0.39
1991	13,086	19.58	108	7.16	12,978	11.98	0.45
1992	48,858	69.44	94	10.70	48,764	58.12	0.61
1993	83,595	123.27	158	11.31	83,437	111.44	0.53
1994	47,646	93.76	97	10.66	47,549	82.68	0.41
1995	37,184	103.21	173	11.29	37,011	91.28	0.64
1996	24,673	81.61	117	7.96	24,556	73.28	0.37
1997	21,138	61.06	137	5.87	21,001	51.00	4.18
1998	19,850	63.20	51	8.39	19,799	52.10	2.71
1999	17,022	52.01	104	8.36	16,981	41.22	2.43
2000	22,347	71.18			22,347	62.38	8.75
2001	26,140	71.98			26,140	69.20	2.78
2002	34,171	84.75			34,171	82.77	1.98
2003	41,081	116.9			41,081	115.07	1.83
2004	43,664	156.59			43,664	153.48	3.11

2005	44,001	192.59			44,001	189.07	3.53
1979–2005	554,625	14,634	1,683	1,385	552,942	1,286	39.2

Total amount of foreign capital actually used

1979–1984		17.14		13.04		3.06	1.04
1985		4.46		2.51		1.66	0.30
1989		10.06		6.29		3.39	0.38
1990		10.29		6.53		3.49	0.27
1991		11.55		6.89		4.37	0.30
1992		19.20		7.91		11.01	0.28
1993		38.96		11.19		27.52	0.26
1994		43.21		9.27		33.77	0.18
1995		48.13		10.33		37.52	0.29
1996		54.80		12.67		41.73	0.41
1997		64.41		12.02		45.26	7.13
1998		58.56		11.00		45.46	2.09
1999		52.66		10.21		40.32	2.13
2000		59.36		10.00		40.72	8.64
2001		49.67				46.88	2.79
2002		55.01				52.74	2.27
2003		56.14				53.51	2.64
2004		64.07				60.63	3.44
2005		63.81				60.33	3.48
1979–2005		781.49		1471.57		613.37	38.32

Source: Statistical Yearbook of China, 2006.

reforms in the current era have concentrated on building a "modern enterprise system" and forcing enterprises to restructure their accounting practices so that they comply with international models and standards.

Both the government and the enterprises recognized the need for foreign capital, advanced management experience, and technology. The desire to attract foreign investment and technology has led to institutional accommodations that support rational-legal accountability and the rule of law within the firm. Coupled with the reformers' intentions, the inflow of foreign capital and global corporations into China exerted significant pressure on the evolution of Chinese business organizations to adapt to the rules of the global market. These influences from foreign investors and global corporations are evident not only in the nation's macroeconomic policies but also in organizational changes that can be observed at the firm level. Western investors—many of whom are more interested in long-term investments to capture market share than they are in cheap labor—generally seek Chinese partners that are predictable, stable, and knowledgeable about Western-style business practices and negotiations.[17] This pressure from international organizations and Western investors has accelerated the rationalization of China's economic system not only at the state level but also within firms.

THE EMERGENCE OF CAPITAL MARKETS

In the 1990s, the focus was on building the institutions that would continue to push along the reforms of the state sector while, at the same time, attracting foreign capital through capital markets (Guthrie et al. 2007; Guthrie and Wang 2007). Accordingly, coinciding with the legislative changes of the 1990s was the founding of the Shanghai and Shenzhen Stock Exchanges. The first of these, the Shanghai Exchange, opened for business on December 19, 1990, with the Shenzhen Exchange opening shortly thereafter. By the end of 2004, the number of domestically listed companies in China had risen to 1371 with a total market capitalization of 525.6 billion US dollars (SSEa 2005; SSEb 2005; Hertz 1998; Gao 2002). Following the gradualist model, the Chinese government's construction of the institutions that govern public ownership has been spread across the period. After a series of regulations such as "the Opinions on Standardizing the Joint Stock Limited Companies" and "the Provisional Regulations on the Administration of Issuing and Trading of Stocks," the *Securities Law of the People's Republic of China* (PRC 1999) was adopted in 1998 at the Ninth National People's Congress and took effect in July of 1999, thus institutionalizing the legal basis for the standardized operation of listed companies. The Company Law (PRC 1994) laid the foundation for this standardization. The law itself contains 12 chapters, covering a range of issues from stock issuance and stock transactions to the rules governing ownership and shareholding of publicly-listed companies. Finally, in 2001, the Central Government passed *The Tentative Measures for Decreasing State Shareholding* (PRC 2001). Yet, as China has been systematically constructing the institutions of a publicly traded economy, even in the area of public ownership of listed companies, we must acknowledge the complexities of enterprise-state relations in the Chinese model, as the government's receding from control over publicly-listed state enterprises has, like every other institutional change in the Chinese economic reforms, been a gradual process. The companies listed on China's domestic stock exchanges are becoming "privatized" in some ways. A typical ownership transformation for a state-owned enterprise would allow the state to retain between 30 and 40 percent of the company's shares; between 30 and 40 percent of the shares are designated for

Table 4.4 Evolution of China's domestic stock markets

	Market capitalization (US$, billion)	Total # of firms	# of firms, Shanghai	# of firms, Shenzhen	# of firms, A shares only	# of firms, A&H shares	# of Firms, A&B shares	# of Firms, B shares only
1990	—	10	8	2	10	—	—	—
1991	—	14	8	6	14	—	—	—
1992	—	53	29	24	53	—	18	—
1993	—	183	106	77	183	3	34	6
1994	—	291	171	120	227	6	54	4
1995	47.65	323	188	135	242	11	58	12
1996	—	530	293	237	431	14	69	16
1997	—	745	383	362	627	17	76	25
1998	—	851	438	413	727	18	80	26
1999	363.45	949	484	465	822	19	82	26
2000	660.30	1088	572	516	955	19	86	28
2001	597.56	1160	646	514	1025	23	88	24
2002	526.29	1224	715	509	1085	28	87	24
2003	583.01	1287	780	507	1146	30	87	24
2004	508.86	1377	837	540	1236	31	86	24
2005	445.28	1381	834	547	1240	32	86	23

Source: Statistical Yearbook of China, 2006.

institutional shares; the remaining 30 percent of shares are designated for public consumption as free floating shares.

THE MACRO-LEVEL IMPACT OF MULTINATIONAL CORPORATIONS

Attracting foreign investment has been a basic part of China's economic development in the reform era. On June 11, 2001, in the City of Shanghai, the multimedia giant Time Warner (at that time known as AOL Time Warner) announced a $200 million joint venture with Legend Holdings, China's largest computer maker.[18] The venture is working toward the development of Internet services that will then be bundled with Legend's computers. (Legend currently holds about one-third of the market share for personal computers in China.) Despite the fact that foreign companies are still not allowed to own stakes in Internet services or Internet content providers, Time Warner has committed $100 million to the development of a venture that will place the company primarily in a position of consultation and technical support. The reasons why the company was willing to accept such a deal likely include the enormous potential of Internet development in China and the fact that the prohibitions against foreign ownership in the telecommunications sector are going to change with China's entry into the World Trade Organization. For China, the positive aspects of this deal are many: it commits a large amount of capital, even compared to other large-scale joint-venture deals;[19] it brings technology to China in an area that is rapidly evolving; and it brings international cache and branding from the largest personal-access Internet services provider in the United States.

Yet, despite these many advantages for both sides of the partnership, both sides also take on significant risk. The risk for Time Warner is largely economic: given that many of the joint ventures involving multinationals in China have reported losses for the entire time they have been in operation in China, it is unlikely that Time Warner will see a return on its investment anytime soon. This is an investment for the future, and the future is always somewhat unpredictable in developing countries like China. The risk for China is, in some ways, more fundamental: when the State Council endorses a deal of this size, it is giving up some amount of control over the development of the sector in which the venture is occurring. In other words, investments such as these pierce the veil of the authoritarian government's sovereign control over the nation and the economy. Presidents and chief executive officers of multinational firms investing large sums of money in China expect to be heard. In Beijing, the mayor has established an advisory council, made up of presidents and chief executive officers of companies with significant stakes in China, so that these high-powered individuals can have an official forum through which to express their views.[20] Sometimes, company executives are afforded even higher access to air their concerns. For example, following an incident that involved theft of intellectual property, DuPont used what bargaining power it had to pressure government officials to set forth policies that would safeguard against the recurrence of a similar incident in subsequent investments. In 1994, on the brink of embarking on another joint venture in China, DuPont's chairman Edgar Woolard met with Chinese president Jiang Zemin to discuss formal policies that would protect foreign investors. It is unlikely that Woolard was able to elicit any guarantees from Jiang or that this meeting was a direct precursor to the law protecting intellectual property, which was promulgated in 1995 (the law had been in the works for a long time prior to the meeting). Yet, as China needs foreign investment to develop, such high-stakes negotiations require the Chinese government to create an environment in which these investors feel that their assets are somewhat protected. This requires giving up sovereign control over industries and sectors of the economy.

There are a number of ways that negotiations over foreign-invested joint-venture agreements have an impact on Chinese state sovereignty. For example, if companies specify arbitration clauses in their joint-venture contracts, the Chinese government no longer has jurisdiction over disputes that may arise in these deals. Beginning in 1979, for the first time since the founding of the PRC, foreign parties have input on decisions that affect Chinese internal affairs. Enforcement still lies in the hands of Chinese authorities. But for a country that only a few years ago operated fully on the institution of administrative fiat, turning over decision-making power to a third party is somewhat problematic. In other words, negotiations with foreign parties require the Chinese government to give up some power and control over Chinese society. The extent to which the Chinese government is forced to give up sovereignty varies with the value of the joint-venture investment: when the Chinese government is facing a large multinational company that seeks to invest a significant amount of capital and technology, both of which China desperately needs, it must give up control over the venture to a significant extent. And if that company uses arbitration clauses in its joint-venture contracts, as most large multinationals operating in China do, the government gives away control of the economic venture in question to a still greater extent.[21]

The Time Warner deal is especially interesting in this vein, because it comes at a time when the government seems intent upon maintaining tight control over the evolution of telecommunications in China. To argue that information technology (IT) plays a causal or even central role in diminishing China's sovereign control over economic development, or the telecommunications sector, specifically, would be an exaggeration of IT's role in what is a larger trend. Foreign investment has played an important role in China's reform effort since it reopened its doors to foreign investment in 1979. From Deng's visit to the United States in 1979 to the Law on Chinese-Foreign Equity Joint Ventures—one of the first laws passed to usher in the economic transition—the attraction of foreign capital and technology has played a central role in the economic changes occurring in China. Table 4.3 puts the Time Warner venture into perspective: despite the size of the venture, this sum of money, while significant, is only one part of an investment trend that has been occurring for the last two-and-a-half decades in China. It is the first venture of its size in the highly guarded telecommunications sector and the first with a major Internet provider, and it will be interesting to see how the Chinese government deals with the inevitable challenges to economic and social control this venture will bring about. But this venture is only the most recent in a long line of investments that have placed the Chinese government in a partnership with Western multinationals. It remains to be seen whether IT matters for encroachments on state sovereignty in the realm of foreign investment, but this challenge to the state is only the most recent in a long line of sectoral transformations that have occurred throughout the economy over the last twenty years.

CHANGES IN PRODUCTIVITY AT THE FIRM LEVEL

In the 1980s and early 1990s, many prominent economists advising nations in the construction of markets assumed that institutional change was a relatively simple process. The institutions of capitalism and democracy reflected the natural state of rational economic actors, and if we could just get the institutions right, individuals in these societies would know what to do. Further, the inefficiencies of state planning and the shackles of an authoritarian government ran counter to this natural state, and there was no way to configure the institutions of planned economic systems to work with the instincts of human nature. Accordingly, during the period of China's transition to a market economy, economists and institutional advisors from the West have advocated the rapid transition to market institutions as the necessary medicine for transforming communist societies. Many scholars have argued that private property provides the institutional foundation of a market economy, and, therefore, communist societies making the transition to a market economy must privatize industry and other public goods. Further, the radical members of this school have argued that rapid privatization—the so-called shock therapy or big bang approach to economic reforms—is the only way to avoid costly abuses in these transitory systems. According to scholars in this camp, the institutional goals of these transitions are clear, and the architects of these transitions should not waste any time in pushing their economies toward these goals (Kornai 1980, 1990; Sachs 1992, 1995a, 1995b; Sachs and Woo 1994a, 1994b, 1997).

Much like the advocates of rapid political reform, those demanding immediate economic reform often take for granted the learning that must take place in the face of new institutions. The assumption among rapid-reform advocates is that, given certain institutional arrangements, individuals will naturally know how to carry out the practices of democracy and capitalism. Yet these assumptions reflect a neoclassical view of human nature in which rational man will thrive in his natural environment—free markets and a democratic system. Completely absent from this view are the roles of history, culture, and preexisting institutions, and it is a vision that is far too simplistic to comprehend the challenge of making markets and democracy work in the absence of stable institutions and a history to which they can be tied. The transition from a system of a planned economy and authoritarian rule to one of free markets and democracy can be a wrenching experience, not only at the institutional level but also at the level of individual practice. Individuals must learn the rules of the market, and new institutions must be set in place long enough to gain stability and legitimacy. These are processes that occur slowly and over a long period of time.

Two sectors of the Chinese economy have outperformed others over the course of the reforms: in the 1980s, it was the township and village enterprises (TVEs) in the rural industrial economy; in recent years, it has been those firms that have been shaped by foreign direct investment (FDI). The first fact corresponds to the changes that have reshaped state-firm relations in the reform era. Even though the command economy is virtually nonexistent today, where a firm was positioned in the industrial hierarchy of the former command economy has had profound consequences for how it experiences economic reforms. The central issue here is the level of attention firms receive in terms of monitoring and support from the state administrative offices to which they report. The second case of elevated productivity corresponds to the impact that relations with foreign firms have on Chinese corporations. Many scholarly and popular accounts have focused on either the exploitative role of foreign firms in the Chinese economy or on the importance of technology transfer in the economy. Here, however, I examine the ways in which a particular group of foreign multinationals is playing a critical role in the transformation of organizational practice in China.

The market economy is not simply a natural state that will magically emerge in the face of private property or "shock therapy." Rather, successful navigation of an emerging market economy is a learned set of practices and behaviors, and actors in transforming economies must be exposed to the models of economic action and the guidance from different organizational actors in the marketplace to institutionalize the successful models of the new economic system. Managers of Chinese corporations learn the rules of the market from the organizations that provide the best lessons for the successful transition to a market economy. As Chinese firms deal with the uncertainties of China's emerging marketplaces, they are influenced by the organizations—whether local state offices or foreign multinationals—from which they learn the successful practices of a market economy. Transfers of knowledge occur in three ways in the development of market economic practices in China's transforming economy. First, they sometimes come from above: local state offices offer guidance to the firms under their jurisdictions, helping them implement the new management practices that are necessary for survival in China's transforming markets. Second, heightened expectations and standards come from close relationships with powerful foreign investors. Chinese managers want desperately to land the lucrative joint-venture deals that will bring access to technology and investment resources, and when they are in a position to compete for those resources, they raise their level of production accordingly. The attention to productivity, quality, and "efficient" management all become signals in the marketplace that these organizations know the meaning of doing business in China's emerging market economy; they know what it means to "link up" with the international world. These kinds of relationships with foreign investors stand in contrast to those in which foreign investors are simply seeking cheap labor. Third, close collaboration with foreign multinationals through the negotiation of joint-venture deals and sitting on joint boards of directors with their foreign partners are also important mechanisms through which transfers of knowledge flow. Interlocking directorates become a conduit through which senior management of a Chinese company has constant access to the input and advice of a successful multinational partner in its own sector. Various combinations of these transfers of knowledge can be observed in the cases described below.

THREE CASE STUDIES OF CHINESE INDUSTRIAL FIRMS
The Shanghai Kang Hua Meat and Foods Company

Originally founded in 1958, this was one of the many factories in China's urban industrial economy that had been expanded to accommodate the need for jobs for people returning to urban areas after being "sent down" during the Cultural Revolution.[22] A small factory located in one of Shanghai's small special economic zones,[23] the Caohejing open economic zone, the factory sits under the jurisdiction of the Caohejing district company, the local district administrative arm of the government for that area. One of the most striking things about this factory is the aggressive development course it has taken since the late 1980s. In the mid-1980s, the factory began to vigorously expand operations, and in 1990, the district administrative office decided to try turning the factory into a company, forming a board of directors and giving the board significant economic freedom to develop and transform.[24] When I first visited the company in 1996, it had just built a new factory facility and expanded operations significantly. As the general manager of the company described the trajectory of his company,

> In 1990 things really started to develop quickly for our factory. Our district office made us into a limited public shares factory, we formed a board of directors, and we started thinking about how to develop within this sector aggressively. Since then we have made

many changes within our organization that reflect our market orientation. I think, maybe, you will find that our organization is quite different from many that you will see in China. Maybe it is a little more like the organizations you have in the United States.

He went on to distinguish the attitude and engagement of his factory from the "old style" organizations of the planned economy:

Old-style organizations of the planned economy don't understand markets. They have no interest at all in developing aggressively. They are not connected to their profits and they can't make decisions on their own. . . . The freedom and competition of the market economy have forced us to develop much more quickly than some other organizations. . . . In 1986 our fixed assets were 590,000 renminbi; in 1992 they were 3,600,000 renminbi; and in 1994 they were 30,000,000 renminbi. This kind of growth is all a result of our aggressive development plan.

(Personal interview, 1996)

This case exemplifies the close relationship some district administrative offices have with the factories under their jurisdiction. Though the factory could not draw on funds from state coffers for bailouts from a very early stage in the reforms, the district administrative office nevertheless was able to provide a resource that was more valuable than redistributive resources: it provided guidance through the economic reforms, helping the senior management of the factory think through and implement new management systems and expansion-oriented development plans. Changing the factory into a "company," setting up a board of directors, and giving management significant autonomy over economic development plans did not mean, however, a lack of attention from the local administrative office. On the contrary, the company's general manager spoke repeatedly about the close alliance between the district office and his company's board. He often referred to the district office as "our leader," noting the care and leadership that came out of the district office as the company experimented with new management systems and new development plans. Thus, the transfer of knowledge and the learning of capitalist practices in this case came directly from the local government, a situation similar to that described in Andy Walder's (1995e) description of the relationship between local township and village governments and the industrial organizations under their jurisdiction. Indeed, the general manager of this factory went on to distinguish between those relationships with other organizations that were valuable and helped in development and those that did not. With regard to the role of foreign investors in these relationships, the general manager was careful to acknowledge those firms that were helpful:

Of course, we want foreign investment, foreign technology, foreign management systems. But we are not just going to wait around for foreign companies to bring their technology to us as part of an investment. This is not the way to develop. So we are working on developing new management systems and technological areas ourselves. . . . This is the main reason, by the way, that I am not very interested in investments with Taiwanese and Hong Kong companies. They are not interested enough in development of technology and managements systems. What they seem to want most is cheaper labor.

(Personal interview, 1996)

Motorola and the Hangzhou Telecommunications Factory

In 1988, Motorola set up one of the first large-scale wholly owned foreign enterprises (WOFEs) in China, Tianjin Motorola. Set in Tianjin's special economic zone, this venture would become one of the early models for companies testing the waters of entry into China's markets in the early stages of the economic reforms. In the early stages, WOFEs were a way of protecting intellectual property. In joint-venture negotiations, one of the key factors of the negotiation in asset or technologically intensive industries is the transfer of technology. For companies that were concerned with the protection of the proprietary technology in the joint-venture entity, it was often a significant challenge to safeguard intellectual property at levels that were common in home countries. In one famous example, when DuPont opened an agricultural chemicals plant in Shanghai, local entrepreneurs infiltrated the company, copied one of DuPont's herbicidal formulas, and brazenly started a rival company to produce it. Despite the passage of the Patent Law of the PRC in 1985, DuPont found that Chinese courts would not protect the intellectual property rights of its products.[25] To avoid such situations, some multinationals set up WOFEs, which can easily protect proprietary technology, and then establish licensing agreements with Chinese factories that produce prepackaged technology. With these arrangements, Chinese factories do the assembly and production, but they do not have access to the technology from start to finish. While the advantage of these arrangements lies in the protection of the technology, there is a disadvantage: if the multinational corporation wants access to internal Chinese markets (as opposed to just production for export), the export ratio is also part of the joint-venture negotiation. Firms that do joint-venture deals generally receive better export ratios (i.e., they are able to sell a greater percentage of their product to internal markets) than those that simply engage in licensing agreements.

Though licensing agreements do not demand the same level of commitment as joint-venture relationships—they are "cooperative" agreements rather than joint ventures (*hezuo xiangmu* as opposed to *hezi qiye*)—they do require a commitment over time. The distinction here is between contractual production agreements that are between a Chinese and a foreign firm that are commitments over time and those contractually bound ventures in which a completely separate legal entity (a joint-venture firm) is established as part of the deal.[26] Thus, on the spectrum of the intensity of the relationship between a Chinese firm and a foreign partner, joint-venture agreements are the most intensive and usually require long-term commitments (most deals are for twenty years); they include the joint establishment of a new entity, which almost always has board members from both contributing organizations, and they usually involve some form of technology transfer. The next-closest arrangement is the cooperative licensing agreements, which are commitments over time but do not include the establishment of a new organization or the transfer of technology. Beyond licensing agreements, farther down the spectrum of Chinese-foreign relations are other types of contractual relations between foreign and Chinese firms that are not commitments over time. For example, the piece-rate production agreements that prevail in the garment and shoe industries tend to be per project and are renegotiated and shopped on a competitive production market in each round of production. Thus, the commitment of a company like Liz Claiborne or the Gap to an individual factory is marginal, as they are always shopping for cheaper production prices. This is fundamentally different from a licensing agreement or a joint venture, as these commitments are long-term agreements.

When Motorola set up its WOFE in 1988, it needed a well-placed partner with which to sign a licensing agreement. Motorola worked with a number of factories, but the one it worked with most closely was the Hangzhou Telecommunications Factory. In terms of this firm's position in the administrative hierarchy of the former command economy, as the name suggests, this organization sat directly under the Telecommunications Bureau of Hanzhou Municipality. The organization was a sprawling factory complex, a classic "little society" socialist work-unit facility under that system—a campus containing all of the necessities of life for the individuals who were employed by this organization in the old system. There are many large-scale factories such as this one throughout China, and many of them are among the group of organizations that are struggling to find the road to efficient production in the era of economic reforms.

The Hangzhou Telecommunications Factory, however, is much different. Walking through the grounds of this factory in the mid-1990s, it was amazing to see just how far down the road of market reform this firm was. Banners and signs hung across the main thoroughfare running through the complex advertised the firm's identity as part of the "modern enterprise system," a catchall phrase indicating an organization's alignment with the institutional changes of the reform era. Similar banners exhorted workers to familiarize themselves with the Labor Law, which had been passed in 1994 and pushed workers and management alike into a new era of intrafirm labor relations. Impressive new buildings stood side by side with old buildings constructed during the prereform era, giving a sense of newness built on top of the old. At each appointed stop within the factory, managers would greet visitors (in my case, an academic researcher) with a friendly seriousness, giving a sense that, while they were very happy

—even proud—to open the doors of their well-run facility, time was money, and there were many things yet to be done in the day. When the tour finally reached the center of the factory, I was ushered into a new building and allowed to slowly browse the assembly-line production going on within. Moving at a rapid clip down the line was their prized product—the Motorola cell phones that were, at that time in the mid and late 1990s, becoming ubiquitous symbols of status and style throughout China. Workers were undistracted by our presence, moving quickly and efficiently as they assembled, tested, and packaged the phones for the outside world.

This factory benefited tremendously from its relationship with Motorola in a number of ways. First, the revenues generated from the production of the cellular phones licensed from the Motorola Corporation made this old state-owned factory wealthy in comparison to other large-scale SOEs in China. As distribution grew and Motorola handsets spread throughout China, as the central node of production for these handsets the Hangzhou Telecommunications Factory gained significantly from the infusion of the cash that came in from these products. The added income, while important, was secondary to the ways the factory changed as a result of its relationship with Motorola. The critical ways the factory changed had to do with a transformation of management practices and the level of standards to which management and workers aspired. Managers spoke openly of their relationship with the Motorola Corporation and how much they had learned about "international business" through that relationship. They spoke of Motorola's role in helping the factory "link up with the international [business] community." At this point, that learning was primarily through advice given and standards set by the Motorola Corporation and, more directly, Tianjin Motorola. Also important, to be sure, was the fact that Motorola had set up an in-house training system, dubbed Motorola University China. Established in 1988, MU-China was established to train senior and middle management from Motorola's suppliers and business partners (Borton 2002). Thus, through active engagement in the education of managers of firms within its supply chain—the Hangzhou Telecommunications Factory among them—Motorola was teaching the principles, practices, and standards of participation in the emerging market economy.

In the mid-1990s, the limited nature of that relationship began to change. After several years of watching Motorola enjoy solid returns for its handset production in China, the Chinese government began to pressure the corporation to expand its relations with its primary partner in China. As mentioned above, the WOFE-licensing agreement configuration allows the foreign corporation to protect intellectual property. However, for exactly this reason, the Chinese corporation is often written out of one of the things it covets most in the Chinese-foreign joint-venture relationship—technology transfer. In the mid-1990s, the government began pressuring Motorola to set up a joint-venture relationship with the Hangzhou Telecommunications Factory. In return for the schedule of technology transfer that would be incorporated into the agreement, Motorola would receive greater access to internal markets and, more important, the corporation would continue to receive "favorable" treatment from the government in matters of approvals and the like. As one highly placed Motorola employee put it to me,

> We really didn't have much choice in the matter. We have been doing well over here for a while, and now the government wants us to share the wealth a little. Ideally, we would keep things the way they are, but, at this point, it's clear that that's really not an

> option. But we will get better market access through it. And
> Hangzhou has been a good partner for us. So it should be fine.
>
> (Personal interview, 1996)

In 1996, the two companies established the Hangzhou Eastern Telecommunications Company, or Eastcom. When I visited the Hangzhou factory in 1995, this deal was already well under way. As such, the top-level managers with whom I spoke had already benefited from extensive experiences of sitting on a joint board with Motorola management and going through the details of negotiating a complex joint-venture deal, not to mention the years of joint work in the production of Motorola handsets through the previous licensing agreement. In many ways, the managers of the Hangzhou Telecommunications Factory had learned the ins and outs of market-driven production from Motorola. The factory had finally been "married off"—a term state officials often used to describe the Chinese-foreign equity joint-venture deal. The joint board and the close contact with their foreign partners facilitated the flow of knowledge between foreign and Chinese management.

The Shanghai Number 10 Electronics Tube Factory

In some industries, however, where the orientation is toward driving down labor costs in piece-rate production scenarios, we find the more familiar pattern of foreign multinationals in the pursuit of cheap labor. Such was the case in the Shanghai Number 10 Electronics Tube Factory,[27] a small, collectively owned factory under the direct jurisdiction of the Shanghai Electronics Bureau. The factory is located on a very small lane not far from Shanghai; it is one of the factories that is located near the center of the city, buried in a labyrinth of lanes that twist and turn until you finally—unexpectedly—come upon a large industrial factory that you would never have known was there. The factory director is a woman, which is somewhat of an anomaly in the urban industrial economy, particularly in Shanghai. It has a feeling like a family-run business. Founded in 1958, the factory was moved under the jurisdiction of the Electronics Bureau in 1977; it employs about three hundred full-time workers.

Walking through the grounds of this factory has a very different feel from the experience of a place like Hangzhou Telecommunications. Though solid in its development over the years of economic reforms—the factory does not represent one of those that has "fallen behind" in the reform era—it is not the type of impressive, seemingly efficient production organization that we find in other transforming organizations. For example, rather than investing in the upgrading of machinery or figuring out how to capture greater market share in the company's sector, the director is quite preoccupied with finding ways to invest that will yield quick returns. One such way that is common in China's reform era is to invest in the service-sector economy. With the rapid growth of the service-sector economy in the 1990s, struggling factories have often capitalized on this growth by investing capital in karaoke bars or restaurants as a way to generate income. Though these investments yield quick returns on investment, they are not a savvy economic strategy in that they have little to do with the industrial upgrading that is often needed to help transforming organizations compete in the new markets of the industrial economy (Guthrie 1997, 1999). It is an investment strategy that does not make a lot of sense in terms of viable capitalist development, but it does pay the bills. As the factory director explained,

> We have a significant investment in the service sector. We are doing really well in these areas. . . . We are an enterprise, and our

main purpose is to search for ways to develop and make money. We have to search for as many ways as possible. China, especially Shanghai, is developing very quickly in the service sector. If I wanted to invest in any other sector, I might not understand the market or the products. But the service sector is not really complicated at all. I just invest some money, place one of our workers in the position as a manager, and I get most of the profits that the company makes. Then I just take these profits and invest directly back into the factory.

While the logic of diversifying to generate revenue for her factory seems sound, this is much more commonly an investment strategy that is adopted by struggling firms in China's industrial economy. When pushed on the question of whether it would be better to organize investments around upgrading machinery to better generate revenues and ultimately increase profit margins, the director defiantly proclaimed,

I am not interested in profits [literally: I don't do profits—*wo buzuo lirun*]. My goal is to raise the living standard of my employees as much as possible. So when we have an excess, I usually just distribute the money evenly among my employees.

(Personal interview, 1995)

Most interesting for this case, however, particularly in contrast to the previous two cases, is the lack of guidance—from either the local state office overseeing them or from formal foreign partnerships—in learning to navigate the market economy. With respect to the former, the factory experienced little oversight from the Shanghai Electronics Bureau. The Electronics Bureau in Shanghai was one of the economic offices that was struggling the most, in terms of governance and guidance of the factories under its jurisdiction. This was in stark contrast to the Hangzhou Electronics Bureau and its oversight of its prize factory, the Hangzhou Telecommunications Factory, and to factories under the jurisdiction of local municipal or district offices in Shanghai. With respect to investment partnerships, this factory had no joint venture partners, though it had, at one point, signed a piece-rate contractual deal with a Taiwanese manufacturer seeking to outsource production to China. As the factory director described the situation,

We did once have a contractual production relationship with a Taiwanese company. But there were many problems with this deal. . . . At that time, our workers' salaries were 400 renminbi per month. So when I took over as director in the middle of this project, I found out that they had agreed in the contract to pay the workers 160 renminbi per month. I thought this was terrible, so I told my workers that I would renegotiate and that I would get them 500 renminbi per month. When I raised the subject with the Taiwanese manufacturer, he would not even talk about it. I tried to explain that it was impossible for our workers to live on that salary, but he would not listen at all. . . . I couldn't allow my workers to work for that kind of money, so I paid the workers the extra 340 renminbi per month from my own factory's funds. . . . When the production began, the company demanded that we produce more than the contract said we had to produce in the first month, and he didn't even import the technology he said he was going to license to us. He was putting us in an impossible situation. I was overseeing the work, and I told my workers that we would just try to do the job the best we could. Even though he was not adhering to the contract, I was not going to be pulled into that. . . . At the end of the month, we actually did produce the amount that he required. When he came to check on production, I pointed out all the places that he had gone against the contract. He didn't seem to care at all. But after I told him that I was going to take him to court for violation of the contract and ask that the contract be voided, he left and I never heard from him again. He didn't even come back to sell the products we had produced in that month. They are still sitting in a warehouse in the Caohejing district. Without the revenues from production, I estimate that we lost about 3,000,000 reminbi in this venture. It's as if we threw the money into the river.

(Personal interview, 1995)

THE UNDERPINNINGS OF SUCCESS

The Chinese government's gradual and methodical experimentation with different institutional forms and the party's gradual receding from control over the economy and political processes has brought about a quiet revolution in the Chinese economy. Recognizing that the transition to a radically different type of economy must occur gradually, the state has allowed for maximum institutional stability as economic actors slowly learn the rules of the emerging market economy. And, to the frustration of many institutional advisors from the West, China has undergone the most successful transformation of any economy making the transition from a planned to market system. While the government has achieved this end by gradually introducing new laws and institutional reforms that have guided the reforms forward, of equal importance to the success of this model is the fact that capitalism is a learned set of practices, where economic actors shape themselves after the available models in the marketplace. In other words, policies of gradual reform have been important, because they have maintained stability in the face of radical institutional change, and they have allowed economic actors to learn the rules of the game gradually, rather than assuming that they know the rules intuitively.

Many state-led development strategies have pushed the

process of economic reform in China forward. The government has been behind the construction of more than seven hundred new federal laws and regulations that govern the economy and society and over two thousand new local laws and regulations (Pei 1994, 1998). It has done this through a process of gradually introducing changes into the economy, experimenting with their implementation through on-the-ground practice, implementing them on a larger scale, and, finally, institutionalizing them in formal declarations through laws and regulations. It has gradually allowed for the emergence of a private economy, slowly moved enterprises off of the dual track system, and gradually rationalized production processes and labor relations within firms (Naughton 1995; Guthrie 1999). While these forces of change have been important in the evolution of the Chinese economy, both types of institutional change—the state-level policies and regulations and the growth of a private economy—do little to explain the ways that firms will actually respond to institutional change or increased competition in markets.

Some firms in the Chinese economy had important advantages. First, some benefited from the changing distribution of responsibilities within the industrial hierarchy of the former command economy, because, at certain levels of the hierarchy, state firms were given the autonomy to take advantage of new opportunities in the urban industrial economy. Second, alliances with foreign firms played a critical role here as well. These two issues will be discussed in greater detail below. The focus of this discussion will be on the ways that relationships within the economy give rise to a transfer of knowledge, helping to guide Chinese firms through the turbulent waters of the transition to a market economy.

THE IMPORTANCE OF STATE STRUCTURE

If we return for a moment to Figure 2.1 (in Chapter 2), we find a key factor that defines state-firm relations in reform-era China. A number of scholars have identified the importance of the industrial hierarchy of the former command economy as one of the key legacies shaping China's path through the economic reforms (Bian 1994a; Guthrie 1997, 1998a, 1999; Oi 1989, 1992, 1995; Rawski 1994; Walder 1989a, 1989b, 1992a, 1992b, 1994a, 1994b, 1995a). One of the key features of the economic reforms that would emerge from the vision of gradual reform was that the bureaucratic sector slowly pushed economic responsibilities down the hierarchy of the former command economy, placing economic responsibilities on the shoulders of local officials and individual managers. As economic responsibilities were shifted onto the shoulders of enterprise managers and the local officials who governed them, local-level economic actors were to be responsible for the industrial upgrading and strategizing of the firms they governed. Those administrative offices that had the fewest factories to govern were also the most subject to tightening fiscal constraints (in large part because of their distance from the central government). The combination of tightening fiscal constraints and the close monitoring and attention these lower-level governmental offices could give to the few factories under their jurisdictions allowed these factories to receive the most hands-on attention and guidance through the turbulent waters of the economic reforms. Oi (1989, 1995) and Walder (1995a) have argued that it is the combination of closer monitoring and tighter fiscal constraints in rural areas that led to the higher levels of productivity among the TVE sector, which was, in many ways, the most dynamic part of the Chinese economy in the 1980s.

Close monitoring by local officials meant a level of security and continuity, even as budget constraints were being hard-ened and the competitive pressures of China's emerging mar-kets were proceeding apace. Walder argues that, as economic burdens are shifted down to local areas, local governments have increasingly acted like local firms. The fact that they were overseeing only a few firms under their jurisdiction gave them the advantage of being able to pay close attention to how firms were strategically making their way through the turbulent markets of China's transforming industrial economy. In stark contrast to the arguments about the impossibility of a gradual transition (Kornai 1990), it was the local officials—the former agents of the planned economy—who were actually the tea-chers (or perhaps collaborators is a better word) of the market economy to the local managers under their jurisdiction. In other words, a firm's position in the industrial hierarchy of the former command economy matters tremendously to the ways that the reform process transpired.

Even though we have not seen equal rates of growth in productivity in the urban industrial economy, there is, never-theless, evidence of similar patterns of state-firm relations. Namely, firms under the jurisdiction of municipal bureaus were much more likely to be losing money and to adopt "life-boat" strategies of economic reform (such as renting out fac-tory space to the highest bidder) than their counterparts under lower-tier urban government offices. The primary issue here was the extent to which firms were able to gain stability from the close monitoring by officials from a local administra-tive office. With hundreds of firms under their jurisdiction, bureau officials had little ability to soften the shock of harden-ing fiscal constraints; however, with only a few firms to watch over, officials from municipal and district company offices were able to provide stability, guidance, and leadership for the firms under their jurisdiction, encouraging them, for example, to focus on upgrading machinery or pooling resources with other firms to avoid shortfalls.

The case of the Shanghai Kang Hua Meat and Foods Company described above provides a good example of this dynamic. The central point that comes across in that case is that where a firm was positioned in the industrial hierarchy of the former command economy had dramatic consequences for the guidance and collaboration it received in learning the rules of the market economy. Although local offices had little to offer firms under their jurisdiction in the way of fiscal bailouts, those with few firms to govern could deliver to their firms another asset—careful guidance through the turbulence of China's emerging markets. This view directly contradicts economists who predicted that state officials would always act in corrupt ways without the incentives provided by rapid privatization (Kornai 1980). In the Chinese case, local officials became collaborators in firms' gradual adaptation to the rules of the market. Following the logic of the above arguments, we might expect that firms under lower-level government offices would have higher levels of productivity.

THE IMPACT OF FOREIGN INFLUENCE

A second key feature driving the learning of successful practices in the market economy among transforming organizations in China was the entry of foreign capital into the Chinese economy. With the passage of the Chinese-Equity Foreign Joint Venture Law in 1979 and Deng Xiaoping's symbolic trip to the United States (discussed in Chapter 2), foreign corporations were granted entry into the Chinese marketplace, and the foreign capital that flowed into the Chinese economy from this point on grew steadily over the course of the economic reforms. From 1997 to 2001, the average annual commitment was on the order of $64 billion, and by 2001, the amount of foreign capital committed to economic projects in China would total over $70 billion annually.

There has been some debate over the impetus behind the dramatic investment in China. On the one hand, Yasheng Huang (2003) has recently argued that FDI has been attracted to China because of a distorted institutional environment: artificial suppression of the private sector in order to protect the state sector has created the opportunity for extraordinary growth in the FDI sector. Others (e.g., Fu 2000) have argued that the state has purposefully set in place the institutions to attract FDI, because of the variety of positive externalities that come along with it: both the government and the enterprises recognized the need for foreign capital, advanced management experience, and technology. In either case, the impact on Chinese business organizations has been significant. While much of the focus on the firm-level impact of foreign investment has been on the issue of technology transfer and the opening of new markets (e.g., Zhu *et al.* 1995; Shi 1998; Fruin and Prime 1999), one of the critical aspects of FDI has to do with the transfer of knowledge in the learning of new economic practices. Much the way certain organizations in the industrial hierarchy of the command economy benefited from different levels of monitoring and support throughout the process of gradual reform, those with direct contact with foreign firms have learned the practices of a market economy as well. It is not simply the opening of markets or the transfer of technology that allows Chinese firms to transform into capitalist entities; of equal importance are the new management practices that Chinese organizations observe in the marketplace, and one of the critical places they learn these practices is through contact with foreign companies (Santoro 1999; Guthrie 1999, 2002b, 2002c). The general impact of contact with foreign investment can be observed in the differing levels of productivity between firms that receive foreign capital or some form of foreign involvement and those that do not. Table 4.2 shows that, according to a number of different economic indicators, Chinese firms that have some kind of funding coming from foreign sources do significantly better on a number of different economic indicators.[28] These firms have better ratios of output to assets, profits to cost, and they are nearly 40 percent more productive than firms with no foreign funding.[29]

Not surprisingly, there is variation across regions of China with respect to this effect, and it may be useful to think about whether the effect of foreign investment is tied to specific regions or sectors of the economy.[30] While there are a few interesting anomalies in the relationship between foreign involvement and productivity, such as in tobacco, where foreign-invested firms do worse than their noninvested counterparts, the relationship generally holds: across a number of economic sectors of the economy, firms that have direct contact with foreign corporations fare significantly better across several key economic indicators. However, we should be careful not to view outliers such as the tobacco industry as simply anomalies in this relationship: indeed, in China today, tobacco is the only industry that, by Chinese law, does not allow a majority stake of foreign ownership in joint-venture firms. Thus, it may be the case that foreign majority ownership is an important factor in the productivity of firms that have foreign involvement. Yet, suggestive as the results are, from this industry-level data it is difficult to interpret the meaning of such a series of relationships.

One obvious argument behind the higher labor productivity among foreign-invested firms is that foreign corporations arrive on China's shores seeking cheap labor, thus inducing firms they have contact with to raise production while driving down labor costs (hence producing higher levels of labor productivity, by these calculations). However, while this view is likely correct for certain sectors of the economy—such as garments, where piece-rate, project-by-project contractual relations prevail—the figures in Table 4.2 also include firms that have joint-venture relationships, which pay significantly higher wages than their peers who have no such relationships (Guthrie 1999). While these figures give us a sense of the sectors of the economy that fare better or worse in terms of productivity, they are aggregate-level data. Aggregate-level data, whether at the sector or regional levels, give us little sense of the changes that are actually taking place at the organizational level. What changes actually occur at the firm level? In what ways does foreign investment matter for these changes? Beyond the type of monitoring activity that occurs through government-state relations, what are the transfers of knowledge that occur between Chinese firms and their foreign partners?

I have argued elsewhere that relationships with foreign investors result in significantly different practices in the ways that their Chinese partners define labor relations and economic practices within their organizations. We might extend this analysis beyond a strict focus on organizational practice to an analysis of how practice translates into productivity. The argument here is that Chinese firms learn from their foreign partners through institutionalized relationships like joint boards of directors, joint decision-making processes, and through the process of negotiating a joint venture deal, as is illustrated in the case of the Hangzhou Telecommunications Factory and its relationship with Motorola. They learn what capitalist firms from advanced market economies look like in terms of internal structures, systems, and norms, and they often implement these changes as a way of attracting further investment from the foreign community.

With respect to the third case described above, the differences between the resources and experiences of the Shanghai Number 10 Electronics Tube Factory and the previous two were extreme. Where Hangzhou's relationship with its foreign partner led to a deeper understanding of quality, "efficiency" in production, and investment in fixed assets (to name only a few of the lessons), Shanghai Number 10 learned a very different set of lessons from its contact with FDI. This relationship was one that did not deliver any of the lessons of how to operate like an efficient production organization but instead the lesson of the risks involved in the pursuit of cheap labor.

CONCLUSIONS

The Chinese government has driven the reform process forward in three ways. First, through gradual reforms, the state has created an institutional environment that has integrated China into the global market, both externally and internally. Externally, the development of an export-led economy—especially in the early years of the reforms through the coastal development strategy—allowed China to emerge as an economic juggernaut, becoming one of the largest suppliers of manufactured goods in the world. Internally, the government opened its markets enough to attract massive amounts of foreign capital. Foreign capital has been important for economic development in China in a variety of ways. Beyond supplying capital and, in many cases, the transfer of important technologies, there is a learning process that has occurred in the transfer of management knowledge across organizations. Aggregate data shows that across a variety of sectors and regions of the Chinese economy, those firms that have benefited from foreign direct investment are significantly more productive than their counterparts that have received no such investments. While one might assume that some of these gains in productivity surely come either from a selection effect or from pressure to squeeze labor for greater production at lower costs, these two scenarios are only part of the story of gains in productivity. Also important are the ways that firms learn to survive and thrive in the market today. Beyond the labor squeeze, it is clear from organizational-level data that, when productivity is measured as output-per-unit labor, firms that have greater exposure to the export market (a proxy for piece-rate contract relations) have significantly lower levels of productivity.[31] Foreign investment of a particular kind—joint venture relationships—helps guide firms through the process of economic development and the learning of the dynamics of a market economy.

Second, decentralization has been a crucial factor in the government's management of the transition to a market economy. In the 1980s, we saw the strength of this method in the rural economy through the thriving TVE sector. But even in the urban industrial economy, we also see the advantages of local government offices taking direct control over the firms they are governing. Following the logic of the previous arguments, local offices have greater administrative resources to help guide the firms under their jurisdiction through the reforms. However, administrative status—that is, the level of government—actually does matter, and perhaps in crucial ways. For example, as described above, the basic levels of Chinese government are the central, provincial, municipal, township, and village governments. Within urban areas, there are also local district governments, but these are ultimately under the primary category of the municipal government. While municipal and district companies in the urban industrial economy have similar monitoring capacities—both having jurisdiction over only a few firms per office—municipal companies ultimately report to the municipal rather than the district government. This difference gives these offices greater administrative clout in their areas, compared to district companies of the same size. Position in the state hierarchy—particularly in a way that allows Chinese firms to receive significant attention from the government offices that oversee them—is a critical factor in the success of firms in the economic reforms.

Third, while the government did not undertake a process of full-scale privatization of the state-owned economy, it did allow a private economy to emerge. This growing private economy has played an important role in the creation of a competitive marketplace in which the state sector must now compete.

One hot day in June 1995, I was conducting an interview at a factory in the Caohejing district of Shanghai, a thriving economic area in the southern part of the city, mostly populated with small, dynamic factories that report to the economic bureaus of the Caohejing district government. As I sat with the general manager of this factory, he spoke at length about how committed he was to living like the workers of his factory. He pointed out repeatedly that his salary was "exactly the same" as that of the line workers in his factory. "I am just like them," he said, "I make the same amount of money as they do. That is what it means to be a socialist factory. . . . We believe in equality." As the interview was drawing to a close, I began to think about my long ride back to the city center on my one-speed bicycle. It was a hot day, and I was dreading it. I mentioned something about this to my host, who then suggested eagerly that I leave my bike at the factory and let him drive me back to the city center, as he had business there anyway. As he suggested this course of action, he pointed across the parking lot to his company car, a large, expensive-looking Mercedes.

I declined the offer. But as I rode back to my dorm room, I thought about the encounter. What do the economic reforms actually mean for individuals working in China's transforming economy? If we measure socioeconomic status by income, as is common in many studies, we may mistakenly think that this general manager does indeed live like the workers in his factory, as he claims. But if we think about access to nonwage benefits, like an apartment or a company car (a Mercedes, no less), the situation might look much different. And how are these factors changing in the era of economic reforms? Who is getting access to more, and who is getting access to less? Who is gaining wealth, and who is falling behind? This chapter will address these questions through an exploration of the changing stratification order of Chinese society in the era of economic reform.

TWO FAMILIES, TWO RADICALLY DIFFERENT TALES

To bring these questions into graphic relief, let us consider the lives of two individuals in Chinese society on the eve of the economic reforms.[2] When China's economic reforms began, Fengtong Liu, a welder from Beijing, and Frank Liu, a university student in Shanghai, were in similar situations economically and socially. By the standards of living in China in 1979, they were both positioned to live comfortable—though by no means luxurious—lives. Fengtong had just landed a job at a large, state-owned coal factory, known as the Beijing Number 3 Coal Plant, where he would meet his future wife, a fellow employee. In the China that these young men came of age in, landing a job such as this placed Fengtong at the top of the socioeconomic heap. With employment at a large, state-owned enterprise came social status; extensive benefits packages, including housing, paid vacations, child care, and early schooling; meal subsidies; and, above all, stability. Wages were not high, but they were not high anywhere in China, and employment came with a lifetime guarantee, so a job in a high-status "work unit" such as this meant long-term security.

At about the time that Fengtong Liu began working at Beijing Number 3, Frank Liu was beginning his studies in management administration at the Shanghai Engineering

Technological University. When he finished his education, he would have a degree of higher education, while his compatriot in Beijing had only a high school diploma; but in pre-economic reform China, this would mean little in terms of potential for income and social status. Indeed, if anything, in the wake of the Cultural Revolution (1966–76), when many from the intellectual class—including Frank Liu's parents—were punished as "bourgeois capitalists," a welder's social position and future might have seemed more secure than that of an "intellectual." According to the rules of communist China, the likely outcome, it seemed at the time, was that Frank and Fengtong would live very similar lives in terms of wealth, material comfort, opportunity, and social status.

The economic reforms would, however, change everything. As the reforms explored in the previous chapters unfolded in the 1980s, the situations of these individuals would shift dramatically. In 1998, after nineteen years of service at Beijing Number 3, Fengtong Liu would lose his job, and his wife Jie would be placed on a waiting list for the same fate. Their secure futures crumbled like the walls of the now run-down, state-owned factory to which they had given their adult lives. That factory was simply one of the casualties of China's transition from a command economy to a market economy: deeply embedded in the inefficient ways of the Soviet-style command economy, this factory, like thousands of other factories in China, would find itself unable to survive in China's emerging market economy. Today, Fengtong works as a dance instructor, making about ninety dollars a month—half of his pay at Beijing Number 3—with no benefits and no job security. He and his family live in a 600-square-foot apartment on the grounds of Beijing Number 3. Today, the dreams of Fengtong and Jie are unassuming: to make ends meet long enough so that their daughter, Wei, can be provided with a solid education and have a secure future—something the couple once took for granted.

Frank Liu's life trajectory proved to be very different. When the economic reforms began, Frank was completing his education, after which he began teaching; he continued to do so for six years. With a degree in management administration, Frank was equipped with the skills and knowledge that would give him an advantage in China's new market economy. Market economies reward skills and knowledge differently than command economies do, and Frank Liu's education positioned him well to reap the benefits of China's changing economic landscape. In 1990, after six years of teaching, Frank found a job in a government organization that manages the development of one of Shanghai's many "free trade zones." This organization is now a semiautonomous "company," and Frank is a vice president, managing the district's development—which means he spends a lot of time working with foreign investors, including such multinationals as Dell, Hewlett-Packard, and Intel. His wife, Lily, who has a degree in engineering from a Shanghai university, works for Intel. Their son attends an exclusive private school, and they just recently purchased a 1260-square-foot, three bedroom high-rise apartment with all the amenities you would expect to find in an apartment of an upper-middle-class family in the United States.

While they began the economic reforms in relatively similar situations, Fengtong and Frank have fared very differently in the economic reforms, and the differences in their experiences bring to light many of the economic and social changes I have been exploring throughout the pages of this book. First, there is the fundamental restructuring of China's economy —the transition from a command economy to a market economic system. Under the command economy, employment in a large, state-owned factory was a high-status position in

Chinese society, in part because of the excellent benefits employees of these units received, but also because these work units were so closely protected by the government. These large factories were the backbone of China's command economy, and they were heavily subsidized by the government; there was never a question of profits, losses, or covering costs. In the era of economic reform, this system has been completely transformed. Now these organizations operate under the constraints of China's newly emerging markets and, in many cases, with no subsidies from the state at all. Many of these factories are struggling to survive, ending the once sacred social contract of lifetime employment and laying off long-time employees such as Fengtong Liu. The restructuring of the command economy in China has been nothing less than a complete transformation of the economics of production and the rules by which production units survive, prosper, and die in China's industrial economy. At the same time, as changes sweep across industrial markets, new markets are opening up. For example, the development of the computer industry throughout China—a sector that Frank and Lily Liu have both capitalized on—is creating new opportunities for individuals who are equipped to ride this wave.

A second shift illuminated by the lives of Frank and Fengtong Liu relates to the impact that foreign capital and globalization are having across China. China's economy is transforming in significant ways, and it is not only because the government has consciously worked to dismantle the command economy and allow markets to emerge. The entry of foreign capital into Chinese markets has also had important consequences for the kind of economy that is emerging in China. As discussed in earlier chapters, foreign multinationals bring with them technology, capital, and, above all, ways of doing business that are shaped by the market economies from whence they came. Chinese citizens who are positioned to be a part of this process have immediate access to higher salaries, benefits, travel, status, and, most of all, on-the-ground experience in the practices of a market economy. That Frank Liu spends much of his time dealing with and courting foreign capital has important implications for his social and economic position in China. Everyone in China is struggling to master the ways of survival in the unfamiliar—and often harsh—realities of the market, and Frank is learning his strategies from executives at Dell, Intel, and Hewlett-Packard. That Frank and his wife Lily have adopted English names and shift easily between Mandarin and English is indicative of their ability to deal in the new global economy.

Third, Fengtong and Frank's stories illuminate fundamental changes in the mechanisms of social stratification, the factors that shape the life chances and outcomes of individuals in China. In the China that Fengtong and Frank grew up in, class credentials were extremely important—intellectuals and capitalists were always at some degree of risk for political persecution. There was little difference in wages across the industrial sector, but stratification did occur—primarily through the benefits a given factory was able to secure for its employees. In this system, factories like Beijing Number 3 were the wealthiest and most powerful organizations in the country, and employees reaped the benefits of working for these high-status organizations. In the China of today, political credentials and class position are of little help in competing in the markets of the transforming economy. Knowledge, educational credentials, language skills, and, above all, the ability to adapt to the new rules of the market are rewarded in the form of high wages and open doors to the wealth of opportunities that exist for the few in the new global economy.

Finally, it is important to note that as different as the stories of Fengtong and Frank are, they do not even represent extremes in the spectrum of possible outcomes for citizens of China. Indeed, the comparison of these two individuals and their families is interesting precisely because their social and economic positions were so similar at the beginning of the reforms. But there are also the millions of indigent farmers in the countryside and nouveau riche of the economic reforms—those who drive luxury cars and have become millionaires virtually over night. There is the so-called floating population—the migrant workers, who are the castoffs of the industrial economy—a population of people estimated at about 100 million. There are more people in this impoverished position in China than there are people in Germany, France, or all of Northern Europe. There are the government bureaucrats, many of whom are struggling to adapt to the rules and necessities of China's emerging market economy and many of whom are making out quite comfortably.

In order to understand how China's reforms have shaped the lives of these different groups of Chinese citizens, we must understand how China's transition to a market economy has unfolded.

EDUCATION

Before 1949, more than 80 percent of the Chinese population was illiterate. In the decades since, the country has made great strides in providing a basic education for a substantial portion of the population, as the substantial gain in literacy of the great masses of its population shows (see Figure 5.1). Shortly after the founding of the PRC, a national system of education was built, and the policy of universal primary education was one of the main agendas of the national education system at that time. In 1955, the state attempted to facilitate literacy by standardizing language

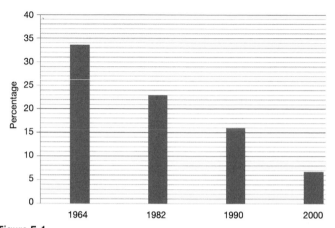

Figure 5.1
Decreasing rates of illiteracy of the total population in China, 1964–2000.

Source: Statistical Yearbook of China, 2002.

(*putong hua*) and creating a common set of simplified Chinese characters.

In 1957, the national education policies took aim at developing professional education institutes, based on the Soviet model, in order to facilitate research in, and the development of, technical areas that would help build the economy. However, the commitment to technical and scientific development was short-lived. The 1957 Hundred Flowers Reform initiated by Mao led to an outpouring of criticism from intellectuals, which gave rise to a deep suspicion of the intellectuals and a radical shift in Mao's education policies. Following that, the goals of education were driven toward political and ideological ends. Mao initiated large-scale social movements and mass campaigns, including the Cultural Revolution, and mobilized the active participation of the masses. Political education would become the primary content in those movements, and Mao's Little Red Book became the most important

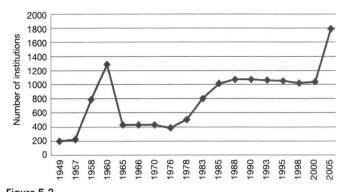

Figure 5.2

Number of regular higher education institutions in China, 1949–2001.

Source: The 1949–83 data from Tsang, M., 2000, "Education and National Development in China since 1949: Oscillating Policies and Enduring Dilemmas," *China Review*; the 1985–2005 data from *Statistical Yearbook of China*, 2006.

textbook. During the Cultural Revolution, an entire generation of college students—Mao's "Red Guard"—was sent down to the countryside for "reeducation" with manual labor. Few from this generation of students would find the opportunity to recapture what was lost in educational opportunities during that period. As Figure 5.2 shows, where institutions of higher education expanded rapidly in the years following the founding of the PRC, most of these institutions were shut down in the years following the Great Leap Forward (1958–60) and during the Cultural Revolution (1966–76).

The education policies of the 1960s and 1970s were reversed in the late 1970s with the launch of economic reforms. While the average amount spent on education amounted to only 6.5 percent of government expenditures in the years 1950–78, that figure rose to an average of 11 percent of total government expenditures in the years 1979–92 (Tsang 1996). The status of intellectuals and professionals has been upgraded in accordance with their better living and working conditions, and they have been able to play more and more important roles in the transformation of China in the reform era. The national examination for merit-based university entry resumed in 1978, and the lower levels of education systems were also reoriented toward improving educational quality. Political ideology is still part of the curriculum at all levels of education and one of the mandatory subjects in the college entrance examination, but it is an area of learning that carries less and less weight today. The emphasis of education today is placed on "expertise" (zhuan), in line with the goals of economic development and the building of a market-oriented economy.

Since 1985, the Chinese government has enforced a nine-year compulsory education policy and expanded the scale of the education system to provide full access to children from various backgrounds. On the other hand, the Chinese government supports a highly stratified education system to prepare people for diversity of vocational tasks that will best serve the goals of economic development (Tsang 2000). Various secondary technical and skilled workers schools have been established to satisfy the increasing demand for technical and skilled personnel in this period of rapid economic growth. One of the key policies in this area sought to merge small-scale universities into more effective, larger universities; it was a policy that led to a slight decline in the number of higher-education institutions from 1988 to 1998. In 1995, Jiang Zemin proposed that the current development strategy "must focus on science, technology, and education." Since then, the education reforms have concentrated on the development of one hundred key universities in key disciplines. Then, in May 1998, after more than a decade of discussion on the topic, a formal reorganization of the higher education system was set in motion. The first change was that ten universities were

Table 5.1 Vital statistics on higher education in China

	No. of univ. graduates per 10,000 pop	No. of faculty (higher ed.) per 10,000 pop.	No. of students studying abroad	No. of students returning from abroad
1980	14.7	24.7	2,124	162
1985	31.6	34.4	4,888	1,424
1986	39.3	37.2	4,676	1,388
1987	53.2	38.5	4,703	1,605
1988	55.3	39.3	3,786	3,000
1989	57.6	39.7	3,329	1,753
1990	61.4	39.5	2,950	1,593
1991	61.4	39.1	2,900	2,069
1992	60.4	38.8	6,540	3,611
1993	57.1	38.8	10,742	5,128
1994	63.7	39.6	19,071	4,230
1995	80.5	40.1	20,381	5,750
1996	83.9	40.3	20,905	6,570
1997	82.9	40.5	22,410	7,130
1998	83.0	40.7	17,622	7,379
1999	84.8	42.6	23,749	7,748
2000	95.0	46.3	38,989	9,121
2001	103.6	53.2	83,973	12,243
2002	133.7	61.8	125,179	17,945
2003	187.7	72.5	117,307	20,152
2004	239.1	85.8	114,682	24,726
2005	306.8	96.6	118,515	34,987

Source: *Statistical Yearbook of China*, 2006.

named as "international-level universities," and the central government would concentrate its resources on the development of these universities. The remaining twenty-six universities under the central government would be gradually turned over to provincial and municipal governments. Within this first-tier group, in addition to the usual funds that the institutions under the central government would receive, the top four universities would receive extra funds to help them develop as international-level universities.[3] Under this reform, universities were now free to raise funds on their own, develop relations with foreign universities, and generally develop the programs that would make them competitive with top-tier research universities around the world. Table 5.1 and Figures 5.3 and 5.4 show the growth and changes in this sector since 1980. Since that time, the number of university students in China has increased by almost 200 percent; the number of faculty in universities has increased by almost 75 percent; the number receiving postgraduate education has increased by about 1,600 percent; the number of students studying abroad has increased by more than 1,000 percent; and the number of study-abroad students who have returned to China has increased by more than 4,500 percent. These changes created a sector that is autonomous from the central

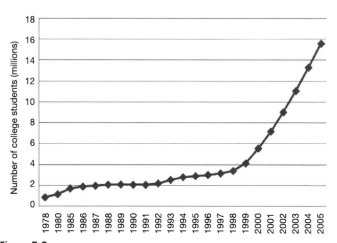

Figure 5.3
Undergraduate enrollments of regular higher education institutions in China by period.

Source: Statistical Yearbook of China, 2006.

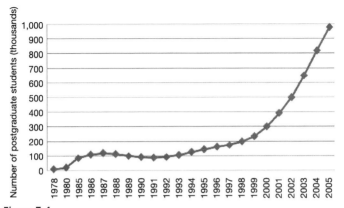

Figure 5.4
Numbers of postgraduates in China, 1978–2005.

Source: Statistical Yearbook of China, 2006.

government in ways fundamentally different from the situation of the pre-reform era. Thus, the 1990s education reforms in the higher-education institutions have substantially brought about massive expansion of college and postgraduate opportunities, as Figures 5.3 and 5.4 show.

Despite these successful achievements in education in the reform era, the Chinese government today is still faced with significant challenges in creating more educational opportunities for its citizens. As of 2005, less than 4 percent of the total population hold a college degree; 38 percent receive only primary schooling, and only half of the population finish the nine-year term of compulsory education; 8 percent of the population have not received any schooling at all. In addition, it is widely noted that the nine-year schooling requirement is difficult to meet in the impoverished countryside, due to a lack of both resources and qualified teachers. About 10 percent of the children in the poor hinterlands—mostly girls —cannot even attend the primary schools.

The Communist Revolution and the decades following changed the roles of women in the Chinese society in unprecedented ways. Women have entered into agrarian and industrial production and into the professional spheres, and the changes have created a relatively high rate of female employment. Women accounted for 8 percent of the total workforce in 1949; this rose to 31 percent in 1978 and reached 46 percent in 1995.[4] Female access to education and income significantly improved as well: the post-1978 economic reforms have greatly shifted gender inequalities by bringing about opportunities to women and men and slowing down the state-driven socialist movement aiming to eliminate the gender inequalities.

The research on gender inequality in the reform era have led to inconsistent conclusions about the direction of change, though all scholarship is clear about the gender inequality that exists in reform-era China. Beyond the widely acknowledged female infanticide driven by the one-child policy (discussed

Table 5.2 Changing percentages of female students in Chinese educational institutions, 1980–2001

% of female students	1980	1985	1990	1995	2000	2001
Total students	43	43.4	44.9	46.5	47.1	47.1
Institutions of higher education	23.4	30	33.7	35.4	41	42
Specialized secondary schools	31.5	38.6	45.4	50.3	56.6	57.4
Regular secondary schools	39.6	40.2	41.9	44.8	46.2	46.5
Vocational secondary schools	32.6	41.6	45.3	48.7	47.2	47.5
Primary schools	44.6	44.8	46.2	47.3	47.6	47.3

Source: *Statistical Yearbook of China*, 2002.

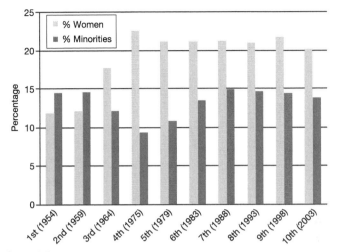

Figure 5.5
Composition of National People's Congresses, 1954–2003.
Source: Statistical Yearbook of China, 2006.

in Chapter 3), some scholars observe the labor-market discrimination against female workers in hiring and layoffs, job
placement, and wages, and the worsening working conditions
for female workers in southern China (Honig and Hershatter
1988; Lee 1995; Liu et al. 2000). Others find that the declining
gender gap in household income contributions—driven by
the off-farm employment opportunities—has improved the
status of rural women in the reform era (e.g., Entwisle et al.
1995; Matthews and Nee 2000). Findings by Yanjie Bian and
colleagues (2000) indicate that in urban China, the gender
gap in earnings and other work status has remained stable
from the 1950s to the 1990s. Despite the indeterminacy of
these findings, there are some clear tendencies of the changing
gender inequalities that help us understand the changing status of men and women in the reform era. First, in recent
decades, with the increase in educational opportunities for the

Chinese population as a whole, the influence of gender on educational achievement has gradually decreased. Table 5.2 shows that the percentages of female students in the total student population, and in each type of educational institution (including regular and specialized institutions), have all increased. Among them, the percentage of female students in specialized secondary schools and in institutions of higher education has increased the most.

The gains in access to education for women have, to some degree, reduced gender inequality, but there are still significant inequalities in the allocation of social, economic, and political resources. For example, a recent study on social stratification of contemporary China conducted by the Chinese Academy of Social Sciences shows the striking gender differences in each of these spheres. According to those findings, men account for about three-fourths of the dominant positions in the most advantageous occupational classes, including state officials (cadres) at the management level, high-level managerial positions in industrial enterprises, and private enterprise owners. At the middle level of the occupation classes —those positions occupied by professional technicians, low- and mid-level functionaries, managerial personnel, and self-employed individuals—the distribution of men and women is relatively even. However, at the upper level (higher-level professional technicians), the ratio of men to women is much higher. For those in social groups with comparatively low social economic status, the distribution of men and women is relatively even, with men holding a higher ratio among industrial workers (accounting for three-fifths). Women account for about 70 to 80 percent of urban unemployed, laid-off, and "half laid-off vagrants." In addition, women face more difficulty than men in being hired and gaining promotion in both public and private sectors. In the public sector, for instance, women are forced to retire at age fifty-five, five years earlier than are men. In many cases women are laid off first by factories and often have to take work outside the regulated formal market.

As to the allocation of political power in today's China, gender inequalities are particularly evident. Among CCP members (who form the major social base of the political elite in China), only 14 percent of the membership is female. And only 7.5 percent of the Central Committee of the CCP is made up of women. Currently the Politburo Standing Committee (PSC)—elected by the CCP's Central Committee at the 2002 Tenth Party Congress—comprises nine members, and all of them are male. Within the current National People's Congress (NPC), about 21 percent of the representatives are female, and only 9 percent of the NPC Standing Committee is made up of women. The most influential woman in China's political hierarchy, Wu Yi, is currently one of the vice premiers of the State Council. Thus, at all levels of the political system, from the highest echelon of government down to that of the townships and villages, women, in general, experience low participation. The policy of early retirement in the government and public sectors also greatly decreases the opportunities for women to get promoted or hold the leadership positions in the political system.

In rural areas, women comprise 60–70 percent of the agricultural labor force. Many women become the heads of their household when their husbands migrate to the cities for work. Rebecca Matthews and Victor Nee (2000) argue that such a position brings greater household decision-making power to female family members. With the development of the private sector in rural China, the opportunities for working in family business have also been opened to women, but men are currently more likely than women to run the family business. The

1995 study by Barbara Entwisle and colleagues finds that households with a large pool of female labor have no advantage in starting and running small businesses. Instead, business involvement depends on the male labor pool—especially the presence of older men.

More traditionally female industries—such as those of textile, shoe, and garment making—have opened up a number of opportunities for off-farm employment for women from the rural areas. With the sizable export economy and the resulting creation of more off-farm employment opportunities for women, especially in the coastal areas, female workers' contributions to household income have significantly increased, and the relative size of contributions to rural household income for male and female nonfarm workers has narrowed (Matthews and Nee 2000). To some degree, this fact may help enhance women's status in Chinese rural households. In addition, the significant migration from inland to coastal areas in the reform era has provided women with more autonomy than they had in previous eras. Overall, however, the situation in reform-era China is still one of significant gender inequality across a number of socioeconomic and political settings.

RISING INEQUALITIES ACROSS SECTORS AND REGIONS

Communist China was a hierarchically organized economy where the government redistributed resources to different levels of organizations and the individuals tied to them.[5] In theory, those resources were allocated and redistributed evenly throughout the society as a whole, such that all individuals were compensated in similar ways. In fact, however, while wages were similar across Chinese society, work organizations varied widely in the nonwage benefits they could offer employees. An enterprise's position in the hierarchy of the command economy was the strongest predictor of the benefits the firm would be able to offer its workers. Those at the upper end of the nested hierarchy—under the jurisdiction of the central, provincial, or municipal governments—were able to extract the most resources from their government offices and were thus able to offer their workers the most extensive packages of nonwage benefits (Walder 1992a). Benefits ranged from housing to localized medical clinics, meal services, kindergartens, and the availability of commuter buses and group vacations.

One of the key changes in the economic reforms sought to relieve enterprises of some of the economic burden of providing social welfare for their employees. As enterprises have looked for ways to cut costs, Chinese workers are no longer guaranteed lifetime employment, as many are placed on fixed-term labor contracts (Guthrie 1998a), and the provision of extensive nonwage benefits has also diminished significantly. Wages are now more directly connected to the performance of the firms. There have been considerable differences in the rise of wages in the reform era. In the urban industrial economy, wage distribution was fairly tight even as late as the early 1990s. However, over the course of the last decade, wages have grown at differential rates. In 1978, employees of state-owned enterprises and urban collectives had average annual incomes of 644 and 506 yuan, respectively (there is no data for foreign and joint venture factories, as they did not exist as a category in 1978). By 2005, individuals in these organizations were making 19,300 and 11,280 yuan, respectively, while individuals in the foreign sector were making just over 18,200 yuan.

Income in urban areas has risen much more rapidly than in rural areas. In rural areas, income has risen from an average household level of 133 yuan in 1978 to 3,250 yuan in 2005; during the same period, the overall average income for urban

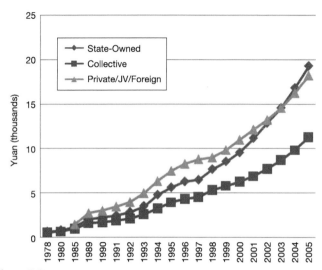

Figure 5.6

Average wages of employees in economic sectors with different ownerships, 1978–2005.

Source: Chinese Statistical Yearbook, 2006.

households has risen from 343 to 10,493 yuan. By official measures (i.e., according to the Chinese government), the proportion of poverty-stricken households—those households that have a net annual income of 600 yuan and below—has decreased from 87 percent in 1985 to about 4 percent in 2000. However, the rise of rural household income is strikingly small when compared to that of urban areas. Rural incomes in China are only 40 percent of urban incomes, when, in most countries, rural incomes are 66 percent or more of urban incomes in the mid-1990s (World Bank Report 1997). Further, this figure is a low poverty-line estimation. Using the international standard of one dollar per person per day would produce a higher figure, as would a poverty estimate based on calorie intake (UN in China 2005).

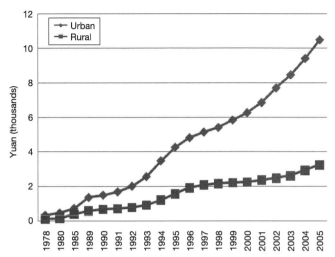

Figure 5.7

Per capita annual incomes of urban and rural households, 1978–2005.

Source: *Statistical Yearbook of China*, 2006.

Regional disparities are also significant in reform-era China. In the communist era, differences between regions were small. However, as economic reforms have concentrated development in the coast region, the uneven development between the coastal and inland areas has been extreme. Per-capita annual income in urban Shanghai in 2001 was 12,980 yuan, far ahead of other urban regions. When we compare the average annual income of high-income provinces, which are located in the eastern region, with those of the lowest income provinces in the western region, the differences are significant. For urban areas in 2001, the lowest per-capita annual income in the nation, that of urban Gangsu, was 5,413.7 yuan, less than half of the per-capita annual income of urban Shanghai. For rural areas, in 2001, the highest per-capita net income in the nation, that of rural Shanghai, was 5870.9 yuan, which is more than four times the per-capita net income of rural Tibet,

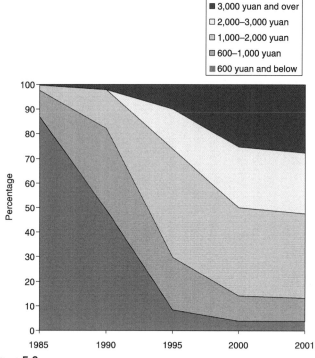

Figure 5.8

Percentage of rural households grouped by per capita annual net income, 1985–2001.

Source: *Statistical Yearbook of China*, 2002.

the lowest in the nation. In each provincial-level region, the per-capita annual income of urban areas is between two and four times that of rural areas. There were nine provincial-level regions where the per-capita annual income in urban areas in 2001 was above the national average of 6,907.1 yuan; these include Beijing, Fujian, Guangdong, Jiangsu, Shandong, Shanghai, Tianjin, Tibet, and Zhejiang. Except for Tibet, which is located in the western region and has received special subsidiaries from the central government, the other eight

China and Globalization

provinces are in the Eastern region. As for rural areas, there are ten provincial-level regions with per-capita annual income above the national average of 2,366.4 yuan. They are Beijing, Jiangsu, Fujian, Guangdong, Hebei, Liaoning, Shandong, Shanghai, Tianjin, and Zhejiang; all except for Hebei are, again, in the Eastern region.

RURAL-TO-URBAN MIGRATION

Throughout the communist era, the household registration (hukou) system has been one of the major tools of social control employed by the Chinese state. Far beyond a system of providing population statistics and identifying individual status, the hukou directly regulates population distribution, blocks rural-to-urban migration, and, most important, defines accessibility to state-provided benefits. In the pre-reform era, economic development strategies placed a high priority on heavy industry and created significant inequality between the agricultural and industrial sectors. The work-unit system of urban industrial economy provided full employment and a range of nonwage benefits to urban residents, while the rural population was basically outside of the state welfare system. To avoid the flows of individuals between industrial and agricultural sectors, as well as between rural and urban areas, the state instituted the hukou system as a strict measure of migration control.

Under this institution, Chinese citizens were forced to live in the place where their "household registration" was kept. Each citizen was required to register in one—and only one— place of regular residence. Prior to 1998, hukou registration was a "birth-subscribed" status inherited from a child's mother. Reforms to the policy in 1998 allowed children to inherit hukou status from either their mother or their father (Chan and Zhang 1999). Once assigned a residential location,

Table 5.3 Per capita annual income of rural versus urban households by region, 2001

Eastern provinces	Rural (yuan)	Urban (yuan)	Central provinces	Rural (yuan)	Urban (yuan)	Western provinces	Rural (yuan)	Urban (yuan)
Beijing	5025.5	11659.0	Hebei	2603.6	6027.8	Shanxi	1956.0	5416.3
Tianjin	3947.7	8999.4	Heilongjian	2280.3	5461.7	Gansu	1508.6	5413.7
Liaoning	2557.9	5832.6	Jilin	2182.2	5361.4	Ningxia	1823.1	5582.2
Shandong	2804.5	7141.2	Inner Mongolia	1973.4	5561.1	Sichuan	1987.0	6406.6
Jiangsu	3784.7	7427.5	Shanaxi	1490.8	5513.8	Yunnan	1533.7	6849.7
Shanghai	5870.9	12981.5	Henan	2097.9	5292.1	Guizhou	1411.7	5467.2
Zhejiang	4582.3	10540.4	Anhui	2020.0	5715.5	Qinghai	1557.3	5883.8
Fujian	3380.7	8384.6	Hubei	2352.2	5888.7	Xinjiang	1710.4	6456.9
Guangdong	3769.8	10534.7	Hunan	2299.5	6832.6	Tibet	1404.0	7912.4
Guangxi	1944.3	6722.8	Jiangxi	2231.6	5545.7	Chongqing	1971.2	6755.5
Hainan	2226.5	5927.4						
Averages	3626.8	8741.009		2153.15	5720.04		1686.3	6214.43

Source: Statistical Yearbook of China, 2002.

individuals cannot elect to change their *hukou* registration. By 1955, all citizens of China were listed with either an urban or rural household registration. This classification was then used to determine whether or not a citizen was entitled to state-subsidized benefits and a variety of other social goods, such as public education. Holding an urban *hukou* gave a citizen access not only to the supply of food, housing, and other basic life necessities provided by the state in the pre-reform era, but also to many types of urban jobs. With proper paperwork, in some instances, individuals could legally migrate to urban areas, for example, but few people would choose to do so because it was so difficult to survive outside their *hukou* registration locations since urban job recruitment and job transfers were controlled by the government. Thus, the *hukou* system was not simply about migration control alone; it was also a fundamental part of the state monopoly over the distribution of goods and services.

In the beginning of the economic reforms, the barriers between urban and rural areas began to break down. There were at least three major reasons for this change. First, the receding state control over economic decisions led to diminishing control over social policies as well. The institutional mechanisms once maintaining the communist order in both urban (the work-unit system) and rural areas (the collective production units) declined with the withdrawal of the party-state's roles in the reform era. The *hukou* system still exists and functions in some important ways even today, but it is not the only channel through which Chinese citizens obtain their resources, goods, and services. The market economy provides more people with these resources outside their place of formal *hukou* registration. In addition, state-subsidized welfare for urban citizens has been greatly reduced when compared to the prereform era. Second, the rapid growth of China's economy has produced increasing need for low-wage, temporary labor in developing urban areas (mainly in construction) and for more permanent labor in the export-led economy. These economic developments have become a significant driving force behind migration between rural and urban areas as well as between inland and coastal areas. Rural population began to migrate to cities for temporary jobs and money, despite the lack of state-guaranteed benefits attached to urban *hukou* status. Third, rapid growth in unemployment in rural areas since the 1980s also accounts for the increasing mobility from the countryside to towns and cities.

By 1984, the central government began to relent on the strict control over population regarding household registration, acknowledging the need for some level of rural-to-urban migration. Key changes were made by the central government to adjust its policies on migration control and household registration. In 1985, the Ministry of Public Security (MPS) published "Provisional Regulations on the Management of Population Living Temporarily in the Cities." This regulation stipulated that people of sixteen years of age and over who intended to stay in urban areas other than those of their *hukou* registration for more than three months could do so by applying for a temporary residence certificate. As an attempt to aid local authorities to monitor and control this temporary population, the 1985 regulation created a new category that fit into the household registration system. One year later, it became legal to sell grain to peasants at work in the cities, and thus this temporary population was allowed to actually live in those cities on a long-term basis. Since then, almost all provincial and city governments have created their own policies for the regulation of the temporary population within their jurisdiction. In 1988, the State Council and the Ministry of Labor recommended that impoverished provinces in the hinterland export their labor to more advanced regions where there was an increasing demand for low-cost labor.

In 1989, the MPS introduced citizen identification cards in order to deal with the new population mobility; it was then mandatory for everyone over the age of sixteen to carry a citizen identification card. For peasant migrants, the citizen identification card has replaced the "introduction letter" from the home village where the citizen's *hukou* is held (Solinger 1999b). Those who legally and permanently change their places of regular *hukou* registration are now required to change their citizen identification cards (Chan and Zhang, 1999). This new system of photo identification provides the local governments with a more efficient way of regulating outsiders within their jurisdiction because the outsiders' statuses are easily identified. In 1989, the State Council permitted state enterprises to sign labor contracts directly with individual workers, as long as they report the employment to the local labor bureau and enter their individual records into the citizen identification databases.

One of the most significant products of the loosening of *hukou* regulations was the emergence of the "floating population"—those urban-dwelling and unlicensed laborers migrating from rural areas (Solinger 1999a). It is estimated that over one hundred million people constitute this floating population in today's China.[6] The existing *hukou* classification between urban and rural citizens has placed peasant migrants at the lowest level of the urban social stratification system, making them "secondary citizens" in urban areas (Solinger 1999a, 1999b). As Dorothy Solinger argues, migrant laborers are not treated like urban citizens there, despite the ability to move and work within the system. The state has allowed them the ability to move, but it does not afford them the "rights" that go along with an urban household registration in a given area. They are ineligible for welfare, medical, educational, or housing benefits to which urban residents of a given area have access. For example, migrant laborers have no access to urban housing allocations, but they are also not allowed to build or buy houses or to occupy land in urban areas; nor do they have access to government-sponsored health care or educational institutions. Since the 1990s, migrant laborers have unofficially bought land and built housing in urban areas, giving rise to growing shantytowns built by migrant laborers in urban areas. In recent years, migrants' shantytowns have begun establishing their own schools, hospitals, and other unofficial institutions. Yet the existence of these shanty towns is precarious at best, as they can be subject to the local government's supervision and even mandatory removal.

CONCLUSIONS

A brief stroll down Huaihai Road, one of Shanghai's posh shopping thoroughfares, gives an immediate sense of the changes that have reshaped life for Chinese citizens. Wealthy nouveau-riche couples stroll down the street, dressed in expensive suits and shopping at Shanghai's most expensive department stores, sometimes holding miniature dogs (a new accessory of the wealthy in China). Some of these people have chauffeurs waiting for them, no more than a block away, in their luxury Buicks. Many of them will return to new homes in the suburbs of Shanghai, or to their large houses within gated communities, with private schools nearby. But in these same blocks, one will also run up against the reminders that capitalist economies are rife with inequality: small children from the countryside will run up, with the signs of poverty written on their faces and on their clothes, hands outstretched for any help that one can give them. They are part of the underclass of rural migrants who have made their way into China's booming metropolises to beg for a living.

Life chances for individuals have changed dramatically over the course of China's economic reforms. Pre-reform Chinese society was one in which wages were very tightly controlled, and there was relatively little variation in annual incomes and little ability for mobility within the society. There were, nevertheless, certain pathways toward elite status. Party membership and government jobs created an administrative class that had significantly greater access to resources and positions of authority in the pre-reform era. In the reform era, party membership is still important, but paths to power have opened up substantially. College education has expanded significantly since 1979, and wages of college-educated individuals have risen significantly as well. And the reforms have opened a number of different pathways to middle-class status throughout the society: state bureaucrats and managers of large enterprises are still powerful in Chinese society, but so are many entrepreneurs who have made their fortunes in China's growing private economy. Individuals with the credentials that have currency in the global economy, such as college educations and English language skills, also have the ability to get ahead in today's China.

The expansion of college education and the private economy have opened up avenues for success for a larger portion of the population, but there is also growing inequality. Those in sectors that are trimming the social benefits they formerly offered people are finding themselves without health-care coverage or without the pensions that they expected would carry them into old age. Those in the countryside and, more generally, in the western provinces, have gained significantly less than those in the eastern urban centers. The loosening of migration laws has mollified these differences to some degree, as individuals from rural areas and from the west can travel to jobs in the export economy of the eastern seaboard. These individuals may do better in eastern factories or in construction jobs in urban centers like Shanghai than they do in their rural villages, but they are nevertheless the system's underclass. As China's economy makes its way on the path toward capitalism there will be many winners and many losers within this system—but then, this is the fate of virtually all market economies around the world.

Economic Reform and the Rule of Law
Six

Doesn't a work unit have to heed national law? We want an explanation. We are just protecting our rights.

> Plaintiff in a Chinese labor dispute (quoted in Rosenthal 1998)

In December of 1999, Bao Zhenmin, a former employee of the Thomson Group Jiadi Real Estate Limited Company (TGL) in Shanghai, sued his former employer for back wages that resulted from what he alleged was an inappropriate dismissal.[1] Mr. Bao had signed labor contracts with TGL in May 1994, January 1997, and January 1998. First introduced into the Chinese economy in 1983 as part of a larger effort to rationalize labor relationships and codify worker rights in the factory, labor contracts are recognized by many workers in China today as a key mechanism for knowing what their rights are in situations such as these. Though many Western scholars of China remain skeptical that reforms such as these actually fulfill their purported purpose, the reality is that many workers like Mr. Bao know their rights and they exercise them. Initially, things did not look good for Mr. Bao in his quest to win compensation. When he applied for a hearing in front of Pudong's Labor Arbitration Commission (LAC), the LAC denied his claim. So he took the only avenue left to him—suing the company in the Pudong District People's Court (Bao Zhenmin v. Thompson Group Ltd. 12/28/1999). After an initial decision, an appeal by TGL, and a second decision by the court, Mr. Bao received a favorable judgment, one that awarded him back wages, two-months living allowance, and economic compensation for lost wages. TGL was also required to pay the costs of the trial. Mr. Bao received his day in court, and he won.

In the early 1980s, the idea of citing national laws and protecting rights would have been absurd. The work-unit system of the prereform era rested on authority relations that left Chinese citizens with little protection against the heavy hand of the state. However, in China today, citizens experience much greater freedom, much more protection from capricious authoritarian rule, and many more avenues for recourse against unfair labor practices. In the area of the institutions that govern the workplace, since the economic reforms began, the Chinese government has been gradually building the scaffolding upon which rational and fair labor practices rest. For example, in the case of Mr. Bao, working in his favor was not only the labor contract he had signed with TGL, but also the Labor Law (PRC 1994), the Regulations of the Shanghai City on Labor and Personnel Administration, and the Measures on Economic Compensation and Termination of Labor Contracts. By the end of the 1980s, Chinese local governments and workplaces had begun adopting the types of systems and structures that are most often found in workplaces of advanced capitalist economies. Chinese workers and citizens today experience the greatest sense of freedom since the founding of the People's Republic of China. These changes in labor relations have important implications for the emergence of a democratic society in China. In this Chapter, I will discuss the first part of this equation—the changes Chinese citizens are experiencing in the reform era—and in Chapter 7, I will discuss the implications these changes have for the process of democratization.

Concretely, three critical factors are shaping the transformation of labor relations in China today. First, state-level institutional changes are the foundation for changing labor relations. From governmental policies propelling the reform of state enterprises to a host of new laws and institutions, reform-minded leaders have set in place the institutional underpinnings of a rational economy, and these changes stand at the center of China's transition from an authoritarian system to one based on rational law. Second, the emergence of a rule-of-law society more generally has provided an ethos of legalism, a context in which workers can now place their understanding of the changing labor relations they experience. Third, exposure to the international community has helped push forward the emergence of a rights-based labor regime in China. Finally, an increasingly fluid and open labor market has meant that workers now hold the most basic form of bargaining power—they have the ability to leave the workplace and find employment elsewhere. While such a right might seem simply inalienable from a Western perspective, this change has been a crucial step in the transformation of labor relations in China.

THE EMERGENCE OF A RULE-OF-LAW SOCIETY

Because of the absence of a clear, radical break with the authoritarian past, China is often portrayed as a place in which institutional change has not yet occurred in any substantive way. It is much more common to speak of corruption and the authoritarian nature of the system than about the fact that these gradual reforms have, in many ways, begun the process of constructing a rational economy.[2] Yet, despite the fact that such changes are dismissed, if not ignored, China has created the foundations for an economy based on rational-legal principles and individual civil liberties. As the state gradually receded from direct control over enterprises, it left in place a rational economy that will eventually govern the decisions of the economic actors that survive the transition. New laws and institutions have created the basis for a new conception of labor rights that few scholars of China acknowledge, much less explore.

In this chapter, I will approach the emerging rule-of-law society in two ways. First, there is empirical reality: an analysis of economic reform in China must begin with an acknowledgment of the changes and progress that have actually occurred there. Of course, it is still the case that abuses of labor, a curtailing of individual freedoms, and many other violations of human rights occur in China. However, this is only part of the story; the other part is one in which the government has sought to create a society in which individual civil liberties and a protection of labor sit at its core. Second, there is explanation: understanding the forces driving these changes forward must avoid the simplistic assumptions of efficiency, the invisible hand, and the progress toward modern capitalist markets and, instead, strive to isolate the institutional forces and actors that are guiding this process of change. More than a simple logic of the freedom to pursue profits, the decisions and practices of managers and entrepreneurs in China are shaped by willful political decisions by the government and the economic models to which Chinese managers and entrepreneurs are exposed. Economic pressures are important in economic decision making, but markets are more than purely economic systems; they are also political and social settings in which actors make decisions based upon the social, normative, and political pressures they experience. As state officials and economic actors are exposed to different models of institutional structures in the global marketplace—and as they receive different kinds of pressure to adopt new models of action—they implement strategies that reflect these pressures. The forces behind the changes occurring in the Chinese economy must be analyzed through this prism. As we observe the emergence of a rational economy in China, we must begin with a social, political, and normative understanding of the origins of these models of economic behavior.

The emergence of a rule-of-law economy in China is not based upon an inevitable march toward rational economic action or the result of some inexorable drive of modernization. Instead, economic actors in China are adopting Western models of economic behavior because of normative pressure to take seriously the new laws and institutions emerging from the government; as a way of attracting foreign investment; as a result of the pressure from international organizations, such as the World Trade Organization; and as a result of the changing demographics and structure of labor markets in China. The Chinese government, for its part, is willfully creating a rule-based economy as an institutional and political project that is shaped by the desire to participate in the global economy and by the success of market systems in the West. Within this framework, modern rational capitalism is not an inevitable outcome of laissez-faire economic systems, as transition economists have argued. It is the outcome of a power struggle among nations (and among ideological camps within nations) in which capitalist nations and powerful economic actors force these models onto the economic agenda. Modern rational capitalism arrives as the result of particular social and political forces in a particular historical moment. The ideas of this economy are, in cases such as China's, exported overseas to governments and economic actors within developing nations.

One might raise the question here of why it would be that capitalist nations, and capitalists themselves, would care about exporting rational-legal capitalism to China. Indeed, there are many examples of development around the world in which Western nations and capitalists have happily undercut the institutional framework as a way of supporting despotic regimes or extracting profits through the exploitation of labor. And the Chinese government has hardly been a champion of rational law—at least in the first thirty years of the PRC. But the case of China, in this particular phase of development and in this particular moment in the global economy, brings together a different set of dynamics and a different set of principles about development and the transition from socialism to capitalism. The point here is that, while it is empirically true that Chinese firms and the labor relations within them are becoming more rationalized, this is not the inevitable outcome of a march toward modernization or the inevitable outcome of market reforms.

Rather, changing labor relations in China are the unintended consequence of a particular set of power relations that involve large-scale Western capitalists, the Chinese government, and the international agencies organizing the global economy. Because Western capitalists are intent upon conquering the Chinese market (it is simply too large and lucrative to cut off, as we have done with Cuba) and they are unwilling to wait until China's authoritarian government collapses, pressuring the government to create a rational economy—one in which rational law and contracts are respected—is the next best thing. The Chinese government and Chinese factories, for their part, know that their own survival lies in continued economic development, which, in turn, relies heavily on the attraction of powerful investors that will bring with them new technologies. Changing labor relations and, more generally, the creation of a rational environment within the firm become important markers and signals that Chinese firms can set in place to attract powerful foreign investors and thereby secure their own future.[3] In the sections that follow, I will first lay out some of the fundamental changes occurring in the Chinese economy.

There are many other critical changes occurring, but due to space constraints, I will limit my discussion here to only a few of the critical changes that are transforming labor relations in China. Following that discussion, I will explain the reasons behind these changes.

THE TRANSFORMATION OF LABOR IN CHINA

Under Mao, labor was organized according to authoritarian principles. Workers were subject to the caprice of organizational and party authorities, and they had little recourse against this system. To the extent that labor relations in market economies are based on "independence, contract, and universalism," labor relations in prereform China were based primarily on "dependence, deference, and particularism" (Walder 1986a, 10). Andrew Walder's study of factories and labor relations in prereform China reveals a system organized around political and social relations in the firm, and central to these relations is the notion that workers are dependent upon management and supervisors. If formal rational (or rational-legal) systems imply a structure in which the benefits and rights of the worker are defined independently of personal ties, factories in the prereform Chinese system were decidedly informal. The relationships among workers and supervisors were personalized, and supervisors had considerable discretion over processes in the workplace.[4] In other words, supervisors within factories made decisions about worker advantages and advancement based on personal relations and personal decisions, unrestrained by formal rules or routinized decision-making systems. This system has changed radically in the reform era. While the transformation is far from complete, the fundamental building blocks for a new set of labor relations have been set in place in China.

Labor Contracts

The transformation of labor relations in China begins with the institutions that are rationalizing these relationships. Labor contracts are the first among several important institutional changes that have transformed labor relations. In Mao's China, under the command economy, employment was guaranteed by the state.[5] Workers were assigned to work units by the Labor Bureau, and, from that point on, the work unit was responsible for dispensing income, benefits, and retirement pay for the rest of the worker's life. In different periods, especially in the late 1970s, a small fraction of the population was classified as "waiting for employment," but for the most part, the state still fulfilled its promise of finding employment for everyone.[6] Although by 1980, state-sector jobs had become more competitive than ever before (only 37 percent of workers were assigned jobs in state enterprises), still 80 percent of workers were assigned jobs in either state enterprises or collectively owned enterprises in that year (Walder 1986, 57, 68–74). Once jobs were assigned, except in rare cases of disciplinary firing and even rarer cases of layoffs (which were often followed by reassignment to another enterprise), the job assignment was for life. This is not to say that workers never changed jobs or resigned from a given enterprise, but once workers were assigned to a work unit, except in exceptional circumstances, they had the option of staying at that organization for life.

Labor contracts began a new system in which enterprises are only responsible to workers for as long as the contract specifies. If the enterprise and individual sign a one-, three-, or five-year contract, the enterprise is only responsible for the worker for one, three, or five years and is under no obligation to renew the contract at the end of this period. At the end of a contract period, the enterprise has no obligation to continue to pay income or benefits to the worker. As one manager in the chemicals sector explained the gravity of this change,

> The labor situation has changed tremendously over the last few years. . . . I think that probably the most significant change is that we have everyone on labor contracts now. Now if workers violate the terms of their contracts, they can be fired. . . . We've never had this type of labor relationship before.
>
> (Personal interview, 1995)

The labor contract was officially introduced in 1986 with Document Number 77 and Decree Number 99, both promulgated by the State Council.[7] Although these institutional arrangements officially emerged in 1986, experimentation with labor contracts dates back as early as 1983, as defined by the 1983 State Council Notice for Trial Implementation (PRC 1983). Following the 1986 documents, the legitimacy of the labor contract was further enhanced by the Enterprise Law (PRC 1988, Chapter 3, Article 31), which states, "The enterprise shall have the right to employ or dismiss its staff members and workers in accordance with the provisions of the State Council." Though such a statement does not sound radical as far as enterprise rights go in market economies, in fact, turning the rights of hiring and dismissing of workers over to the enterprise was extremely radical in the context of China's recent institutional history. Other institutional changes, such as the establishment of unemployment and social security funds, set up to protect workers in the event that their organization would let them go in the "re-optimization" movement, have also given legitimacy to the use of labor contracts.[8]

The proportion of the industrial labor force on contracts has risen steadily and significantly since 1984. In 1984, 1.8 percent of workers were on labor contracts.[9] By 1994, about

26 percent of workers were on labor contracts. By sector, the labor contract has been most readily adopted in manufacturing, where 41 percent of workers were on labor contracts in 1994.[10] What this means is that a large percentage of employees are no longer guaranteed lifetime employment by the work units at which they are employed. While I have argued elsewhere that labor contracts are adopted by managers and factories as a way of protecting themselves from the economic duress of supporting a labor force with lifetime employment—in other words, they are adopted to end lifetime employment and therefore are not in the interests of workers (Guthrie 1998a, 1999)—there are positive unintended consequences of this transformation for the rights of workers. This is a common theme that will come through in many of the transformations occurring with regard to labor in China: while a series of changes have been adopted for a variety of reasons, there are positive unintended consequences for the emergence of a rational economy, in general, and the rights of the worker, specifically. Despite the fact that factories have adopted labor contracts as a cost-cutting measure, they have rationalized the labor relationship in fundamental ways. These contracts provide workers with an institutional basis upon which employment relations are defined. They lay out the terms of the labor relationship, forcing workers and managers to acknowledge that labor relations have taken on a formal, rationalized, contractual quality. If workers want to file grievances about their treatment in the firm, they can rely on a formal document to present their case. In the past, the rules of the workplace were defined solely on the caprice of authoritarian rule; today, they are increasingly based upon previously agreed-upon terms that are depicted in a formal document.

Transformation of the Firm

Another way that labor relations have been transformed in fundamental ways lies in the transformation of the workplace itself. A process of rationalization is occurring in the workplace, as well, where Chinese companies are adopting a number of the rational bureaucratic systems that are most often found in Western organizations, such as grievance filing procedures, mediation committees, and formal organizational rules and guidelines. Evidence from urban Shanghai shows that Chinese factories and companies have been experimenting with a number of formal institutions in the workplace (Guthrie 1999, 2002b). Figure 6.1 shows that more than 60 percent of workplaces in industrial Shanghai have adopted formal organizational rules, formal grievance filing procedures, and formal pay scales. More than 80 percent have institutionalized worker representative committee meetings, which many workers and managers informally refer to as "our own [factory's] democratic institutions" [women zijide minzhu zhidu] (personal interviews, Shanghai, 1995, 1996). And more than 50 percent have institutionalized formal job descriptions and mediation institutions within the firm. The emergence of some of these changes is remarkable, given that many of these formalized institutions only emerged in American firms in the 1970s (Dobbin et al. 1993; Sutton et al. 1994).

Foreign investment—specifically in the form of joint venture relationships between foreign firms and their Chinese business partners—has played a crucial role in this process of change. Joint venture relationships have a statistically significant and consistent effect on the rationalization of organizational decisions and practices of Chinese factories. Also, factories and companies that have formal relationships with foreign firms are significantly more likely to have formal organizational rules (Guthrie 1999). They are about seventeen

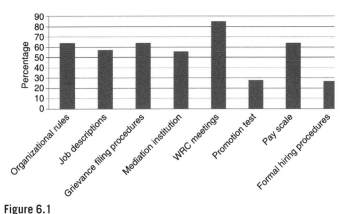

Figure 6.1

Percentages of firms in Shanghai institutionalizing formal labor reforms, 1995.

Source: See Guthrie 1999, chapter 3.

times more likely to have formal grievance-filing procedures, about five times more likely to have worker representative committee meetings, and about twice as likely to have formal hiring procedures. In addition, these companies that have foreign partners are more likely to adopt the laws and regulations the Chinese government has constituted to create a rational-legal economic system—for example, the company law—that binds them to the rules of the international community. This relationship amounts to a significant positive effect of foreign joint ventures pushing their partner organizations to adopt stable rational-legal structures and systems in their organizations. More important, the Chinese partner companies in these joint-venture relationships are also changing as a result of joint-venture negotiations.[11]

While these stable, rational-legal systems are adopted more often to attract foreign investors than they are for the good of workers, they nevertheless have radical implications for the structure of authority relations and, therefore, for the lives of individual Chinese citizens. Compared to the state sector and urban collectives, the average wages in foreign-sector and joint ventures are significantly higher and have increased much faster, especially after 1993. The visible internal-structure changes in Chinese workplaces are affecting millions of Chinese citizens on a daily basis. The workers in those business organizations have greater bargaining power within their own workplaces and now are entitled to numerous human rights (except for the right to independent unionization) guaranteed by the Labor Law (1994). Examples in this realm include the right to file grievances with Labor Arbitration Commissions (LACs), the right to a fair hearing at the LACs, and the right to a minimum wage. With respect to grievances filed with the LACs, by 2000, workers were winning, on average, about 60 percent of the cases brought before the LACs.[12]

Other Institutional Changes: the Labor Law and Labor Arbitration

Beyond the emergence of a rationalized and formalized labor relationship within the firm, other formal institutions have emerged to create an environment outside the firm that further rationalizes the labor relationship. The Labor Law (PRC 1994) and the LACs are two governance structures that have had the largest influence on firms' institutional environments and, by extension, the internal practices firms adopt in the period of economic reform. For example, Chapter 10 of the Labor Law, titled "Labor Disputes," is specifically devoted to describing the process laborers are legally entitled to follow should a dispute arise in the workplace. The law explains in an explicit fashion the rights of the worker to take disputes to outside arbitration (the district's LAC) should she be unsatisfied with the manner in which grievances are being handled within the organization. These institutional shifts have exerted pressure on organizations to alter their internal structures, much as changing institutional environments in the 1960s in the United States forced U.S. organizations to alter their internal structures by experimenting with job ladders, employment tests, job descriptions, and the like (Dobbin et al. 1993).

The LAC is an institution under the jurisdiction of the Labor Bureau. There is an LAC in each urban district and county. The emergence of the institution of labor arbitration in China is directly related to the issues of economic transition and the emergence of a market economy. As one official who now oversees the Labor Dispute Office in Shanghai's Labor Bureau explained this relationship,

> The need for arbitration in China grew as we moved away from the planned economy. In the planned economy, everything was fixed and decided by the government. No one could be fired from his/her job, and everyone was secure. In the early 1980s we started to move into a market economy. With this came the labor system reform. . . . At the same time as we were introducing contracts that allowed factories to only hire workers for a fixed amount of time, we realized that the labor relationship would become much more complicated with this change. We realized we would need a way to settle labor disputes. So also in 1987 we formed the first Labor Arbitration Commission.
>
> (Personal interview, 1995)

The emergence of the LAC is grounded in a number of legal and institutional changes of the period of reform. What first defined these changes were the State-Owned Enterprises Labor Dispute Resolution Temporary Rules, which were adopted by the State Council in 1987. While these rules dealt only with dispute resolution in state-owned organizations, the 1993 PRC Labor Dispute Resolution Regulations expanded the rules to include all types of labor relationships. Later, the Labor Law solidified the role of the local LACs as an institution for labor dispute resolution, as Chapter 10 of the law is devoted exclusively to labor disputes and the use of these local institutions. Finally, the Arbitration Law (PRC 1995) established the practice of arbitration as a formally supported legal structure in the governance of labor relations in China's economic transition.[13]

Within the LAC, there are two divisions: the arbitration court and the labor section, which primarily takes care of labor disputes. One group within the labor section is made up of volunteer workers, while the other group is ruled by the presiding official. The volunteer system is dependent upon the participation of workers (they are not paid). Basically, the labor union at each organization submits names of potential individuals to occupy this position, and the LAC chooses from this list of names.[14] Three groups are represented in the labor arbitration process: the government is represented by the Labor Bureau, the organization is represented by the Economic Commission in the Central Economic Administrative Unit, and the worker is represented by the organization's labor union.[15] This governmental unit actually only represents state-owned organizations; if the dispute is with a private company, a separate governmental department represents the organization.

There are basically three types of problems that go through the LAC. The first relates to disagreements over contractual issues surrounding firing or quitting. The second type of dispute relates to salaries, insurance, and benefits. The third type of problem relates to vacation days and work leave. These three kinds of problems are each handled by three different sections within the LAC. The greatest problem area for applications to the LAC is contractual disputes, which comprised over 50 percent of the applications to Shanghai's LACs as of 1995. Most often, the problem is that people have signed contracts and the work unit is not adhering to the terms of the contract; these cases are usually decided in favor of the workers.[16] The state has created this system, in conjunction with the Labor Law, as an institutional structure to help facilitate due process in the workplace. One official in the Labor Bureau explained the goal of this system, saying, "Our main focus in creating this system is to build a system of legal structures that will make all labor relationships the same. If there is a problem, we want all resolutions to be simple and straightforward" (personal interview, 1995).

Thus, among the Labor Law, the LACs, and the institutional changes within the workplace, an infrastructure is now in place to institutionally protect workers from the whim of authoritarian rule. Do these institutional changes matter? That is a more difficult question to answer. However, over the course of the 1990s, cases brought before courts and arbitration boards have been steadily on the rise. In 1999, more than 115,000 cases were brought before LACs throughout the country. Of these, workers won more than half outright, while only about 10 percent were decided fully in favor of the firm (about one-third of the cases were partially decided in favor of both parties). Table 6.1 shows the breakdown of these cases for 1999 by organizational type and outcome. Firms owned and run by overseas Chinese have the highest number of disputes and the greatest number of cases won by laborers. Following in descending order are state-owned enterprises, urban collectives, private firms, rural collectives, joint ventures, and government organizations.

Despite the gradual nature of their emergence in Chinese society, these changes mark a radical break from the past. From the national-level institutional changes that have redefined workers' rights to the institutional changes that have rationalized labor relations within the firm, Chinese workers

Table 6.1 Labor disputes by outcome and organizational type

	Totals	SOE	Urban coll.	Rural	Overseas Chinese*	Private	JV	Govt	Other
Won by Firm	15,674	4,836	3,028	1,972	2,013	876	1,046	335	1,379
Won by Laborer	63,030	12,742	9,613	5,156	16,317	8,411	3,411	1,014	5,018
Partial victory	37,549	7,560	4,867	2,685	9,313	4,235	1,904	777	5,469
Totals	116,253	25,138	17,508	9,813	27,643	13,522	6,361	2,126	11,866
Percent won by workers	54%	48%	53%	52%	59%	62%	53%	47%	42%

Note:* Taiwan and Hong Kong owned firms depicted in this category.

Source: *Statistical Yearbook of China,* 2000, pp. 750–751.

have more access to rational institutions and rational law than ever before. As important as the empirical reality of these changes, however, is an understanding of the forces driving this process of change. As mentioned above, if it is true that Chinese workers are experiencing a rationalized economic system, it is an anomaly for developing economies, in general, and for authoritarian societies, in particular. What particular circumstances in the Chinese case have led to the emergence of a rational economy there?

THE DYNAMICS OF CHANGE

Market transition in China has been informed by a particular dynamic that amounts to a struggle between a government that wants to stay in power and an international community that wants access to that mythical market of a billion consumers. The Chinese government has resisted rapid economic and political change. The Communist Party made it resoundingly and brutally clear in 1989 that it would not undertake a path of rapid political and economic reform. Instead, the government has maintained political control—at least to the extent that China is still a one-party system—while gradually reforming the economy. Why, then, do proponents of an international economy not simply write China off the way they have Cuba and North Korea? The answer here is that there is simply too much to gain in China; the prospect of access to the internal market there is too enticing to ignore. So the U.S. government and Western capitalists find themselves in a position of wanting to invest in this gradually transforming economy, but, at the same time, they are forced to deal with an authoritarian government that, at least when the economic reforms began, was unpredictable at best. The Chinese government, for its part, recognizes the importance of Western capitalists and international markets on at least two levels.

First, since the economic reforms began, the architects recognized the need for a "modern" rational economy. From Zhao Ziyang to Zhu Rongji, the leaders of this reform have clearly focused on the creation of a rational accountability and the embracing of international standards. Indeed, the "modern enterprise system" and all of the accounting practices that stand behind it are based upon international models and standards of firm management. Second, the government and enterprises themselves recognize the need for foreign capital and technology. The desire to attract foreign investment and technology leads to institutional accommodations that support the role of contracts, rational-legal accountability, and the rule of law within the firm. The rationalization of labor relations is an unintended consequences of this larger dynamic.

As we examine the changes behind the transformation of labor in China, our focus will be on three critical factors. First, contrary to representations of the Chinese government as an unchanging, unresponsive, authoritarian government, China's leaders have aggressively enacted state-level institutional changes that have formed the basis of the rationalized economy emerging in China. Second, pressure from international organizations and Western investors has led to a rationalized economy not only at the state level, but also within firms. Third, changing labor markets and opportunities have transformed the bargaining power of workers in the economy. All these factors have come together to facilitate the emergence of a rule-of-law ethos in China, which has changed the extent to which workers approach the issue of rights. We will explore each of these changes in greater depth here.

Transformation from Above

Economic reform in China has been a state-driven process, as the architects of the reform have aggressively led this transition. Despite the fact that markets have steadily emerged in China, the gradual creation of the new institutions within the market—including the experimentation with these institutions and their measured, steady implementation in the reform-era economy—has been a process that emerged from elite ideologies and reform-minded leaders. At the center of their strategies has been the gradual freeing of firms from reliance on the planned economy, and the implementation of a rational economy. Both Zhu Rongji and (before him) Zhao Ziyang have been fundamentally focused on the creation of a rational economy in China, one that operates by independent, transparent accounting systems and respects formal rational laws and contracts. However, where Zhao's goal was to help newly autonomous enterprises survive in the face of economic uncertainty, Zhu's goal has been to create a stable investment environment that will help further integrate China into the global economy. Zhu knows all too well that China's only hope for such integration lies in the creation of an institutional framework that will put corporate investors from advanced capitalist nations at ease; for with these corporate investors comes much-needed technology, and critical technology transfer is now, more than ever, a central part of China's transition plan.

In the early years, the institutional changes were about experimentation with new forms of enterprise management, the creation of a rational economy at the firm level, and the weaning of firms from the purse strings of the state. However, if the 1980s were defined by the creation of a rational economy, the 1990s were defined by the creation of laws that will govern this society for years to come. Since the economic reforms began, the National People's Congress has passed over seven hundred new laws, and local people's congresses have passed an additional two to three thousand. An estimated half of these laws are directly tied to the creation of a rational economy. The Company Law, the Bankruptcy Law, and the Joint Venture Law are the most famous among these, but there are many more laws and resolutions that have reshaped the economy in fundamental ways. Several of these laws have had fundamental consequences for labor relations in the economy. The important point here is that despite the depictions of a stolid, unresponsive, and unreformed government in China, the last two decades of reform have, on the contrary, been marked by an activist approach to economic and social reform, one that brought about many new economic practices inside the firm and many new laws to govern the economy in which these firms were embedded.

The Rule of Law

The specific changes in labor relations should be viewed in the context of a wider movement toward the rule of law in Chinese society. The last decade has seen amazing changes in this area. In the Spring of 1999, several relatives of students who were killed in Tiananmen Square in the early hours of June 4, 1989 decided to sue the government for the slaughter of their children. They invoked two relatively new laws, the Administrative Litigation Act, passed in 1990, and the National Compensation Law, passed in 1995, which effectively allows Chinese citizens to sue the government for compensation for restitution for past wrongs. Passage of this law seemed to occur as a matter of course, as the National People's Congress passed many rights-based legal institutions in the mid-1990s in China, including a Labor Law, a Prison Reform Law, and many others. Yet, while the government may not have anticipated such an employment of these laws, the event marked a dramatic step forward in the evolution toward a rational-legal system in which the government is held accountable for its actions just the same as individual citizens are. In 1989, the participants in the Tiananmen Square movement were operating completely outside of the institutional system they were criticizing; they were branded "counterrevolutionaries," "hooligans," and "enemies of the state." A decade later, their relatives are employing the legal system to criticize the state for its actions.

These events are important for two reasons. First, it is important to understand the extent to which this society is indeed evolving in a dramatic fashion, despite the fact that the evolution (instead of revolution) make changes seem all too slow to come about. That individuals can now sue the government for past wrongs stands in stark contrast to the society that existed even a decade ago. Second, the creation of a predictable, rational-legal system has been a central part of the Chinese government's path toward the creation of a market economy; it has also been a necessary part of China's transition to a global market economy. A number of scholars have argued that the construction of a rational-legal system to ensure market transactions that match the standards of the international community is a necessary precondition to participation in the global economy. It is possible to have an economic system that is not based on rational-legal principles—for example, an economy could be based on social ties and particularistic relations—but this type of economy is unlikely to attract significant amounts of foreign capital, as investors from overseas will be at a disadvantage in this type of market. Yet, a market still requires enforcement mechanisms for meting out justice, and if cultural norms and social ties cannot serve this function, other institutional standards must form the basis for the governance of the market. In the mid-1990s, the National People's Congress adopted a certain urgency with respect to legal reforms, affirming that legal reform would be the backbone for a stable and regulated marketplace. As Minxin Pei (1995, 68) puts it, the rule of law is "the institutional foundation of a market economy and a constitutional government," and China is hurtling headlong toward this type of institutional system.

In the two decades since the economic reforms began, the National People's Congress has written and passed literally hundreds of new laws, resolutions, and policies that gradually move the country away from the governance of capricious leaders and toward a rational-legal system in which newly defined laws and market institutions govern society. New laws, such as the National Compensation Law and the Labor Law (1994), which rationalizes the labor relationship in significant ways, have fundamentally changed the structure of Chinese society, at least on an official level. These laws and many others have dramatically transformed the institutions and rules that define labor relations and economic transactions in China's reforming economy. With regard to the Administrative Litigation Act (1990), the case of the Tiananmen Square suit is only the highest-profile example of a trend that is actually quite common in China today: with the passage of the act came a rush of suits against the government—about 25,000 per year. Perhaps more amazing is that the courts ruled with the plaintiffs in about 28 percent of the cases (Pei 1995). Also in line with the high-profile Tiananmen case, there have been many cases in which political dissidents have filed suit against the government for violation of their constitutional rights.

We might ask, at this point, whether the creation of all these new laws and institutional frameworks is having any impact on the way Chinese society is actually governed. Indeed, it could very well be the case that while these new laws and institutions exist on paper, they have little impact in practice.

Table 6.2 shows evidence of the rule of law in everyday governance in a number of different spheres. At this point, China only has one-tenth the number of lawyers that we have in the United States. However, for the number of professionals in this field to have tripled over the course of a decade suggests dramatic growth in the litigiousness of this changing society. The number of cases brought before the Chinese legal system has increased by about sevenfold over two decades of economic reform. Most remarkable is the emergence and dramatic rise of economic and administrative cases: in the prereform era, these two spheres were simply not subject to law in any way, yet they have emerged as central features of the Chinese legal system in the reform era.

In discussing the rule of law, it is also worth considering the transformation of the prison system in China, for this is one of the primary targets of allegations about human rights abuses. The most systematic assessment of the prison system in reform-era China is presented in James Seymour and Richard Anderson's *New Ghosts, Old Ghosts: Prisons and Labor Reform Camps in China* (1998).[17] As the common form of incarceration in China, the Chinese *laogai* (literally, "reform through labor") is a network of up to 1,250 labor reform prison camps, housing perhaps 1.5 million offenders (other estimates are much higher but do not stand on the quality of research that Seymour and Anderson's estimates do). Though prisons have existed in China for thousands of years, this specific institution has its roots in Chinese communism, as people were expected to change themselves by engaging in hard labor. Corruption and a lack of state regulation in the 1960s and 1970s made this system one of the most abusive prison systems in the world, and, as a result, it was often held up as the Chinese equivalent of the Soviet gulag. Seymour and Anderson's study sets out to examine the state of this institution in the

Table 6.2 Evidence of the rule of law in China

			# of First Trial			
	# of Lawyers	Cases	Criminal	Civil	Economic	Administrative
1980	NA	763,535	197,865	565,679	NA	NA
1985	34,379	1,319,741	246,655	846,391	225,541	916
1990	90,602	2,916,774	459,656	1,851,897	591,462	13,006
1995	NA	4,545,676	495,741	2,718,533	1,275,959	52,596
1996	100,198	5,312,580	618,826	3,093,995	1,515,848	79,966
1997	98,902	5,288,379	436,894	3,277,572	1,478,822	90,557
1998	101,220	5,410,798	482,164	3,375,069	1,450,049	98,350
1999	111,433	5,692,434	540,008	3,519,244	1,529,877	97,569
2000	117,260	5,356,294	560,342	3,412,295	1,290,867	6976
2001	122,585	5,344,934	628,996	3,459,025	1,149,101	6891
2002	136,684	5,132,199	631,348	4,420,123	NA	NA
2003	142,534	5,130,760	632,605	4,410,236	NA	NA
2004	145,196	5,072,881	647,541	4,332,727	NA	NA
2005	153,846	5,161,170	684,879	4,380,095	NA	NA

[1] Source: *Statistical Yearbook of China*, 1999, 2000, 2006.

mid-1990s, exploding myths about the institution with empirical information.

With a total prison population of about 2 million (including jail populations), the rate of incarceration is about 166 individuals per 100,000 people. Even in the mid-1990s, there were still horrific conditions in some parts of the prison system, such as in the Xinjiang system. Yet, the system is improving under the new laws and regulations that emerged in the 1990s. The rule of law is changing the situation in the Chinese *laogai* in fundamental ways. While a great deal of abuse still occurs in the *laogai*, the situation is apparently changing in response to the reforms enacted by the 1994 Prison Reform Law. Institutional change is an incremental process, and if we are going to apply political pressure for reform in China, we must also recognize progress when and where it occurs. As one former prisoner put it, "Since the prison law . . . prison conditions have improved greatly. Now the *duizhang* [wardens] no longer beat prisoners, because they also study the prison law" (Seymour and Anderson 1998, 180). Rule of law is the one true hope for human rights in China, and this study makes that point convincingly.

The rule of law, which many scholars have argued is a centerpiece of the transition to a market economy, is also the foundation of a rights-based society and the gradual transformation of an authoritarian political system. The Chinese government has institutionalized so many new laws—those that govern the economy and extend to the level of individual civil rights—that it has obviously made great progress toward the creation of a rule-of-law society. Skeptics might still argue that change has not come quickly enough, that the laws are a formal shell, more symbolic than substantive, or that the only true marker of political reform is a dismantling of the authoritarian one-party system itself. To some extent, this view is right: there have been many accounts of the ways that new laws have been ignored or openly defied in practice, and, although the rule of law is often bandied about as evidence of true change, constitutional rights can still be overthrown at the party's whim. However, deeming this fledgling system a failure also places unrealistic expectations on the process of institutional change in China—which is, necessarily, a gradual process—especially given that the country was devoid of such formal institutions when the economic reforms began. In addition to the construction of new legal institutions, it is also necessary for norms, legal cultures, and general public awareness to follow these changes. These norms and cultures are being built in China gradually and over time, and they have significant implications for the rights of the population, in general, and for workers, specifically.

Western Systems in Chinese Companies

While an activist state has been crucial in setting the institutional framework of changing labor relations in place, equally important are the face-to-face negotiations in the marketplace with the very economic actors the government seeks to attract, as Western investors pressure Chinese firms to take seriously the institutional changes the government has set in place. These negotiations play out differently in the "old" and "new" economies, but they play a central role in the ways these economies are taking shape. The transformation of Chinese factories has been dramatic, and policy makers in debates over trade with China often ignore the radical changes occurring in this sector of the economy. Policy makers focus almost exclusively on issues such as regime type and treatment of political dissidents, but, meanwhile, a "quiet revolution from within" has been occurring in the Chinese workplace.[18] As I have described above, a process of rationalization is occurring in the

Chinese workplace, where companies are adopting a number of the rational bureaucratic systems that are most often found in Western organizations, such as grievance-filing procedures, mediation committees, and formal organizational rules and guidelines, among many others. It is striking to see these kinds of changes in Chinese factories, given that this type of legalization within the workplace only occurred in American firms as recently as the 1970s.[19]

Foreign investment and, more important, joint-venture relationships play a crucial role in this process of change. In my own study of Shanghai's industrial economy, I have shown that joint-venture relationships have a statistically significant and consistent effect on the organizational decisions and practices of Chinese factories (Guthrie 1999). This relationship amounts to a significant positive effect of foreign joint ventures pushing their partner organizations to adopt stable rational-legal structures and systems. In other words, it is not only joint-venture firms that are different from classical, old-style Chinese factories, but the Chinese parent companies in these relationships are also changing as a result of joint-venture negotiations. While these stable rational-legal systems are adopted more often to attract foreign investors than they are for the good of workers, they nevertheless have radical implications for the structure of authority relations and, therefore, for the lives of individual Chinese citizens.

Chinese factories that have formal relationships with foreign firms are significantly more likely to have formal organizational rules, are almost twenty times more likely to have formal grievance-filing procedures, and are more likely to have worker representative committee meetings and formal hiring procedures. They pay significantly higher wages (about 50 percent higher), and they are more likely to adopt China's new Company Law, which binds them to the norms of the international community. Those with Western partners are significantly more likely to have arbitration clauses in their joint-venture contracts, which subject them to the authority of international legal institutions, such as the Chinese International Economic Arbitration and Trade Commission. I have had many conversations with managers in which they openly acknowledge that the changes they have set in place have little to do with their own ideas of efficient business practices and much more to do with pressure brought on them by their foreign partners.

Human-rights advocates, as well as others who are knowledgeable about the alliance between capitalists and repressive regimes in developing countries, often remain skeptical of these developments within China. However, the Chinese case is different than that of most circumstances of labor exploitation in the developing world—at least with regard to Western investors, who tend to bring large-scale, high-profile investment projects to China. It is rarely the case that corporations are the leading advocates of civil liberties and labor reform, but they push for these reforms in China for a couple of reasons. Because many foreign investors in China are often more interested in long-term investments to capture market share than they are in cheap labor, they generally seek Chinese partners that are predictable, stable, and knowledgeable about Western-style business practices and negotiations. They want partners who will understand the issues at stake in contractual law and arbitration clauses. In short, they seek partners that have familiarity with Western laws, institutions, and negotiations.

Chinese factories, for their part, want desperately to land these partnerships, and they position themselves as suitable investment partners by adopting a number of the practices that Western partners will recognize as stable, reform-minded business practices. Among the basic reforms they adopt to show their fitness for partnerships with international corporations are labor reforms, as they are often the most visible internal-structure changes Chinese factories can make. Thus, Chinese companies signal a commitment to stable Western-style business practices through making a visible commitment to labor reform. Foreign investors and Chinese firms are not interested in human rights, per se, but the negotiations in the marketplace lead to transformed workplaces, which affect millions of Chinese citizens on a daily basis. As one general manager of a large industrial factory in Shanghai put it,

[These practices are a] very important part of the economic reforms happening in China. . . . It's a way of linking up with the international world. If a foreign company comes to China and wants to invest, who are they going to look for? They are going to look for the organizations with the most progressive and most Western ways of management and organization. . . . It's a way of acting the way the foreign companies act, so they will see what kind of organization we are.

(Personal interview, 1995)

The implication here is that Chinese factories are not simply adopting the practices that are most efficient in the market; rather, they are imitating the models of economic practice that are most respected and admired in the marketplace as a way of attracting foreign investment. With joint ventures, the stakes are often very high, so the pressure from foreign investors for a rationalization of economic processes is not surprising. However, the new legal institutions are also touching the piece-rate economy, as Western businesses seek to avoid public-relations debacles such as Adidas, the Gap, and Nike have experienced. As one senior manager of an American garments company, who spends much of his time inspecting the labor and human rights situations in the factories he uses, explained to me,

> We're not trying to make [managers of Chinese companies] do anything that they don't already have on the books over here. We just want them to follow the laws that the Chinese government has already set up. The fact is, the Chinese government has set in place a good number of laws and institutions that protect the interests of workers. . . . We think we can play a positive role by emphasizing the importance of these laws. If we don't like the way they're running things, we can take our business elsewhere. They need the business, so they're generally pretty cooperative. . . . Believe me, we have our own interest in this. The last thing we want is the public relations disaster of allegations that our products are manufactured by a factory that violates human rights. It's just best for everyone that we do these visits.
>
> (Personal Interview, 1995)

Even within China's emerging new economy, which is much younger and more fluid than the industrial economy, though the players are different, the basic issues are the same. For example, in the industrial economy, where we see powerful industrial giants from the West working to shape Chinese markets in their images, in the new economy, companies like Chinadotcom, Eachnet, and Sina.com have a great deal invested in creating a market that is viable for the virtual economy—one that makes foreign investors feel secure. And where investment banks have played critical roles in helping to finance major projects in the industrial sector—like the initial public offering of shares of Petro-China—in the new economy, the important players are as likely to be the venture capitalists who are setting up incubators to help in the development of a Chinese high-tech economy. Nevertheless, despite the differences in who the players are, the themes of bringing capitalism to China from the players who are most powerful in the international economy are ever present in the emergence of these new Chinese markets.

New Labor Markets and New Freedom

Workers in China today are also exposed to changing labor markets and a greater autonomy within these markets than ever before. As I discussed in Chapter 4, in the planned economy, workers were placed in jobs by the Labor Bureau. This fact, combined with the reality of lifetime employment, meant that there was very little movement in the labor market. Workers had few options for new employment and, therefore, no bargaining power in the labor market. Further, as I discussed in Chapter 3, with the state control over the allocation

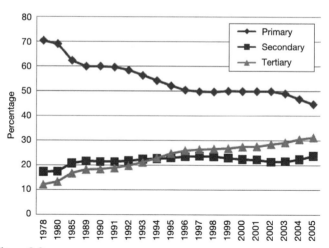

Figure 6.2
Percentage breakdown of the labor force across key economic categories.

Source: Statistical Yearbook of China, 2006.

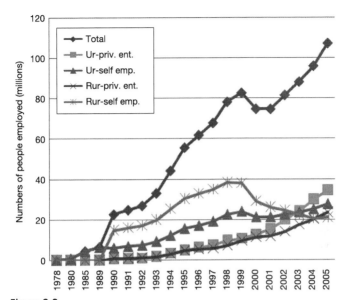

Figure 6.3

Growth of China's private sector.

Source: Statistical Yearbook of China, 2006.

of jobs, there were significant incentives against dissention with party officials and managers of state enterprises. But over the course of the economic reforms, these incentives keeping workers beholden to the state have withered away. The emergence of true labor markets in China means that individuals have greater bargaining power within their own workplaces. Ultimately, the increasingly autonomous labor markets mean that workers can vote with their feet, as it were, if they do not approve of the way they are being treated in their workplace. In other words, autonomous labor markets mean that laborers are free to exit the firm and find new employment elsewhere. Figures 6.2 and 6.3 show the changes in the labor market for different sectors of the economy. As of 2005, the service sector represented more than 30 percent of the total jobs in

China, and there were over 107 million workers working in the private sector. (If you recall our discussion of expansive definitions of state versus private economies in Chapter 4, I have used the conservative definition of the private economy here. By the more broadly conceived private economy, which includes joint stock companies and the like, the number would be much higher than 107 million.) These labor markets provide significant outlets for workers to seek employment beyond the reach of the state. But more important than whether there are jobs in these emerging sectors is the fact that they exist, and that workers are no longer tied to their workplaces with no options elsewhere.

CONCLUSIONS

The changes in China in the last two decades have been dramatic and deep, and these are changes that extend beyond the economy into the realm of labor relations and society in general. There are three central implications to the changes discussed above. First, while economists want to imagine that economic actors simply gravitate toward the type of economic practices that are the most efficient in the face of market constraints, the reality is that the shape of a market is the result of a variety of pressures, and efficiency is only one of them. Also important are the types of economic leverage that are brought to bear in the negotiations of the marketplace and the political actors shaping these institutions. Powerful actors in the marketplace often push Chinese companies to take seriously the very institutions that the Chinese government has set in place to govern the market. Second, because of the uncertainties in the Chinese legal system itself—and the uncertainties of investing in a country that is ruled by an authoritarian government—economic negotiations in China have a more positive outcome for workers than is often the case in overseas investment. Corporations push for stability and commitments to Western institutions—including labor laws—as a way of ensuring that their partners understand the workings of the global economy. In 1998, the United States surpassed Japan as the largest foreign investor in China, both in terms of capital and number of ventures. It is crucial that we understand the implications of the U.S. presence there. Corporations must always be monitored, just as repressive governments must, but in the case of China, the pressure to adopt Western-style economic systems is overwhelmingly positive for the legalization and rationalization of Chinese labor practices. Labor relations are being transformed in fundamental ways in China, and an activist government, self-interested foreign investors, an open labor market, and the emergence of a rule-of-law society in general are all behind these changes.

Third, an institutional framework has emerged that allows workers to seek rational-legal protection from capricious authority. The fact that workers can file grievances against employers in an institutional context separate from the firm is a radical departure from the employment relations of the past. Some concerns still exist in this realm. Namely, LACs are institutions of a still-authoritarian government, a fact that may reduce our confidence in the extent to which these institutions are actually set up to protect workers. And, not surprisingly, workers have the least chance of winning cases that are filed against state-owned enterprises and governmental organizations. Yet, across all other organizational types, the majority of cases filed against workplaces are won by laborers. In addition, if their cases are not handled to their liking, citizens like Mr. Bao (described above) can take their employers to court. And finally, individuals in China have greater freedom to move throughout the economy than they have had for fifty years. This is perhaps the greatest leverage that workers have over their workplaces: with the end of the job assignment system and the new freedom that workers have to participate in open labor markets, they can now vote with their feet.

The concerns over abuses of human rights and labor that are inextricably tied to China's reputation in the global economy are significant, and it is not my purpose here to dismiss the importance of the harm that the Chinese government has inflicted on its people. However, it is also the case that gradually implemented reforms have transformed labor relations in China in fundamental ways, and it is important to depict an accurate and empirically grounded picture of those changes. By looking beyond the workplace, we can begin to understand the forces pushing these reforms forward. The programs of reform-minded elites, who are creating the "quiet revolution" occurring within China, are reshaping the institutional terrain within which labor relations occur. Pressure from foreign investors to show commitments to the rational principles of the international economy are reshaping the normative environments in which managers make decisions about labor. Changing labor market dynamics afford the most talented workers to test the boundaries of the rational-legal reforms that are transforming labor. As China continues to evolve under the normative pressures of the international economy, these changes are likely to become even more widespread.

Seven

Conventional wisdom of reform in China depicts a country that has taken strides in the area of economic reform yet remains steadfast and unbending in the area of political change. In this chapter, I offer a more nuanced view, not only in terms of the reality of change in China, but also in terms of how we should actually think of the issue of democratization.

What do we mean when we refer to the question of democratization? According to the *Dictionary of Modern Sociology*, the concept of democracy entails a philosophy or social system

> based on the principle of [equality], the principle being
> particularly applicable in political aspects of life . . . in any social
> system, rule by majority, usually with regard to certain rights of
> minorities; a form of government wherein supreme power is held
> by societal members in general, such members typically
> exercising their power in a system of representation involving
> periodic free elections.
>
> (Holt 1969)

Most observers would agree with this framing of the concept. Yet, it is also important to acknowledge here that the process of democratization is complex. While many observers view political reform as nonexistent (or significantly lagging behind economic reform), in fact, a gradual and measured political transformation has been underway in China for well over a decade. We typically define democracy as the right to freely elect political leaders within a multiparty system, but the institutions that support democracy are significantly more complex than this simplistic democratic ideal. Creating these institutions and implementing democracy at the local level are challenges that Western advocates often assume to be pro forma events in the process of democratic reform. However, democracy is a learned process, just as capitalism is, and implementing the institutions can occur only as these institutions become stable and individuals learn what they actually mean. If we were to break down the critical developments that would lead to a functioning democratic system, what would we want to look for? We might want to examine the free flow of information; the emergence of autonomous associations and organizations; a bureaucratized governmental system in which institutions operate independently of individuals and where the key institutions of democracy can act independently of other branches of government; an emphasis on the rule of law; the grassroots implementation of democratic elections; and elite support. In China today, significant progress has been made on each of these fronts, and as evolution continues in each of these areas, the gradual path toward democratization in China will become ever clearer.

In the late 1980s, after nearly a decade of economic reform in China, many observers believed that political evolution would be part of an inevitable process. The liberalization of the economy had led to a new and dramatic sense of freedom in Chinese society. New laws brought a new sense of structure to social and political worlds, which only two decades before had been dominated by totalitarian caprice. Although the political elites in China maintained that they were not sure where the reforms were headed, it seemed increasingly clear what the endpoint would be. The direction of the reforms was toward a liberal economy and a democratic political system. And, although the world did not know it (though perhaps many sensed it), 1989 would be a watershed year in the transformation of political systems around the world. After a decade of economic reform in China, the country, like those in Eastern Europe, was poised for a radical transformation, one that would redress the ills that had been visited upon the population by the capricious authoritarian rule of the 1960s and 1970s.

In 1989, these visions were crushed by the images of tanks rumbling through the streets of Beijing, unleashing a destructive terror on student activists who had pushed the regime one step too far. In response to their bid to push this regime through the door of democratic reform, the Chinese government showed the students—and the world—that democratic reform was nowhere on the agenda. We were reminded with clarity that this was still a totalitarian regime and that its leaders would do as they pleased on the road to economic and political reform. As victorious images of peaceful regime changes in Eastern Europe followed in the wake of the Tiananmen Square massacre, the world was left to wonder what the fate of political reform in China would be.

When I was living in China in the mid-1990s, I constantly ran up against the contradictions and tensions of a radically changing system built on the foundations of an authoritarian regime. Sometimes, it would seem that I could move about with the same freedom that I could in any democratic society. But then, when my comfort had risen to a level that would allow me to forget that I was living in an authoritarian society, a warning would come from some quarter, that I was being tracked by the Public Security Bureau. These experiences were always profoundly disturbing, as they often left me wondering who among my acquaintances was reporting on my behavior to higher authorities. Most foreign researchers have a similar sort of tale. Yet, I could not deny the fact that the China I was operating in was so much freer than the closed society foreigners had begun to enter in the late 1970s. It was a place where I was able to visit factories without a chaperoning government official, and the authorities would not restrict or limit my behavior. Still, they would watch very closely. It was a society with many new formal laws and regulations, where managers of state-owned enterprises were exhorted to take advantage of new opportunities—to "link up with the international community"—but their actions would be monitored by the watchful eye of the state.

This is the way of reform in China; a gradual measured process that begins with broad, sweeping changes from above, as the state reshapes the institutional frameworks that govern society. But these broad, sweeping changes are often vague and experimental, and they have always stopped short of a program that might threaten the one-party government. And within the context of these new institutional frameworks, the party-state itself remains conservative and seemingly averse to change. But these institutional changes have also created the space for a gradual and incremental transformation of the world from below. In our desire to see something dramatic, as we did in Eastern Europe in 1989, we have ignored the extent to which, and the ways that, political change has come about in China. In this chapter, I will examine the political changes that are occurring within the country. I will look at the process of democratic reform, in general, but I will be especially concerned with how this process is related to the economic reforms. The economic reforms are, in a very basic sense, the catalyst that set this "quiet revolution" in motion.[1] And while the state took a very strong—and brutal—position against radical political change in 1989, the transformation of Chinese politics and society has continued unabated since the economic reforms began in 1979.

While my focus throughout this chapter will be on the relationship between economic and political change in China, I will begin with a discussion of the Tiananmen movement of 1989, as any discussion of the transition to democracy in China would seem incomplete without a discussion of the Tiananmen movement and the subsequent governmental crackdown. I will follow that discussion with a more general examination of the relationship between economic and political change and will then explore other areas of institutional change, including the emergence of new legal regimes and the emergence of democratic institutions and practices at the local level and, finally, the role of political elites within these processes of change.

POPULAR MOVEMENTS FOR DEMOCRACY IN CHINA

China has a long history of agitation for democratic reform from below. Since the May Fourth Movement of 1919, when some 3,000 students organized a protest in Tiananmen Square objecting to the Warlord government's acceptance of the terms of the Treaty of Versailles, public demands for political and social reform have been an integral part of the Chinese political process. Indeed, on the eve of the economic reforms in China, Deng Xiaoping actually rode one such popular movement to power, the Democracy Wall Movement of 1978–79, until the movement turned a critical eye on Deng himself, at which point Deng turned on the movement. As Deng was securing his position of power, the most radical participants in that movement, which included the now-famous dissident Wei Jingsheng, were extending the protest beyond a call for economic reforms to a criticism of China's ruling elite and the political system. While a call for economic reform benefited Deng Xiaoping as he shored up his position of power over Hua Guofeng, a call for democratic reform was a threat, and the radicals of this protest were jailed.

In 1989, a protest for democratic reform followed in this tradition, but it was a protest that substantially diverged from its predecessors. In the spring of that year, as the world's attention turned toward Beijing, we watched, riveted, as a million Chinese students occupied Tiananmen Square in a struggle for democracy.[2] At first glance, this student-led movement looked simply like another movement in a long history of student-led advocacy for democratic reform, dating back to the May Fourth Movement. But the broad participation and sustained activism of this movement was of a different order of magnitude than the recent movements of 1976, 1979, and 1986. More important, beyond the students themselves, this movement engaged millions of "ordinary citizens" (Strand 1990) in ways that previous movements had not. The result was a political movement of unprecedented proportions in the People's Republic of China.[3]

In the aftermath of this movement, as its images spread across the globe—images of the young dead, of bloody students being carried to makeshift ambulances, of giant tanks rolling callously over bicycles and the other articles left behind by the student demonstrators—the world was left to wonder what the events of 1989 meant for China. The issues I raise here are useful starting points for a general discussion of democratic development in the era of China's economic reforms, for several reasons. First, an understanding of this specific social movement is critical for a discussion of the emergence of democracy in China because it was, by its very nature—both in terms of its content and the state's ultimate response to this movement—about the road toward democratic reform. Understanding what happened in this movement brings to bear many of the issues that surround democratic reform in China's transforming economy and society. Many of these issues have been explored by prominent scholars who have studied this moment of social protest. Second, the symbols and images of this movement have become inextricably linked to the struggle for, and transition to, democracy. The images have, for many, been etched in our minds: Tiananmen Square overflowing with more than a million students, all committed to waiting there until the government heard their cries for reform; the students standing by as the "Goddess of Democracy" was installed in Tiananmen Square; the student hunger strikers, tired, ragged, and hospitalized; the People's Liberation Army marching on Tiananmen Square; and a lone student staring down a phalanx of tanks on Changan Avenue. Third, and perhaps most important for my discussion here, this movement itself is a window into the societal transformation that occurred as a result of the reforms that had taken place over the first decade of economic transition in China. A decade after Tiananmen Square, it still seemed, on the surface, that little progress had been made. The summer of 1999 saw the crackdown on the religious movement Falun Gong and the jailing of Democratic Party organizers Xu Wenli and Qin Yongmin. During that decade, China was subjected to the annual wrangling over its trade status with the United States. In many ways, this movement reveals fundamental things about the structural changes in Chinese society over the course of the 1980s and beyond.

A Timeline of the Events of the Tiananmen Movement of 1989[4]

The 1989 Tiananmen movement erupted with the death of Hu Yaobang, a former handpicked successor of Deng Xiaoping and the governmental scapegoat for the 1986–1987 democracy demonstrations. Because of Hu's political demise in 1987, many in China viewed him as a symbol of democratic reform, and his death brought about a groundswell of renewed support for reform. On April 17, two days after Hu's death, a group of students marched to the National People's Congress with a list of demands, which included restoring Hu Yaobang's reputation, guaranteeing freedom of speech, freedom of the press, and the right to peaceful demonstrations, and ending corruption among party officials. Over the next week a number of small demonstrations occurred: one was linked to Hu's memorial ceremony on April 22; one involved a sit-in at Xinhuamen, the governmental compound, and ended in police beating the students; and one was a gathering of some ten thousand students at Beijing University to discuss strategies. On April 27, the movement took on a scale of a different order, as protesters led 150,000 students through police lines to Tiananmen Square; according to some reports, some 350,000 Beijing residents lined the streets offering support for the students (Shen 1990). On May 4, several hundred journalists from several Beijing publications joined the students in a march to the square, calling for freedom of the press; the occupation of Tiananmen Square extended from this point onward. That same day, intellectuals from several universities submitted a written manifesto in support of the movement. On May 13, some three thousand students began a hunger strike in the square, stating that they would fast until the government met them in equal dialogue. Crowds swelled, and by May 17, estimates placed the number of protesters in the square at around one million. The movement at this point was not limited to students, as workers and "ordinary citizens" were now participating in the movement in large numbers. A meeting between Wuer Kaixi and Li Peng, which was broadcast nationally, occurred on May 18. That same day the independent Workers' Autonomous Federation officially declared itself part of the movement. Li Peng declared martial law on May 20, and on May 22, journalists and intellectuals demonstrated in the square, calling for Li Peng's resignation. On May 26, Zhao Ziyang was labeled an instigator of the movement and dismissed from all of his Communist Party positions. On May 29, the students brought "The Goddess of Democracy" statue into the square, and on May 30 the government issued an official statement that condemned the statue and the movement as a whole. On June 3, the government issued an ultimatum saying that if the people did not leave the Square, they would suffer the consequences. The government carried out a military crackdown on the night of June 3 and in the early hours of June 4.

INSTITUTIONAL CHANGE AND THE DECLINE OF PARTY POWER: UNDERSTANDING THE TIANANMEN MOVEMENT OF 1989

While the events of the Tiananmen movement are fairly straightforward, understanding the underlying societal changes that caused this movement—or, rather, that allowed such a movement to emerge on such an unprecedented scale—is ultimately a much more fruitful task for our understanding of the changes occurring within Chinese society. The scale and scope of this movement were intimately tied to the changes that had been occurring over the course of a decade of economic reforms in China. Andrew Walder's (1994a) essay articulating an institutional theory of regime change in transforming communist societies is relevant to the discussion here. Walder points out that while the emergence of civil societies, public spheres, economic grievances, and political instability may have contributed to movement activity in communist societies in the late 1980s, these phenomena were nothing new to these societies. And while these elements were important for the groundswell of support for movement activities in these societies, deeper changes were occurring that made these movement activities possible in the first place. As Walder puts it,

> [A] theory of political order is a necessary starting point for any theory of change. There must have been institutional mechanisms that served to maintain order in the old regime in spite of longstanding and obvious economic problems and political liabilities; and these institutions must have been eroded in ways we do not yet understand. The current emphasis upon the triumph of "society" over "the state" tends to obscure the logically prior question of how such a triumph, if it is that, could occur. . . . [W]hat changed in these regimes in the last decade was not their economic difficulties, widespread cynicism, or corruption, but that the institutional mechanisms that served to promote order in the past—despite these longstanding problems—lost their capacity to do so.
>
> (1994a, 298)

Economic grievances and political struggles have played long-standing roles in communist societies, and they therefore cannot be viewed as causal agents in unprecedented movement activity or social change. The point here is that an analysis of regime change must begin with the underlying mechanisms that kept these regimes stable and, as they changed, eventually allowed for large-scale social upheavals. Walder goes on to specify the mechanisms that were crucial for maintaining order in communist societies as (1) hierarchically organized and grass-roots mobility of the Communist Party and (2) the organized dependence of individuals within social institutions—particularly workplaces. With the beginning of the economic reforms in China, both of these institutional bases of power began to erode. In the first case—the decline of party power—there are two ways this change had profound implications for the organization of Chinese society. First, the party no longer had strict control over its own agents. Party cadres operated with an autonomy that increasingly grew in scope throughout the 1980s. This was, in large part, a direct consequence of the movement away from the central planning of the command economy. As the reforms progressed, the new economic policies of the 1980s essentially mandated that local-level bureaucrats assume administrative and economic responsibilities for the firms under their jurisdictions (Walder 1995e; Guthrie 1997, 1999). As administrative and economic responsibilities were pushed down in the hierarchy of the former command economy, local-level bureaucrats exercised more and more power in the struggle to control resources and survive in the markets of China's transforming economy. In many cases, local-level bureaucrats abused this new autonomy, leading to the corruption that was one of the central problems in what has been called the crisis of succession (Calhoun 1995); this corruption was a central complaint of the student leaders in 1989. Thus, the institutional changes of the reform economy led to the decline of central party control over its own members.

Second, and perhaps more important, the party no longer exercised grassroots control over individual citizens. In prereform China, the party meticulously exercised grassroots control through local party meetings, usually conducted through an individual's work unit or neighborhood association (Whyte and Parish 1984; Walder 1986a). In the reform era, this centrally mandated practice eroded quickly. Managers and administrators no longer required their workers to attend meetings for the dissemination of party ideology. This change is closely related to the institutional changes of the economic transition described above: as economic imperatives replaced strict compliance with detailed directives of the party, managers and administrators began to run their organizations less around the dissemination of party ideology and more around the ideals of performance.

Dingxin Zhao (1997) makes a similar point in his study of the 1989 Chinese movement. Arguing that it is problematic to place causal primacy on China's nascent civil society, Zhao, like Walder, pushes the analysis to the underlying mechanisms that allowed a civil society to emerge in the first place: the declining control of the party on university campuses, as well as in the workplace.[5] Zhao argues that "the political control system in Chinese universities was greatly weakened between the mid- and late 1980s. This weakening had changed patterns of student interaction and the nature of the control system itself; in turn, it facilitated the rise of the 1989 [movement]" (1997, 161). Craig Calhoun (1995), a firsthand observer of the movement, notes that the university campuses themselves had become an important part of the "free space" that facilitated the students' organizational activities—a situation that was very different from the era before the economic reforms began. It was only through the institutional shifts, of which the declining power of the party-state apparatus were a part, that the use of such state-controlled spaces as "free spaces" could be possible. An emphasis on the structural decline of party control over students' lives is not to eschew the importance of student agency in this movement: central to the students' understanding of democracy was an active rejection of the Communist Party's invasion into private life, and, chafing under the lingering (though much diminished) effects of party control, the students rebelled against it.

In addition to the declining role of the party on university campuses, one of the major mechanisms weakening the sanctioning power of the party was the rise of alternative paths to status attainment, which came with an expanding economic sphere (Walder 1994a; Zhao 1997). Under the command economy, students entering the labor market were assigned jobs by their municipality's labor bureau, an administrative office of the party-state. The system was highly political, and the most prestigious jobs were jobs in the party-state bureaucracy. This included upper-level management jobs in enterprises, as virtually all organizations in the command economy were state-run and university appointments; prestigious jobs across all of these sectors were essentially political appointments. Thus, the party not only had a highly functioning monitoring system on university campuses, but the incentives against rebellion were very strong: consequences were nothing less than a blocked career path for life, regardless of a student's academic performance.

With the economic reforms came alternative paths to status attainment. The growth of private, foreign, and joint-venture economies offered students many options for employment, and the managers of these organizations cared little about a student's adherence to political norms. Of the six movement leaders jailed after the Tiananmen Square protest who were interviewed in Zhao's study, none reported difficulties in finding jobs in the aftermath. In addition, Zhao reports that many other student leaders had simply left Beijing and moved to the prosperous southern provinces to find work.[6] In another example, Shen Tong (1990, 142–145, 209), a student leader in 1989, who wrote a confessional statement for his participation in earlier political activities and fretted about the effects of his political activities on his career, openly defied the government's attempt at controlling his activity in the 1989 movement. The main point here is that with the declining monitoring capacity of the Communist Party and the erosion of the party's sanctioning power, the primary incentives against political activity were largely gone by 1989.

Thus, the causal mechanisms through which we should understand the explosion of this protest for democracy are broad-based institutional changes that came with economic transition. Turning administrative and economic responsibilities over to the individual managers and workers, a coinciding decline of grassroots party organization and surveillance, and the rise of alternative paths to status all changed the equation of protest participation. In other words, while the content of this movement—the demand for democratic reform—is important and noteworthy, the very size, scale, and form that the movement could take on in its cry for democracy were intimately tied to economic reforms themselves. With these fundamental institutional changes came a few other ancillary changes, which were critical facets of the movement that emerged.

ALTERNATIVE FORMS OF ORGANIZATION

In a tightly run command economy such as that of prereform China, the party-state apparatus pervades society. As the party-state receded from economic and social control, it is in the void left by declining Communist Party power that we began to see autonomous organizations and the makings of a civil society. In other words, it was a many-year trend of declining Communist Party power that led to increasingly autonomous organizations among students and citizens alike. Since the mid-1980s a number of different informal student organizations emerged to chart the path to democratic reform. "Democracy salons," "democracy associations," and various "action committees" were proliferating on college campuses at least as early as 1986; informal "conversation associations" began emerging even earlier (Shen 1990, 113–150). These informal organizations served to create an indigenous organizational structure that would allow this movement to mobilize much more rapidly and gather much greater momentum than had movements of the recent past. Beyond helping to foster a type of civil society that stood outside of the party structure, these organizations prepared students for more concrete organizational activity when the movement began. And at the movement's beginning, many of the students who were involved in these informal networks and organizations stepped into leadership roles in the Beijing University Student Association, the Dialogue Delegation, the United Leadership Federation, the preparatory committees from numerous university campuses, and the student-run journalism bureau (Shen 1990; Guthrie 1995). Further, these organizational structures not only allowed the students to conduct crucial practices such as fundraising but also allowed them to strategize and deploy symbols and signals that fostered a more widespread mobilization among the citizens of Beijing (Guthrie 1995).

The rise of private entrepreneurs and enterprises also played a crucial role as organizational forces outside of the party-state apparatus. The state's decision to allow private enterprises and entrepreneurs to enter the economy in the reform era also helped foster the autonomous public sphere that was emerging in the mid-1980s. These individuals stood outside of the party-state and they were prepared to support and foster movement activity when the opportunity arose. The state had no control over their resources, and there were no disincentives against this group maligning the state, as they had already rejected the mechanisms and channels through which individuals are typically rewarded by the party-state. As the movement got under way, private corporations, such as the Stone

Corporation, one of the largest private enterprises in Beijing, contributed significant material resources—money and electronic equipment—that proved crucial to the widespread mobilization that occurred (Perry and Wasserstrom 1991).

THE FREE FLOW OF INFORMATION

In any society, access to information has a significant impact on general perceptions of the social and political world. In a one-party system such as China's, where an authoritarian party-state kept strict control over the media, information did not flow freely. On the contrary: in the years before the economic reforms began, the state controlled all media, so the only information available was the information that the government wanted its citizens to know. Over the course of the 1980s, the state's grip on the media—and therefore on information—began to loosen. In the Tiananmen movement, access to information proved to be pivotal in the large-scale mobilization that occurred in the spring of 1989.

The 1980s saw a dramatic rise in alternative sources of information. Access to information is important because it allows individuals to find and adjudicate among different accounts of events. More than this, however, access to alternative sources of information encourages opinions. The fact that individuals had access to accounts of the student-led democracy movement that varied from the accounts portrayed in the state media allowed citizens to decide for themselves whether they believed the students' intentions were noble and good. In this particular movement, there were two additional instances of the free flow of information that proved pivotal. First, in the 1989 movement, the state-controlled media itself was not unified on its reporting. As elite factions within the party leadership struggled over how to deal with this movement—one faction, led by reformer Zhao Ziyang, sought to use this event to accelerate the pace of reforms, while another faction, led by hardliner Li Peng, sought to use this event to roll back the pace of reforms—the media were paralyzed over which party line to follow in their reporting. The result was, for a brief moment, a state press that reported as objectively and sympathetically as possible. As Walder (1989a, 38) has noted, the media's "detailed and sympathetic reporting" on the hunger strikers "riveted the city's attention on the drama . . . building a huge groundswell of popular support." Second, and perhaps more important, there was, quite coincidentally, a large contingent of foreign media present in Beijing to cover the summit meetings with Russian premier Mikhail Gorbachev and the Asia Development Bank meetings. These members of the media played a critical role not only in broadcasting the images of the movement to the world but also in spreading information and images of the movement to people throughout China. In that sense, the presence of a global media machine played a crucial role in facilitating the flow of information about the movement, thus allowing the movement itself to spin beyond the control of party officials.

While the causal roots of this movement lay in institutional changes that had been occurring for a decade, the free flow of information was also important in the evolution. In a certain sense, though, by allowing foreign media to cover the Gorbachev summit and the Asia Development Bank meetings and by giving the population access to technology—fax machines, telephones, and so on—the Chinese government had inserted itself into a global information network, and its inability to control the flow of information had important consequences for the extent to which it could control the movement. The Chinese government had, in effect, armed its opposition with the tools of resistance, and when the movement occurred, the government could not stop the flow of information beyond its borders, a fact that had profound consequences for the scale and scope of this movement.

More recently, a number of social and political occurrences involving the Internet have illuminated the new role that this form of information technology (IT) might play in the state's ability to control information. In one incident, when China's top official from the State Administration of Foreign Exchange apparently jumped from his seventh-story window on May 12, 2000, government officials were caught completely off guard as the story was posted almost immediately on a bulletin board on the widely visited Sina.com website. According to Elisabeth Rosenthal's report in the *New York Times*, "The government was clearly not prepared to release the news today, and confusion reigned for much of the day."[7] A similar incident occurred when the story of a Beijing University student who was murdered appeared on a Sohu.com bulletin board on May 19, 2000. In the latter incident, students from all over the country staged a "virtual" protest, forcing officials to allow them to openly mourn and memorialize the student, despite the disruptions officials feared the event would cause. In both of these cases, it was clear that the government's mentality regarding control over the flow of information was lagging significantly behind the current reality in this realm. This is a new frontier for outright resistance, and it will be interesting to see, over the coming decade, what role the Internet plays in the government's ability to control the spread of information and the organization of popular movements.

ECONOMIC CHANGE OF POLITICAL REFORM IN CHINA: LESSONS FROM TIANANMEN SQUARE

What, then, does this movement tell us about the prospects for democracy in China and the extent to which these changes are connected to the economic reforms? While the majority of scholarship on this movement has focused on what it reveals about divisions within the government and the ways that the students mobilized on such a massive scale, I find the movement most revealing about the nature of the economic reforms themselves. These reforms have laid the groundwork to make political reform all but inevitable.

First, as I discussed in Chapter 2, economic decision making and autonomy in markets had to be handed over to economic actors in China's newly emerging marketplaces. This was a necessary step in the reform of the command economy: if managers of state enterprises were ultimately going to survive in markets without the insurance and expectation of state subsidies, they would have to learn to make economic decisions themselves. A corollary of this economic necessity, however, was that the party was forced to remove itself from the micro-level political control it carried out in workplaces. Managers could not be expected to take seriously the notion of economic independence from the state if party officials remained present in the workplace, looking over their shoulders at every step. The thinking in Beijing was that the party's function and capacity as the nation's political institution would remain as before—that economic reform need not lead to political reform. However, a declining role of the party in workplaces meant a declining capacity of the party for micro-level social control.

The declining role of the party as an agent of social control was also a necessary precondition for the emergence of a civil society in China. Calhoun's analysis of the emergence of civil society in China prior to 1989 makes a compelling case for the inverse relationship between civil society and state control. According to Calhoun (1995, 167),

The 1989 protest movement was possible because students

were able to deploy existing organizational networks for purposes quite contrary to official policy. They were able to do so partly because individuals and groups within the government and party encouraged them, protected them, or turned a blind eye to their activities. . . . These middle-level officials were central to the organization of society.

But in the years preceding this movement, the students not only benefited from the existing organizational structure of Chinese society but also created civil society through alternative forms of organization. Student leader Shen Tong's report of the movement tells of many organized groups that fostered the insurgency that occurred in 1989: there were the Beijing University Student Association, the Dialogue Delegation, the United Leadership Federation, and Preparatory Committees on numerous university campuses. Perhaps more important, there were "democracy salons," "democracy associations," and "action committees" that were emerging at least as early as 1986 (Shen 1990). The gradual recession of the party-state apparatus left an opening that allowed citizens of China to create this kind of civil order.

Second, a central component in the course of China's economic reforms was the emergence of a private economy (also discussed in Chapters 2 and 4), and with the emergence of a private economy came alternative career paths for individuals (see also Figure 6.3). People no longer had to rely solely on the state for the allocation of prestigious jobs; instead, they could look to the private sector for opportunities. This change further eroded the party's capacity for social control, as it struck at the primary mechanism through which the party exercised that control. To be sure, terror has played an important role in the party's capacity for social control in China. Indeed, every decade since the founding of the People's

Republic of China has been marked by at least one campaign in which innocent individuals have been crushed by the government for showing even nominal opposition to the party-state. However, the deeper level of control within the system came not from terror but from everyday incentives that worked at the individual level. Thus, when people chose not to rebel within this system, they were choosing not to sacrifice their path or opening into the institutions of the party-state system, such as employment and lifetime security. But as the party-state's monopoly over paths to employment eroded, the government lost another critical node of micro-level social control. As individuals began making money within this new private economy, we eventually saw the emergence of what amounts to an economically secure, autonomous middle class (Goodman 1999).

The final element that was crucial in the Tiananmen movement, but is also fundamental on a more general level, is access to, and the free flow of, information. In a tightly controlled command economy such as China's before the economic reforms began, the party-state's control over the flow of information is absolutely crucial to its monopoly as a political system. However, a market economy cannot exist without the free flow of information: people not only need access to multiple sources of information to make choices and comparisons in the marketplace but also must understand that the free flow of information has become institutionalized as a feature of the social system in which this newly emerging market is embedded. But as the party-state's monopoly over information erodes and the free flow of alternative sources of information becomes institutionalized, a third crucial element of the party's program of social and political control becomes compromised as well. Over the last two decades of reform in China, there has been a dramatic proliferation of alternative sources of

Table 7.1 The flow of information

	1980	1985	1990	1995	1997	2001	2005
# of magazines published	2191	4705	5751	7583	7918	NA	NA
# of newspapers published	188	698	773	1049	1077	NA	NA
# of books published	21,621	45,603	80,224	101,381	120,196	NA	NA
News programs (radio)	NA	65,995	135,550	353,368	429,069	483,631	1,066,800
News programs (TV)	NA	7,444	28,593	80,800	116,593	235,336	637,956
Entertainment programs (TV)	NA	6,957	22,096	109,322	225,124	191,154	382,350
TVs per 100 households	0.4	17.2	59	86	90	NA	NA

Source: *Statistical Yearbook of China*, 2006.

information. Table 7.1 shows not only the rise in access to alternative forms of information outside of the party-state's control, but also in the types of information and media that are available in China today. It is striking to note that as television news programs have increased significantly in Chinese society (from 7,000 in 1985 to 638,000 In 2005), access to these programs has increased in the same dramatic fashion.

Another example of the politics surrounding the evolution of information in China has to do with the extent to which this sector has remained under tighter control than in other rapidly developing industries. This sector is monitored closely by the central government for a variety of reasons. First, it is a sector in which very significant technological transfers are occurring in joint-venture deals between foreign and Chinese firms. The Chinese government knows all too well that as big as the Chinese market for IT portends to be, it is this market that foreign investors are after. Hard-line leaders would like to limit the extent to which foreign producers, such as Motorola and Nokia, are able to control that market, and the state's plan is for Chinese companies, such as Huawei and ZTE, to eventually be able to compete with these foreign companies. Yet, the government also knows that it needs the technology that companies like Motorola and Nokia can deliver. As a result, the close monitoring of this sector has become a central part of the process of development occurring within it. And when it has become apparent that certain companies are doing too well, it has not been beyond the government to step in and level the playing field some.[8] Second, and perhaps more important, because the telecommunications industry provides an infrastructure for the spread of information, the government is clearly afraid of completely losing control over individuals' access to information. Accordingly, telecommunications is the last sector to be closed to foreign capital, as Chinese law still forbids foreign capital in this sector.[9] It is for this reason that exceedingly complicated deals have been worked out in the establishment of companies in this sector, as in the case of Sina.com.[10] In addition, telecommunications is the sector that has been the target of the most aggressive regulations, the most recent occurring in October 2000.

There has unquestionably been a great deal of activity in the IT sector in recent years. However, before looking at the development of new information technologies, per se, let us first take into account the spread of information more generally. Table 7.2 presents some indicators of the growth in access to information in China over the last two decades. For both newspapers and magazines, the growth has been exponential over the two-decade time frame, with the number

Table 7.2 Access to media of information in China

	Magazines	Newspapers	Television
1978	930	186	—
1980	2,191	188	—
1985	4,705	1,445	38,056
1986	5,248	1,574	—
1987	5,687	1,611	—
1988	5,865	1,537	—
1989	6,078	1,576	—
1990	5,751	1,444	91,572
1991	6,056	1,524	—
1992	6,486	1,657	—
1993	6,486	1,788	—
1994	7,011	1,953	—
1995	7,325	2,089	383,513
1996	7,583	2,163	—
1997	7,918	2,149	616,437
1998	7,999	2,053	477,893
1999	8,187	2,038	526,483

Source: *Statistical Yearbook of China*, 2000, pp. 712–714.

of newspapers expanding from 186 in 1978 to 2,038 in 1999 and magazines expanding from 930 to 8178 over the same period. Television programs have seen greater than exponential growth over this period, with 38,056 programs in 1985 growing to 526,043 programs in 1999. While these media are not typically placed in the category of new IT, they are indicative of an important trend of growing access to information and thus relevant for any discussion about information and social change.

Table 7.3 shows the growth in IT since the economic reforms began two decades ago. Use of pagers, mobile telephones, e-mail, and the Internet, and the development of optical and digital cable lines—all important aspects of a growing IT economy in China—have expanded dramatically in this period. The growth in pager and mobile phone use has been rapid in the last decade: both of these forms of technology were basically nonexistent in China in the mid-1980s and have grown to 46 and 45 million registered users in 1999, respectively. The use of mobile telephones has undergone another period of extreme growth since 1999, growing to approximately 116 million subscribers as of June 2001, according to Lou Qinjian, vice minister for China's information industry.[11] The penetration of these technologies, while dramatic, is not surprising: in developing societies around the world, as mobile technology has grown, it has been much faster and easier to implement mobile technology as the primary form of communication than it has to lay grounded lines. Given the recent introduction of mobile phone technology into China, the growth in this area has been truly dramatic—25 percent of the 175 million phones in China are mobile phones—and virtually all industry experts agree that the country will very soon become the largest market in the world for mobile telephones. It is also likely that the figures for

Table 7.3 Growth of information technology in China[1]

	Email Subscribers	Internet Subscribers	Pagers	Mobile phones	Land-line phones	Optical Cable Lines	Digital Lines
1978	0	0	0	0	3,868,200	0	0
1980	0	0	0	0	4,186,400	0	0
1985	0	0	0	0	6,259,800	0	0
1986	0	0	0	0	7,059,100	0	0
1987	0	0	30,900	0	8,057,200	0	0
1988	0	0	97,200	3,200	9,417,900	2,717	0
1989	0	0	237,300	9,800	10,893,300	5,670	0
1990	0	0	437,000	18,300	12,313,300	11,453	0
1991	0	0	873,800	47,500	14,544,300	23,613	0
1992	0	0	2,220,200	176,900	18,459,600	51,352	109,300
1993	0	0	5,614,000	639,300	25,673,500	162,861	298,045
1994	2,329	0	10,330,000	1,567,800	38,018,600	330,359	518,915
1995	6,068	7,213	17,391,500	3,629,400	53,993,200	484,231	677,672
1996	10,107	35,652	23,562,000	6,852,800	70,467,500	754,143	965,263
1997	15,246	160,157	32,546,100	13,232,900	87,878,300	935,835	1,139,476
1998	20,959	676,755	39,081,600	23,862,900	107,371,500	1,351,665	1,560,201
1999	19,855	3,014,518	46,744,700	43,296,000	132,378,400	—	—
June 2001[2]	—	—	—	116,000,000	—	—	—

Sources: [1] Statistical Yearbook of China, 2000, pp. 543–546, except where otherwise noted.
[2] China Daily, June 26, 2001, p. 5.

mobile phones are underrepresented, as the numbers listed here are those of subscribers to official services, and the unregistered mobile phone market is huge in China. Estimates on just how big this market is do not exist, but one need only go through the process of buying a secondhand phone and setting up an unregistered account to understand just how popular this practice is.

With the relatively low level of personal computer use in China, it is somewhat surprising that there are more than three million registered Internet users. Yet, as with the mobile phone reports, it is also likely here that the figures on the Internet are underrepresented, as the most popular Internet web sites in China are those that do not require subscriber registration.[12] Instead, the majority of Chinese gaining access to the Internet today do so through a pay-per-minute service provided by their phone company, in which a user can log on anonymously from any phone and access the Internet or publicly maintained e-mail accounts on one of the main Internet portals. For example, "163," "263," and "169" all allow users to gain access to the Internet without establishing a subscriber account. Table 7.3 also shows the developmental trends of the infrastructure that supports such IT as the Internet and optical cable and digital lines; the growth has been from nothing to more than a million lines each, in just over a decade.

The bird's-eye view of the information presented above tells us quite a bit. First, the spread of information more generally in China has occurred in dramatic ways over the course of the economic reforms; second, IT itself is spreading in significant ways in Chinese society, and this spread includes both individual users' access as well as the hardware and infrastructure that is necessary for the further development of the industry. Taken together, this means that access to information and the high-tech vehicles that facilitate communication and the sharing of information are significant forces in Chinese society. In addition, the high-tech sectors of the economy, including telecommunications, are among the most active in terms of foreign investment. The question before us now is what, if any, implications do these changes have for Chinese society, for the capacity of the Chinese state to control its population, and for the process of democratization in China?

OTHER ELEMENTS OF INSTITUTIONAL CHANGE

To this point, I have described the critical elements of the economic reforms that have led to a decline in the level of political and social control that China's one-party government is capable of. To summarize these: (1) economic autonomy yielded to enterprise managers led to a necessary decline in the Communist Party's capacity as an agent of microlevel social control; (2) the emergence of a private economy allowed for alternative career paths outside of the system of state allocation; and (3) the free flow of information allowed individuals to have access to images and knowledge from the world outside of China's borders. These key changes have had cascading effects that have led to changes in the composition of society, all of which make the continuing evolution toward political reform inevitable at this point. However, other major institutional changes have also worked hand in hand with these economic changes, and they, too, have been a necessary part of the reform process. In the sections that follow, I will discuss these critical changes and their role in what Minxin Pei (1995) has called "creeping democratization in China."

BUREAUCRATIZING GOVERNMENT INSTITUTIONS

The National People's Congress (NPC) and its local branches, the People's Congresses (PCs), are China's legislative organizations. In a democratic system of checks and balances, like that found in the United States, the legislative branch operates autonomously from the executive branch, a key factor in the balance of power that defines the system. One question we might be concerned with in the gradual evolution of a democratic system in China is whether governmental organizations are operating with more autonomy than in years past. Founded in 1954, the NPC was a central institution of China's governmental system, and in the early years of the reforms, the NPC was little more than a rubber stamp for the party, much the way legislatures often behaved in Leninist political systems. Indeed, the NPC became such a pro forma institution, passing whatever legislation was brought before it by the party, that Chinese people referred to it as a "hand-raising machine" (Tanner 1999), and it seemed to operate in much the same way that it did prior to the reforms. In the 1990s, however, we saw the maturing of this institution in its capacity to operate independent of—and sometimes in opposition to—the party government. Debate has become so common in the workings of this institution that it seems, in fact, to operate in many ways like a legislature of a full-fledged democracy (O'Brien 1990; Pei 1994, 1995; Tanner 1994, 1999).

While the evolution of the NPC as a democratic institution has been gradual and incremental—as has the evolution of the Chinese economy—the changes are fundamental and real, and they amount to nothing less than the gradual transition to a democratic legislature in China. As political scientist Kevin O'Brien (1990, 11) puts it, "A changing legislature attests to a changing polity. . . . Altered legislative involvement in law making, supervision, representation, and regime support signals a system-wide redivision of political tasks." The first major change in the NPC relates to the liberalization of the legislature from the broader political system. This is a crucial step in the democratization of a country, because a democratic government must have independent branches that act as a system of checks and balances on the decisions of any powerful group within the government. In the case of China, this transformation is essential for the continued evolution of the political system, because the party has traditionally wielded so much power in the structure of the nation's society and that power has been completely uncontested in the past. As the economic reforms have progressed, the NPC and the local PCs have slowly moved away from blanket support of the party. At the Third Session of the Eighth NPC in March 1995, fully a third of the deputies voted against or abstained from voting during the passage of the Central Bank Law, "feeling that the law would give the State Council too much power over the Central Bank and the country's monetary policy" (Pei 1995, 72). Similar numbers refused to approve the Education Law. The NPC has also, in recent years, taken a more activist approach to legislation. NPC officials have been instrumental in passing laws that protect individuals and the lawyers that defend them. In some local areas, PC officials have helped push through environmental legislation (O'Brien 1990; Pei 1995). In the 1990s, the NPC became very much a "legislative agenda-setter" and "reform activist" (Tanner 1999, 109), particularly in the area of economic reforms. The more this institution acts like a legislative body—allowing debate of legislation and setting a legislative agenda that is independent of the party leadership—the further the government will evolve toward a collection of democratic institutions.

A second major change in the NPC as a democratic institution also relates to autonomy from the party government but extends beyond the realm of legislation into the realm of elections. If the litmus test of true democratic liberalization is a regime's willingness to permit multicandidate and multiparty elections among the general electorate, China is not yet there. However, the NPC has helped to push the country in the direction of fair and open elections—while at the same time asserting its independence from the party—by encouraging the election to government positions of candidates who were nominated by the local PCs rather than the candidates designated by the party. In the highest-profile cases, candidates nominated by local PCs defeated two party-nominated candidates for provincial governor (in Guizhou and Zhejiang). It has done the same by encouraging local PCs to nominate their own candidates for membership in the NPC rather than simply relying on those individuals who were handpicked by the party (Pei 1994, 1995). These changes should not be mistaken for a truly open democratic system; members of the NPC and the local PCs are very much entrenched members of the government, and this system is far from one that allows for fair and open multiparty elections. However, it is one in which the NPC is, in a variety of ways, establishing itself as a governmental body that is independent of the once-ubiquitous Communist Party, and this step is a critical one in the gradual evolution of this system.

SELF-GOVERNANCE AND GRASSROOTS DEMOCRATIZATION

Beyond the transformation of the NPC, there have been other fundamental changes in the institutions of governance, especially at the village level. Outside of the urban centers in China, there has been an extreme breakdown of party-state institutions. Corruption among local officials—which has followed somewhat naturally from the lack of party control—has been rampant, and the general characterization of the Chinese countryside is one of chaos rather than reform. However, two things have occurred in the Chinese countryside to make this part of the society worthy of special note in an analysis of social and political reform. First, full economic autonomy has been a transition that has come much more quickly in the countryside than in the urban areas. When decollectivization occurred in the early 1980s, individuals were given direct control over the means of production on their land.[13] As a result, self-governance has rapidly become a way of life for Chinese farmers, who have control over what they produce, what prices they will sell their goods for, and what they choose to do with their land—all with little or no intervention from the state. They are still, in many cases, bound to selling some portion of their agricultural goods to the government, but anything they produce beyond this amount is theirs to use as they please.[14] This notion of self-governance in economic activity—along with the collapse of the institutions of the party infrastructure—has had a large spillover effect for the operation of political institutions in rural areas as well.

Somewhat in response to (and somewhat in anticipation of) the rise in corruption that has followed the breakdown of party institutions in rural areas, in 1987 the NPC established the Organic Law of Villagers' Committees, which effectively gave adult villagers the right to vote, stand for election, and run committees of self-governance (Lawrence 1994; Li and O'Brien 1999). This was a necessary step in cauterizing the wounds left by the failing party infrastructure in rural China. Placing accountability and control in the hands of rural dwellers, it was hoped, would lead to a more transparent and stable political system. For example, Article 22 of the Law on Villagers' Committees requires that elected officials openly publish financial accounts every six months. This type of institutional change forces local officials to be accountable for the ways in which they are spending local funds. The fact that they are now elected rather than appointed means that their actions must be accountable to an electorate. In many villages across

rural China, individuals are forcing elected officials to participate in open planning processes. In November 1998, after
eleven years of practice and experimentation with village-level
elections throughout China, the Law of Villagers' Committees
was given the status of permanent law. No accurate numbers
are available on how many villages have held genuinely competitive elections; however, with about 930,000 villages in
China, some official estimates state that half of the country's
villages have implemented elections in accordance with Chinese
law (Jakobson 1998). Today, village elections occur in some
700,000 villages across China, reaching 75 percent of the
nation's 1.3 billion people. Twenty-five of China's thirty-one
administrative regions have promulgated local laws and regulations to facilitate implementation of the law on villagers'
committees.

International institutions also play an important role in this
transition. For example, the Ford Foundation provided a grant
in 1993 to China's Ministry of Civil Affairs to help develop
and monitor fair elections. Following the Ford grant, grants
also came from the United Nations, the European Union, the
Carter Center, and a number of other foundations. In 1997,
the Carter Center signed an agreement to observe village
election procedures; to provide assistance in gathering election data, educating voters, and training election officials; and
to host Chinese officials to observe U.S. elections. After the
center's completion in 1999 of a successful pilot project, the
Carter Center and the Ministry of Civil Affairs signed a three-
year cooperation agreement. The Carter Center also began
observations of township elections—that is, elections above
the village level—in conjunction with the National People's
Congress in 1999. In December 2002, the center observed
elections at the county level for the first time. This observation
followed a Chinese delegation's visit to the United States in

November 2002. The impact has been dramatic: in parts of rural China, village elections have become commonplace in the 1990s; villagers have concrete experience with the process and demands of self-governance; and the gradual movement toward democracy has led to a stable learning process and an institutionalization of the norms of a democratic society.

Compared to those in rural China, the political reforms in urban areas have been much more limited.[15] This is largely because the central institutions of social control in urban areas, the industrial work unit and the neighborhood association, have remained intact throughout the economic reforms. Yet, major changes are occurring in this sector of Chinese society as well, though they are more subtle changes in the political realm than are the fundamental political reforms occurring in rural areas. First, while the rise of self-employment, private enterprises, and other forms of employment outside of the state sector have eroded the centrality of the industrial work unit in the organization of urban life in China, this institution is still one of the pillars around which urban society is organized. This fact makes the changes that are occurring within and around the industrial work unit all the more important. Within the work unit, labor relations have been formalized, as work units have adopted formal organizational rules, formal grievance-filing procedures, worker representative committees (which create a democratic process in the restructuring of the firm), and formal hiring procedures. Many state-operated enterprises—the old work units that were at the core of the social security system that was constructed under Mao—have placed all of their workers on fixed-term labor contracts, which significantly rationalize the labor relationship beyond the personalized labor relations of the past. Outside of the work unit, these internal changes are supported by new institutions, formed in the late 1980s, like Labor Arbitration Commissions. This bundle of changes, which includes fundamental changes to the nature of the labor relationship (they are now formal and rationalized through labor contracts) and the mechanisms through which authority can be challenged (grievance-filing procedures and mediation committees within the firm), teaches democracy and democratic processes from the ground up. It is now possible in China for workers to file grievances against superiors and have these grievances heard at an institution outside of the workplace. In 1997, out of 51,551 labor disputes that were settled by arbitration or mediation, 40,063 (78 percent) were decided in favor of the workers filing the suits. This is a truly radical change.

Second, there are also more general changes afoot within the urban population outside of the work unit. In the only systematic study conducted on democratic participation in urban China, Tianjin Shi (1997) finds that urban residents are anything but removed from, or apathetic about, politics and political participation. After a decade of reform, Chinese citizens clearly recognized that they were participants in a slowly changing system, but that they were willing and active participants in such a system. Forms of political participation that can be found in urban China today, according to Shi, include participation in elections (of local PC deputies and village or work-unit leaders); boycotting unfair elections; appeals through the bureaucratic hierarchy; complaints through political organizations, trade unions, or to deputies of the PCs; and letter writing to government officials. Shi finds strong evidence for high levels of participation in all of these acts and many more. The changes that might help explain the political assertiveness that Shi finds surely include the growing middle class, which can increasingly afford to act independently of state directives and demands. As was discussed earlier, the changed career choices available to individuals in urban China make this population ever less reliant on the good will of the government for life and livelihood. But beyond these changes in material reliance on the government, after two decades of economic reform in China, there is a deepening culture of democratic participation and gradual political reform there.

REFORM-MINDED ELITES IN THE GLOBAL ECONOMY

Any discussion of economic and political transformation in China would be incomplete without a discussion of the role of political elites in this process. Indeed, this process would not have begun were it not for Deng Xiaoping's political will in steering China onto the road of economic reform. Yet, in the wake of Tiananmen, few would claim that Deng Xiaoping was a backer of political reforms. In addition to Deng, however, other critical players in the government, such as Jiang Zemin, Li Peng, Zhao Ziyang, and Zhu Rongji, as well as the elite political actors below them, have all been instrumental in the pace and direction of economic reform. The struggles among political elites always seem to circle around basic ideas about the nature and pace of economic reforms in China, with liberals ("reformers") championing radical change in the organization of the economy and conservatives ("hard-liners") attempting at every stage to hold back the process of change. Elite politics certainly matter in the course of economic reforms in China.

However, as we are particularly interested in the relationship between economic and political reform here, it is relevant to ask who among these elites has had any impact on political reform. On the surface, while party elites in the National People's Congress are pushing for gradual political reform, it seems clear that the true elites of the government are united in their resistance to political reform. Historically, when party elites have gotten too close to explicitly supporting political reform, the rest of the elite circle has closed ranks on them, immediately purging them from their positions and stripping them of any political power whatsoever. Hu Yaobang and Zhao Ziyang both suffered this fate when they became associated with the democracy demonstrations in 1986 and 1989, respectively. Yet, I would like to argue here that reading China's economic reforms as a case in which political elites are willing to induce economic change but unwilling to implement changes in political realms is a simplistic understanding of the process of political reform in China. It also dramatically oversimplifies the relationship between economic and political reform and the extent to which political elites in China are using economic reforms as a way of accomplishing political reform. There have been repeated messages from antireform elites within the party that explicit suggestions about political reform will lead to retribution from the party, and the cases of Hu Yaobang, Zhao Ziyang, and, more recently, the jailing of Democratic Party founders Qin Yongmin and Xu Wenli, have made this point clear. However, certain reform-minded elites have brought about significant political change without ever mentioning political change directly. They have accomplished this through global integration and the rationalization of the Chinese economy and society.

Deng Xiaoping and Zhao Ziyang brought about radical economic change by pushing the country toward constitutionality and the emergence of the rule of law. This process, which was marketed ideologically as a set of reforms that were necessary for economic development and change, fundamentally altered the role of politics and the role of the party in Chinese society. In regularizing the economy and the state's relation to it, the architects of China's reform set in motion changes that are forcing the emergence of a more rational political system. As Joseph Fewsmith explains it,

The recognition, even in principle, that there were laws and principles that even the party had to obey implied the end of solipsistic knowledge as a legitimating principle. It also laid the basis for later efforts to separate the party from the government, an effort that has gone forward only with great conflict and tension precisely because the principle inherent in bureaucratic rationality conflicts with the privileged claim on truth on which the party originally based its legitimacy.

(1999, 55–56).

In other words, as reform-minded elites emphasized the need for a rational economy for economic development, they were also altering the politics of the party system. The rationalization of the economy and society led to a dramatic decline in the party's power to rule as an authoritarian government.

In recent years, the next step in this process has come from global integration and the adoption of the norms of the international community. The emphasis here is still always on economic norms of the international community, but many social and political norms also come with this project. Zhu Rongji stayed away from discussions about democratization. However, by championing global integration and the rule of law, Zhu brought about gradual political change in China, just at Zhao Ziyang did in the first decade of economic reform in China. Zhu's strategy has been to ignore questions of political reform and concentrate instead on the need for China to adopt economic and legal systems and norms that will allow the country to integrate smoothly with the rest of the international community. Yet Zhu clearly recognizes that the adoption of the norms of the international community will continue to push China down the road of general societal transformation. In other words, Zhu's objective is to deepen all of the reforms that have been discussed above, all of which have, and will continue to, reform China's political system in significant ways. This view has many skeptics among Western academics. However, it is important to note that many of the laws passed under Zhu Rongji's watch, while purportedly about global integration, had at their core an emphasis on individual civil liberties. The Chinese Company Law (1994), for example, is in many areas more aggressive on affirming workers' rights vis-à-vis the corporation than American corporate law is today. Zhu avoided marketing this aspect of the reforms, at least in part, because his political career unfolded in the shadow of Zhao Ziyang's fate. However, it is undeniable that Zhu Rongji and Jiang Zemin, who incorporated entrepreneurs into the Communist Party (discussed below), have pushed forward reforms that have had an impact on political reform in China.

With his seemingly authoritarian stances on a number of issues, many have worried that Hu Jintao would leave his once-liberal image behind, showing instead his true colors as the leader of "China's new authoritarianism." But under Hu Jintao we have seen a fundamental transformation of private property rights and the right to form independent unions, two issues which have been central to criticism of China's political reform process. And, perhaps, most profoundly, it was under Hu Jintao that the Party, in the fall of 2006, literally wrote Mao out the history of the PRC: as Shanghai's high school students returned to class that fall, Mao had been reduced to little more than a brief mention. And, contrary to his predecessors of the 1990s, Hu is not afraid to talk about democratization, as he showed in his speech for the 17th Party Congress in October of 2007. The main point here is that, in the post-Zhao Ziyang era, an outwardly conservative façade has allowed Zhu Rongji, Jiang Zemin, and now Hu Jintao to push forward a reformist agenda of institutional change. As each of these reform-minded elites emphasized the need for a rational system for economic development, they were also altering the politics of the party system.

BUSINESS AND COOPTATION

In 1988, the Chinese government began to exert control over social organizations, including various business associations, by creating an official registration system for such organizations. A newly established Social Organization Management Department within the Ministry of Civil Affairs would enforce it. One year later, the Regulations on Registration and Administration of Social Organizations were issued by the State Council, along with the Measures on Management of Foundations and the Interim Rule on Management of Foreign Chambers of Commerce. These guidelines essentially stipulate that all social organizations must be sponsored by government or party organizations, even though they all have the right to independent legal status. After a period of rapid proliferation, by the end of 1992 the number of established and registered social organizations settled at around forty thousand. In 1998, two new sets of regulations were issued—the Regulations on Registration and Administration of Social Organizations, and the Interim Regulation on Registration and Management of Private Nonprofit Organizations.

The 1990's laws on social organization aimed to incorporate governmental supervision and control while transferring the function of governmental monitoring to a separate governing body. A large body of work on China's reforms has emphasized the "corporatist" model of social organization and control or "embedded" relations between social organizations and their governing agencies.[16] And beyond the formal ties between business associations and the governing system stipulated by law, there are various informal ties between entrepreneurs' groups and the state officials that directly influence the ways such business associations are run.

It is still too early to draw conclusions about the degree of independence of entrepreneur groups and business associations that are emerging in China's reform era. The reality of China's position as a still-authoritarian regime and the Chinese Communist Party's (CCP's) status as the most powerful organization in China suggests significant limitations on the relative autonomy of these groups. However, the emergence and growth of those new social groups have brought about social and political implications that cannot be ignored in today's China. While the wealth attached to the economic elites running new business organizations has not led directly to democratic values or to pressure on the CCP for radical political reforms, these economic elites have become one of the most important social groups that have begun to exert pressure on China's political regime.[17] Perhaps the most critical evidence of the importance of this social group comes from the government's embracing of Jiang Zemin's "three representatives" policy, discussed in Chapter 4, which permits private entrepreneurs to be members of the CCP. Proposed by Jiang in 2001, this policy was incorporated into China's Constitution at the Sixteenth Party Congress in 2002. This policy is a direct outcome of the rapid growth of private economy in the 1990s. Thus, the cooptation model becomes clear: a major part of China's economic growth and transformation has been to bring the private economy and democratic reforms into the fold of the current one-party system. By incorporating private entrepreneurs into its political camp, China's only ruling party is now announcing that it not only continues to represent the workers and peasants but all of the people's interests, including those of the capitalists, the so-called advanced social productive forces. In doing so, the CCP has ended a half century of exclusionary policies aimed at private entrepreneurs. While these entrepreneur groups only occupy a small part of the Chinese population, the inclusion of private entrepreneurs is a clear statement by the CCP and the Chinese government that the business groups can no longer be ignored within the political community.

CONCLUSIONS: IS DEMOCRACY AN INEVITABLE OUTCOME OF ECONOMIC REFORM?

A decade after the Tiananmen Square massacre of 1989, several relatives of students who were killed in the early hours of June 4, 1989 decided to sue the government for the slaughter of their children. They invoked two relatively new laws, the Administrative Litigation Act, passed in 1990, and the National Compensation Law, passed in 1995, the latter of which effectively allows Chinese citizens to sue the government for compensation for restitution for past wrongs. Passage of this law seemed to occur as a matter of course, as the National People's Congress passed many rights-based legal institutions in the mid-1990s in China, including the Labor Law, the Prison Reform Law, and many other laws. Yet while the government may not have anticipated such an employment of these laws, the event marked a dramatic step forward in the evolution toward a rational-legal system in which the government is held accountable for its actions, just as individual citizens are. A decade ago, the participants in the Tiananmen movement were operating completely outside of the institutional system they were criticizing; they were branded "counter-revolutionaries," "hooligans," and "enemies of the state." A decade later, their relatives were employing the legal system to criticize the state for its actions.

These events are important for two reasons. First, it is important to acknowledge and understand the extent to which this society is indeed evolving in a dramatic fashion, despite the fact that the evolution (instead of revolution) makes changes seem all too slow to come about. That individuals can now sue the government for past wrongs stands in stark contrast to the society that existed even a decade earlier. Second, the creation of a predictable, rational-legal system has been a central part of the Chinese government's path toward the creation of a market economy; it has been a necessary part of China's transition to a global market economy. A number of scholars have argued that the construction of a rational-legal system to ensure market transactions that match the standards of the international community is a necessary precondition to participation in the global economy. It is possible to have an economic system that is not based on rational-legal principles—for example, an economy could be based on social ties and particularistic relations—but this type of economy is unlikely to attract significant amounts of foreign capital, as investors from overseas will be at a disadvantage in this type of market. Enter the rule of law. In the mid-1990s, the National People's Congress adopted a certain urgency with respect to legal reforms, affirming that such reforms would be the backbone for a stable and regulated marketplace. As Pei (1995, 68) puts it, the rule of law is "the institutional foundation of a market economy and a constitutional government," and China is hurtling headlong toward this type of institutional system.

In this chapter, I have argued that China has moved down the path toward democratic reform on two levels. First, the basic economic changes that the party government set in motion at the beginning of the economic reforms moved the society toward a level of autonomy that undercut the party's ability to exert the control it did in the pre-reform era. This package of changes, which was enacted in an effort to "marketize" the Chinese economy (but not necessarily for the goal of political reform), was a necessary precondition for political reform. Autonomy from the party came in a number of different forms, but most important among them were economic autonomy in the marketplace and within firms (and on university campuses) and the opening of alternative career paths. As the party receded, alternative forms of organization emerged, and information began to flow more freely. All of these factors followed on the declining power of the party, and all were important preconditions for gradual change—referred to as the "quiet revolution" from within China's existing system.

Working in concert with what may very well have been unintended consequences of economic reform in China are more explicit institutional changes that are working in a gradual way across the country. These include the growing autonomy of China's main legislative body (the National People's Congress), the increasing emphasis on governance by the rule of law, and experiments with democratic participation at local levels across urban, and especially rural, China. These changes have been gradual, but their aggregate effect over the last two decades has been dramatic. Even as China's Communist Party government has been apparently (and austerely) averse to political reform, it has allowed the "creeping" democratic changes from below. The contrast between what has actually occurred in China over the last two decades and what is often depicted as a complete lack of change is so stark at this point that the two pictures appear to have little in common. While democratic reform may not in all cases be an inevitable outcome of economic reform, it is, at this point, an inevitability in China. A truly democratic political system may be decades down the road, but the party is now at a point where there is no turning back. In Chapter 8, I will examine the implications of this argument for human rights in China and for China's role in the global economy.

Eight

Since the first missionaries and explorers arrived on China's shores, Westerners have gazed upon East Asia with a mixture of awe, quizzical scrutiny, and even disdain. The West has long held this part of the world as a distant other, where riches and potential abound, but where differences are great enough that the cultural divide always looms in the background, threatening to swallow even the most amicable trade relations. In recent years, as China has emerged from its isolation and entered the global economy, debates over how to view, acknowledge, and accept Asian differences have taken on a pitched tenor, as the realms of economics, politics, military prowess, and human rights have all become intertwined in a discussion of weighty questions. Is democracy a universal ideal to which all nations should aspire? What individual rights should we consider inalienable? To what extent should economic and political relations among nations be intertwined? Will China ultimately be friend and economic partner, or military foe? And to what extent do cultural differences—particularly differences between East and West—play a role in how we address these issues?

The courses of development in East Asia have belied standard assumptions about how we should answer these questions. In different ways, China and the East Asian newly industrialized economies have shown the benefits of a strong state-led development, and the economic success of these development projects has provided concrete evidence against the neoliberal alternative of rapid privatization. If a strong authoritarian state can deliver economic prosperity to its people, do Western democracies have a legitimate position in advocating liberal democracy for these countries when the cost may very well be the economic success the countries have achieved? As the largest remaining communist regime, China is often lambasted by human rights advocates—not to mention the U.S. government—for its record on human rights, and many argue that a country's poor human-rights record should be at the center of any bilateral relationship with an authoritarian government. In addition, China is fast-emerging as one of the key geopolitical powers that will offset U.S. hegemony as the military force policing the world. Will China's integration pose a threat, as many hawkish members of Congress would have us believe? Or will tensions with the United States and the rest of the Western world rise as China rises? Will the country continue to evolve in the realms of human rights and political reform?

ENGAGEMENT AND GLOBAL INTEGRATION

In this book, I have advanced the view that China's transformation has fundamentally been a global project. Reformers have used the country's need to develop economically as a force to push the country down the path of economic and political reform. Even those who have been against the reforms have had to accept that China needed to grow in the economic sphere. From the time of Deng Xiaoping's visit to the United States in January 1979, the orientation has been toward the global economy. In the early years of the reforms, it was about cash and technology. The coastal development strategy helped turn China into an economic juggernaut, one of the most active producing and trading countries in the world, and it has generated a tremendous amount of economic growth in the process. With foreign firms also came the transfer of needed technologies and management practices. In later years, this integration came to be about more than cash and technology. Reformers like Zhu Rongji used the pressures and standards of the global economy as a means for social reform. The laws that were passed under Zhu's watch were not only helping to create a stable institutional infrastructure for investment in China but were also creating the institutions of social change. In this final chapter, I turn to the issue of what China's integration into the global economy will mean for the rest of the world. Drawing upon the information and arguments of previous chapters, I will discuss China's emerging role in the constellation of powerful nations around the world.

THE CHINA THREAT

A recent issue of the Atlantic Monthly presented a picture of a sinister-looking member of the People's Liberation Army and a jingoistic title, "How We Would Fight China: The Next Cold War." The article within, penned by Robert Kaplan, is the doomsday China scenario at its worst:

> The Middle East is just a blip. The American military contest with China in the Pacific will define the twenty-first century. And China will be a more formidable adversary than Russia ever was. . . . If not a big war with China, then a series of Cold War-style standoffs that stretch out over years and decades.[1]

Unfortunately, this type of irresponsible rhetoric is not uncommon, and it is not confined to irresponsible reporting. Indeed, the much trumpeted Cox Report, issued in 2001, warned,

> The PRC began developing its ballistic missile system in the early

1960s. The first missile, the CSS-2, showed strong Soviet design influences. Launched from mobile launchers, it has a range of up to 1,926 miles. The CSS-3 was the PRC's first intercontinental range missile, but with a range of 3,417 miles it cannot reach the United States. The CSS-4 is the PRC's main ICBM threat against the U.S. With a range in excess of 7,457 miles, it can hit most of the U.S. During the 1990s, the PRC has deployed approximately 20 CSS-4s in silos, most of which are targeted at the U.S. An improved version of the CSS-4, known as the CSS-4 Mod 2, could allow the PRC to deploy multiple warheads.

And U.S. Secretary of Defense Donald Rumsfeld (citing no evidence) recently speculated that China's military budget is actually much higher than it officially acknowledges, ominously stating, "Since no nation threatens China, one must wonder: why this growing investment?"[2]

But what is the truth? Does China pose a serious threat to the military order of the world? Has it undertaken a level of activity that is significantly different from that of other powerful nations? One of the key issues that is often pointed to in doomsday scenarios is the rapid rise in military spending that has occurred in China since the economic reforms began. As Figure 8.1 illustrates, China's defense spending has indeed increased more than tenfold in the two-and-a-half decades since the economic reforms began. From spending less than $2 billion on national defense in 1978, that commitment has risen to nearly $20 billion by 2002. One thing we might first ask to contextualize such a figure, however, is whether this spending has outpaced the growth of the economy overall. In other words, has China's commitment to the military grown more rapidly than its overall rise as an economy and society in the reform era? As the second axis in Figure 8.1 illustrates, in fact, since the 1980s, China's spending in this area has

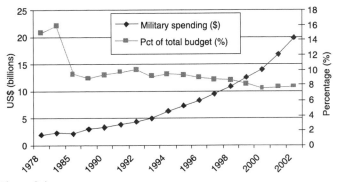

Figure 8.1
Military spending in China, 1978–2002.

remained relatively stable, at about 8 percent of the national budget. A second, and perhaps more important, question we might ask is: Compared to what? How does China's military spending measure up to other countries' spending? On this point, a comparison with the United States reveals an interesting story. As Figure 8.2 shows, in 2001[3] the United States spent nearly $300 billion on national defense—a figure more than seventeen times larger than what China spent in the same year, and a figure that is greater than the combined military spending of all other countries in the world. And in terms of percentages, the U.S. allocation for national defense is more than twice that of the Chinese (16.4 percent, compared to 7.6 percent in 2001).

China is certainly growing in power, and its strength as a nation will extend well beyond the economic realm into the world of geopolitics. However, from these figures, it is not obvious that China's expenditures are unreasonable given the size of the nation, the size of the economy, and what other large nations spend on national defense. The real issue behind the concerns over China's military spending is that hawks in

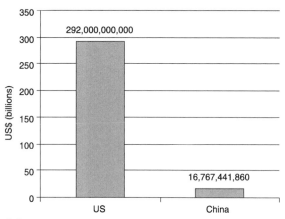

Figure 8.2
Military spending, 2001.

the United States want to ensure that China does not emerge as a credible counterbalance to U.S. military hegemony. Whether the United States merits, or should strive for, the role of unopposed military power in the world is not the subject of this book. However, it is important to note that China's military activity pales in comparison to that of the United States.

These days, the hawkish rhetoric over China's military buildup has subsided somewhat (though not completely), but it has been replaced by an equally loud din of concern over China's impact on the global economy and the corresponding dangers for international business. On July 23, 2007, the cover of *BusinessWeek* gloomily asked "Can China be Fixed?," and spent many pages in the magazine documenting the looming crisis. The article summoned images of Gordon Chang's 2001 screed *The Coming Collapse of China*, which predicted a collapse that never came. The recent press over lead paint in Mattel toy products, poison in dog food, endemic corruption, and the threat to the global environment has made the issues omnipresent in the public consciousnesses. It is an odd juxtaposition: on the one hand we have the most dramatic success of the transition from communism to capitalism; on the other we have visions of the aggressively expansionist military power that is on the verge of collapse due to endemic corruption. The irony, of course, is that China is far more stable (and likely more committed to peaceful global integration) than the nations that have followed US prescriptions and made the rapid transition to a democracy without gradually building institutions to support this system first.

THE HUMAN RIGHTS DEBATE

An equally significant debate over engagement with China has been around the issue of human rights and questions about engagement with an authoritarian government. Starting in 1986, China actively campaigned to resume its status in the General Agreement on Tariffs and Trade (GATT), the predecessor of the World Trade Organization (WTO), which was established in 1995.[4] However, following the Tiananmen Square massacre in 1989, the logic of the Jackson-Vanick Amendment guided U.S.–Chinese relations for more than a decade.[5] The basic position was that the United States would agree only to have normal trade relations with China on an annual basis, depending on an annual review of the country's record on human rights. At the time, following the language of Jackson-Vanick, this was referred to as Most Favored Nation status (MFN), and then later as Normal Trade Relations. Each spring, a group of politicians, pundits, and lobbyists would converge on Washington to debate the merits of engaging in trade relations with China. Behind the annual debate was a set of issues that are intimately tied to larger theoretical questions about the relationship between economic and social reforms. On one side of the divide sat the proponents of engagement, who argued that social change would follow from economic engagement. The view among many in this group was that liberal markets create a kind of freedom that transforms authoritarian systems from within. As U.S. president Bill Clinton, who was a proponent of this view, once put it,

> In the new century, liberty will spread by cell phone and cable modem. . . . We know how much the Internet has changed America, and we are already an open society. Imagine how much it could change China. Now, there's no question China has been trying to crack down on the Internet—good luck. That's sort of like trying to nail Jello to the wall.[6]

And scholars like Michael Santoro (1999) have argued that American firms were really playing a significant role in changing China from within. On the other side of the divide sat opponents of engagement. Individuals in this camp believed that engaging with an authoritarian regime (1) rewards the very systems they believe should change; (2) actually strengthens the regime in question; and (3) gives away the one bargaining chip we have to force social and political change in the world today. Opponents of engagement also remained very committed to the view that, while the reforms have clearly transformed the economy in fundamental ways, little has changed in social and political realms in China and it is still the same despotic and corrupt place it was twenty years ago. On this side of the debate sat a diverse political alliance, which included labor and liberal politicians like Nancy Pelosi and the late Paul Wellstone and hawkish politicians like Jesse Helms and Christopher Cox.

Opponents of engagement misunderstand the situation in China today. First, while change has been gradual, over the course of two-and-a-half decades of reform, we have seen radical changes that make China a fundamentally different society than what it was before the reforms began. Statutes like the National Compensation Law, which allows Chinese citizens to sue the government for past wrongs, and the Prison Reform Law—which, according to most extensive research on the topic, has fundamentally altered the treatment of prisoners—have radically reshaped the reality of human rights in China. In the area of legal institutions and labor, the Labor Law and the Labor Arbitration Commissions are radical steps toward a rational, rights-based workplace and society. These changes amount to nothing less than radical social change. Reform in China has been a gradual process, and in our desire to see something dramatic like the fall of the Berlin Wall, we have imperiously ignored and arrogantly dismissed the radical changes that have evolved over the course of more than two decades of reform.

Second, as was discussed in Chapter 6, it is on the factory floor where the emergence of a rights-based workplace is the most apparent, and it is here that we can see the direct impact of foreign (particularly Western) investment. Those who blithely state that foreign direct investment has resulted in no increased protections for human rights in China simply have no idea of what is going on there. In my own research, I have visited hundreds of factories, spent hundreds of hours interviewing hundreds of managers and workers, and systematically studied the impact of foreign investment on the transformation of labor relations. I watched these factories transform over the course of the 1990s. The emergence of rights-based labor practices is easily apparent to anyone who cares to look, but it is the Chinese firms that are engaged in relationships with Western investors who are leading the way in these changes. The findings of this body of research speak to the real issues before us—the impact of foreign investment on the transformation of Chinese society.

Formal relationships with foreign firms have a significant impact on the ways in which enterprises are changing in China's urban industrial economy. As I described in Chapter 6, Chinese factories that have formal relations with Western MNCs are significantly more likely to have formal grievance-filing procedures and a variety of other intra-organizational structures that protect workers' rights. They pay significantly higher wages, and they are more likely to have adopted institutions that put them on track with other firms in the global economy. Managers trace these rapidly changing practices to their relations with foreign firms, arguing that, although they are primarily motivated by the prospect of attracting foreign investment with these changes, the changes may, at the same time, be radically altering the lives of workers in their firms. Partnerships with foreign MNCs are fundamentally altering the lives of citizens in the Chinese economy.

As I argued in Chapter 6, foreign investment—and therefore engagement—has influenced this process of change in China in fundamental ways. Corporations are rarely the leading advocates of civil liberties, human rights, or labor reform. However, the Chinese case is special for a couple of reasons. Because many MNCs in China are as interested in long-term investments as they are in cheap labor, they most often seek Chinese partners that understand the needs, goals, and desires of MNCs investing in China. They seek long-term partners that have embraced a rational-legal approach to doing business—partners that are predictable, stable, and knowledgeable about Western-style business practices and negotiations. These partnerships are important to Chinese factories—with them come an infusion of capital, access to international markets, and often technology transfers—and they want desperately to land these partnerships. They position themselves as suitable investment partners by adopting a number of the practices that Western partners will recognize as stable, reform-minded business practices. Among the basic reforms they adopt to show their fitness for "linking up" with the international community are labor reforms, and the adoption of these reforms has fundamentally changed the lives of workers and citizens throughout China today. Thus, commitments to stable Western-style business practices and to labor reform have led to key changes in the labor relations in the Chinese workplace. These changes have had radical consequences for human rights across China.

There is also a good deal of evidence that the sanction-and-isolation position does not work in any except the most extreme circumstances. What do the forty-four-year-old embargo of Cuba and the ten-year embargo of Iraq (before the recent war) tell us about the usefulness of isolation in toppling despotic regimes? Has isolation done anything to transform North Korea? If anything is clear, it is that the citizens of these countries suffer while the resolve of their leaders is strengthened. The only case in which a successful international coalition has brought a country to its knees for social change is South Africa, and this case is so different from that of China that the comparison does not even merit discussion. (There will, quite simply, never be an international coalition united to isolate China the way there was in the case of South Africa.)

Those who advocate isolation (in the name of human rights) should look closely at whom they are aligning themselves with in China: the true despots of Chinese society are the ones who would like to roll the clocks back on the economic, legal, and political reforms in China—and they would welcome the isolation position, because they know that the WTO will further erode their dictatorial power in China. In the 1980s, Zhao Ziyang was focused on reform and the opening up of China, and he knew that the further integration of

China into the international community would bring this about. Jiang Zemin and Zhu Rongji followed Zhao, focusing on further integrating China into the international community. (Where Jiang and Zhu diverged from Zhao's path was in being open about any goals of political change.) These leaders have been changing China from within, and they have been using the arguments about stability and global integration to do so.

China's current President, Hu Jintao, has adopted an even more complicated balancing act, on the one hand striking the pose of the strong authoritarian, while on the other pushing forward very progressive institutional reform. Pushing forward institutional changes like the new rights for independent unionization and the new property rights reforms is clearly a progressive agenda about institutional change. However, unlike his predecessors, Hu has not been silent on the issue of democratization, vowing to expand democratic rights and processes in his 17th Party Congress speech in October of 2007. Skeptics dismissed his speech (which mentioned democracy over sixty times) as empty words; Hu's own track record on institutional change belies this view.

INTEGRATING CHINA INTO THE GLOBAL COMMUNITY

Although there is much hand-wringing about the China threat among hawkish writers and politicians and an equal amount of concern from more liberal camps about China's human-rights record, the likely scenario is one of continued integration rather than conflict. The main reason has to do with the fact that economic integration has already occurred to such an extent that it would be simply too costly for any parties to go down the road of conflict.

As I described in Chapter 4, since the early 1990s China has become a major recipient of foreign direct investment (FDI), which occupies the major part of total foreign capital (along with foreign loans and other investments) that China has received. In 1993, China received more FDI than any other country, and since then, China had been the second-largest recipient in the world of FDI, behind only the United States. By early 1999, FDI in joint ventures and wholly foreign-owned companies exceeded US$250 billion, several times larger than cumulative FDI since World War II in Japan, Korea, and Taiwan, combined (Lardy 2002). In 2002, China's total inflow of FDI reached US$400 billion, making it the world's largest recipient of FDI. According to Nicholas Lardy (1995), four factors contributed to the dramatic increases of the FDI China attracted in the early 1990s: (1) the increasing magnitude of aggregate FDI flowing to developing countries in the 1990s; (2) China's political stability in the post-Tiananmen square era, combined with the explosive growth of domestic economy, rebuilt the confidence of foreign firms and investors; (3) after a decade of economic liberalization and the practice of coastal developmental strategies, China's foreign investment regime had been systematically liberalized by then and more sectors had been opened to foreign investors; and (4) Chinese firms disguised their money as "foreign investment" to take advantage of the special policies only provided to foreign-invested enterprises.

It is less widely known that China has also become an increasingly important FDI-exporting country in the reform era. Figure 8.3 shows the growth pace of China's FDI outflow from the late 1970s until 1996. Before the late 1970s, China's outward FDI was minimal, and even in the early years of the open-door policy, China's outward FDI was insignificant. In 1984, China invested about US$134 million dollars abroad, and in the early years of China's economic reform, most of its investment projects were, to a great extent, motivated by

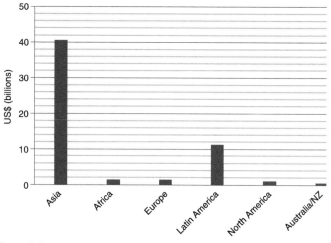

Figure 8.3

China's FDI outflows (cumulative), 1979–2005.

Source: Statistical Yearbook of China, 2006.

political rather than commercial interests (Cai 1999). Starting in the mid-1980s, China's outward FDI began to develop, and investment projects became more business oriented. In 1985, China's FDI outflows reached $628 million, and five years later this figure was $830 million. In the 1990s, China's outward FDI quickly escalated, and in 1992–93, the annual FDI outflow surpassed $4 billion before settling back to just over $2 billion. By this time, China had become the largest outward investor among developing countries and the eighth-largest supplier of outward investments among all countries (Lardy 2002).[7] The rapid growth of China's outward FDI in the reform era has been caused not only by the growing economic strength of the nation as a whole but also by the increasing integration of China's economy into the global community, particularly with neighboring countries. Although China's outward FDI flows are still quite small relative to the largest

Table 8.1 The ten largest trading countries in the world, 2001 (US$, billions)

Country	1990			2001		
	Total	Imports	Exports	Total	Imports	Exports
United States	910.6	517.0	393.6	1911.0	1180.2	730.8
Germany	756.3	346.2	410.1	1056.8	486.3	570.5
Japan	523.0	235.4	287.6	752.6	349.1	403.5
France	451.0	234.4	216.6	586.6	292.5	294.1
United Kingdom	409.7	224.4	185.3	588.3	321.0	267.3
China	115.5	53.4	62.1	509.8	243.6	266.2
Canada	250.9	123.3	127.6	487.2	227.3	259.9
Italy	352.5	182.0	170.5	474.9	236.6[1]	238.3[1]
Netherlands	258.3	126.5	131.8	410.5	194.4	216.1
Mexico	84.2	43.5	40.7	341.2	182.7[1]	158.5

Note: [1] Data refers to 2000.

Source: *Statistical Yearbook of China*, 2002.

economies in the world, the current trajectory is further evidence of the growing links between China and other nations in the global economy.

Perhaps more important than the trade issues, however, is China's economic support of, and integration with, the U.S. government. Few people understand the extent of the integration of our economies, but suffice it to say that trade is only one part of this equation. For the last several years, China has been the largest purchaser of U.S. Treasury Bonds, making it second only to Japan in its holding of such bonds. It is difficult to get exact numbers on the amount of U.S. securities held by China, but industry insiders place the magnitude at several hundred billion dollars. This is China's trump card. If the country decided to suddenly dump a significant portion of their bond holdings, it could wreak havoc on the U.S. economy, sending ripples throughout the world economy. It is difficult to predict what the true effects would be, but there would certainly be an impact on U.S. stock markets, interest rates, mortgages, and, eventually, consumer spending. Some industry insiders predict that it would undoubtedly lead to a recession. As one bond trader who does significant business with China put it to me, "if they started suddenly dumping bonds, they could turn our economy upside down in a day. It could all come tumbling down if they did that. I don't think people realize what is at stake here. And it would hurt us a lot more than it would hurt them." One analyst described the potential impact in a similar fashion:

> What would happen if China decided to dump, say, $100 bn of U.S. government bonds on the market all at once? The effects on the U.S.'s financial markets would be immediate, though possibly only short-term. The U.S. stock market would tumble. I would find it easy to believe that a one-day rise in long-term rates of 1% could easily trigger a stock market fall of 10%. The dollar would also immediately fall. . . . If these changes in asset prices persisted for a period of some weeks, we would then expect there to be noticeable effects on the real economy [as] the sharp jump in U.S. government bond yields would feed through to mortgage and consumer rates.[8]

Another point of economic integration lies in the Chinese purchasing of U.S. corporations. The recent bid to purchase Maytag by Haier, the takeover of IBM's computer business by Lenovo, and the bid of the China National Offshore Oil Corporation to purchase Unocal are key examples of the global integration of U.S. and Chinese corporations. Chinese corporations are no longer simply the second-class partners in joint-venture relationships with U.S. multinational corporations; today, they are emerging as the potential owners of these corporations. The U.S. and Chinese economies are, at this point, intimately intertwined, and the ironies here are many: as the U.S. Treasury blusters about "forcing" China to revalue its currency, it is increasingly China that holds the cards in the stability of our interdependent economies. As the U.S. government has plunged into fiscal irresponsibility over the last seven years, it is China that has softened that decline through its voracious appetite for U.S. bonds. And as U.S. consumers and labor leaders complain about the trade deficit, it is the U.S. consumer who drives that deficit by shopping at Wal-Mart, which is the single-largest contributor to it. Our economies are far too interdependent at this point to talk of coming conflicts with China. We are not even in a situation any longer in which we can dictate the terms of this relationship. Instead, it would behoove all hawks in Congress and in the American media to figure out how we can constructively coexist with China.

As a final note on integration, it is important to briefly address the area that often causes the greatest concern as a potential catalyst for a pending conflict between China and Taiwan and Tibet. But even here, it increasingly looks like integration is largely being guided by economic integration. In the early 1990s, an important shift in Mainland China–Taiwan relations occurred (Hsing 1998). After 1989, many countries in the Organization for Economic Cooperation and Development pulled out of China; foreign investment dropped from US$2 billion in the fourth quarter of 1988 to $900 million in the first quarter of 1990. In order to win back foreign capital, China appealed to Chinese investors from Hong Kong, Macao, and Taiwan by offering favorable investment conditions. Among these were several industrial zones in Fujian Province, the ancestral birthplace of many Taiwanese citizens that were designated for Taiwanese investors. As a result, direct Taiwanese investment in China increased by 75 percent in 1990. Taiwanese linguistic and cultural affinity with Mainland China made it relatively easy for small- and medium-sized investors to cross the straits. And in 1990, under pressure from Taiwan's business communities and industrial organizations, the Taiwan government finally allowed Taiwanese firms to conduct indirect investment in China. Taiwanese investments in China have been small in terms of the size of the project (average investments are less than US$1 million); however, by 1992, Taiwan had become the second-largest investor in Mainland China, behind Hong Kong. This economic interdependence, combined with the weakening of the Taiwanese economy over the last decade, has rendered the economic viability of an independence bid feeble. Before the Asian financial crisis of 1997, Taiwan might have been in a position to push the issue of Taiwanese independence, but not today. Even politicians like Chen Shuibian, who was once bullish on the issue in years past, backed away from explicit conversations about independence as soon as he was elected. And immediately after winning the election in March of 2008, President-elect Ma Ying-Jeou pledged to forge closer ties with Beijing. Taiwan's economic fate is now heavily dependent on good relations with Mainland China, and it is likely that both countries will simply continue to move down the path toward integration.

This discussion would be incomplete if we did not touch on the issue of Tibet. Recently, I was sitting in a Shanghai hotel room, watching a CNN feed on the March 2008 repression of demonstrations in Tibet. Suddenly, in the middle of the report, the screen went black. I fooled around with the remote control until I realized that every other channel was fine. This happens in China sometimes, more often on the Internet than TV, but it happens in both media: critical or provocative media will abruptly disappear. There is no doubt that China has exercised abusive control in annexing and subduing Tibet since 1951. However, it is important to put this into some of the historical and comparative context that we put Taiwan in above.

First, a little history: the first invasion of Tibet by China came in the year 1720 under the leadership of Emperor Kangxi (1661–1722). China continued to expand its reach during the Qing Dynasty under the reign of Emperors Yongzheng (1723–35) and Qianlong (1736–99). Even as the Qing Dynasty was in decline in the first decade of the twentieth century, the regime had successful campaigns to reestablish its authority in Tibet. However, with China descending into Chaos (following the fall of the Qing Dynasty, and the uncertain future of the Nationalist Revolution), in 1913, Britain took advantage of this weakness and sought to ensure Tibet's independence. As the colonial power of the region, Britain's main motivation seemed to be the establishment of an independent buffer between China and India. By 1938, with the Japanese occupation of China, the Chinese Empire that had been united under the Qing fragmented with Xinjiang, Taiwan, and Tibet all asserting independence. Tibet was reoccupied in October of 1950 by the Communists, who claimed they were occupying Tibet to "liberate" it from foreign imperialism, though there was no foreign presence in Tibet at the time. The UN did nothing to stop the occupation. In addition, the only country that had been active in asserting Tibetan independence was Britain, and because of Indian Independence in 1947, Britain no longer had need of Tibet as a buffer between India and China. The Chinese occupied key points in the country within a year and pressured the Dalai Lama's advisors into general acceptance of China's sovereignty over the region. In March of 1959, after a decade of occupation by the Chinese government, a surge of protests against the Chinese occupation turned into armed rebellion. Many Tibetans were killed by Chinese troops in bitter fighting, and some of the most beautiful monasteries were destroyed by the Chinese. The Tibetans' spiritual leader, the Dalai Lama, fled to India where he was given sanctuary despite Chinese protests. Eventually, in the 1980s, Beijing would impose martial law in Lhasa to control the region, as well as a news embargo (no foreign journalists were allowed to enter the region). Chinese citizens have been indoctrinated to believe that they are carrying out patriotic duty by migrating to Tibet to help "develop" the region.

Although Beijing has worked hard at economic integration, it has not been as successful as the dependence that has been created with Taiwan. However, in assessing Tibet (and Taiwan's) claims of independence and China's claim of sovereignty, it is important to acknowledge that these are complicated matters, and we should be careful in thinking about parallels in our own history before being too judgmental of Beijing on its claim to sovereignty over Tibet. The annexation of Hawaii in 1898, which began with the forcible surrender of Queen Liliuokalani in 1893, is not as different from the situation in Tibet as we might like to think. And of course, after the Jackson Amendment was signed into law in 1830, the acquisition of all land west of the Mississippi amounted to an illegal annexation of land (according to the Jackson Amendment) on a much grander scale than that of Hawaii or Tibet.

The point here is not to justify China's actions with the citation of past wrongs by other nations like the United States. However, it is important to keep perspective on the complexities of state sovereignty and the strategic claims to land. In the end, China has embarked on a path of economic Integration with Tibet, much like its plan for dealing with the tensions over Taiwan, though the process is at a much earlier stage in Tibet. However, global integration is also in play here: the international media, Beijing's concerns over potential Olympic protests, and Gordon Brown's ability to weigh in on the issues with Premier Wen Jiabao are all issues that speak to China's relative openness compared to a decade ago.

A final note on the censorship of these events: during the week of March 17, 2008, the censorship worked like clockwork—as soon as Wolf Blitzer (or anyone on CNN) mentioned the violence in Tibet, the screen would go blank. It was interesting to note, however, the extent to which Beijing's censorship of the violence and repression in Tibet became as much a part of the story as the violence itself, a fact that became a significant embarrassment for Beijing. As the week wore on, the story shifted to the ways in which citizens in China could navigate around the firewalls on the Internet to see what was happening in Tibet. As we discussed in Chapter 7, there is so much more information available in China today than there was a decade ago fully that controlling the flow of information is impossible for Beijing at this point.

THE IMPACT OF CHINA'S ENTRY INTO THE WTO

It is one of the most common statements you will hear in conversations with managers across China: "We are getting on track with the international community." And entry into the WTO has been a focal point of this process of "getting on track." After fifteen years of arduous negotiations with the United States and other Western nations, China reached an agreement with the WTO on September 17, 2001, becoming the 143rd member of the WTO on December 11, 2001. By becoming a full member of the WTO, China has made commitments on three levels: (1) a commitment to the objectives of the WTO, such as free trade among all member nations;

(2) a commitment to the international rules governing trade for specific sectors, such as agricultural and textile goods or information technology and telecommunications; and (3) a commitment to bilateral agreements that China signed with its major trading partners, without whose support China's accession to the WTO would have been impossible. The protocol of China's accession to the WTO provides for "additional liberalization of China's trade regime and further opening up of opportunities for foreign direct investment" (Lardy 2002, 65). Around these provisions are two broad categories of issues: market access and evolution of the institutions that govern the market within China.

The issues around market access are substantial. For agricultural products, China has pledged to reduce tariffs from an average level of 31.5 percent to about 15 percent. It will eliminate export subsidies and rapidly increase the volumes of tariff-rate quotas on most imports. For industrial products, China has pledged to phase out restrictions and cut the average tariff from 24.6 percent to 9.4 percent by 2005. China has also agreed to sign the WTO Information Technology Agreement, which will result in the elimination of all tariffs on telecommunications equipment, semiconductors, computers and computer equipment, and other information technology products. The most far-reaching change, however, is expected to take place in the service sector, which has largely been closed to foreign competition. China has promised to open important service markets, including those of telecommunications, banking, insurance, securities, and many other professional services, to foreign service providers. Foreign firms will be granted trading and distribution rights, and thus they can engage in wholesale and retail trade, transportation, service, and maintenance, as well as import and export.

Besides these commitments in the area of market access,

China has pledged to comply with almost all provisions set forth in the WTO agreement, with the aim of increasing transparency in China's trade and investment regimes. The country has agreed to eliminate all prohibited subsidies (including those to state-owned enterprises), liberalize trading rights, and standardize the operations of state trading companies. Perhaps the most significant commitment within the WTO agreement is that China has consented to accept the provisions of trade-related aspects of intellectual property rights, among the thorniest of issues in U.S.–Chinese trade relations in the last decade.

The depth of China's WTO commitments compare favorably with those of other WTO nations (Lardy 2002). Both market access and rule-based commitments far surpass those made by founding members of the WTO and also go beyond those made by countries that have joined the WTO since 1995. What, then, has been the incentive behind China's pursuit of WTO membership in the last decade? First, as a result of China's WTO accession, the United States has granted China permanent, normal trade-relations status, ending the decade-long annual conflict over considering China's trade status under the Jackson-Vanick Amendment. Second, several of China's trading partners will have to lift most of their restrictions against China on a range of products. According to the Agreement on Textiles and Clothing, for example, all quotas on China's textiles and clothing will be phased out. Other quotas will also be phased out in accordance with negotiated schedules. This is actually an important point in understanding the politics behind the United States blocking China's entry into GATT and the WTO since 1989. To wit: every year, U.S. Senator Jesse Helms, from North Carolina, was one of the loudest proponents of blocking China's bid for Most Favored Nation (and later, Normal Trade Relations) status on the grounds that the United States should not be doing business with an authoritarian government that brought on such human-rights abuses as China did in Tianenmen Square in 1989. However, the jingoistic Helms could hardly claim a long-standing position of advocating for human rights around the world. What was behind this? Economic interests, plain and simple. North Carolina is one of the largest producers of textiles in the United States, and the phasing out of the "multi-fiber" agreement meant that North Carolina would be hurt most by growing competition from China. The other sector that would be threatened by China's entry into the WTO would be tobacco, also a mainstay of the North Carolina economy.

There is little doubt that WTO accession will benefit Chinese consumers and lead to greater economic efficiency, even though some heavily protected sectors will suffer as trade barriers fall. For China's labor force, increasing unemployment will be unavoidable in a few state sectors, but the opening of the service sector will likely generate some employment in the near term. Finally, with WTO membership, China can now resort to the WTO dispute settlement mechanism to protect its own trade interests, as well as participate in multilateral negotiations on trade rules and future trade liberalization. Another potential benefit of WTO membership is the opportunity for China to play a role in shaping the rules of the international trading system over time.

Probably the most important motivation behind China's joining the WTO is rooted in the realization among liberal reformers that the country needs greater external impetus to overcome domestic obstacles to further reform. During the past two-and-a-half decades, China has experienced dramatic institutional change in almost every field. The country has come a long way in liberalizing and opening up its economy, but some of the most difficult structural adjustments still lie ahead, especially in the highly protected industries. WTO membership will inevitably exert increasing pressure on the measures China will take shortly in the areas of institution building and in continuing to reform the state sectors. There is little doubt that China's WTO membership will further push the nation toward broader and deeper integration into the global economy.

The implications stemming from China's accession to the WTO and, thus, greater integration into the international community lie on three levels. First, on the level of the international economy, the implications of China's membership in the WTO are immense. China's emergence as one of the largest players in the global economy will inevitably lead to shifts in world production, trade, investment, and employment. China's economy and foreign trade are so large that the growth of global trade and the pace of expansion of global output will undoubtedly be affected. Not surprisingly, concerns have been raised in some developing countries that global demand for their exports will shrink and their FDI inflow will fall due to China's vast market and great potential in the production of labor-intensive exports. Advanced industrialized nations worry that China's exports will flood their domestic markets. The reality, however, is that the way in which China's WTO accession and relative openness affect other countries is a much more complex issue than simple FDI and exports statistics reveal. China's accession to the WTO will definitely strengthen trade and investment ties with its Asian neighbors and, thus, provide them with a more stable external environment. The newly industrialized economies of Asia are likely to benefit the most from China's WTO accession, given their heavy investment in China in the past two decades. China's WTO membership also brings many opportunities and challenges for the United States and other advanced industrial economies. Over time, the opening up of China's services sector should offer these countries large trade and investment opportunities. Most advanced industrial nations are expected to increase their exports of capital and technology-intensive manufactures to China. In addition, as the only major trading nation that is not an advanced industrial economy, China will bring "a distinct perspective to the negotiations" and will "be influential in future rounds of WTO trade negotiations" (Lardy 2002, 134), and will thus be able to exert greater influence over the multilateral trading system.

Second, with respect to China's macroeconomic policy, it is likely that China will rapidly dismantle its remaining central planning mechanisms, formulate more laws and policies consistent with its WTO commitments, and enforce uniform rules through the country. In the past two decades, foreign capital and global corporations that have moved to China have exerted considerable pressure on China's economic reforms, mainly concentrating on driving economic organizations within China to adapt to the rules of the global market. Starting in the early 1990s, the government has made greater strides in creating a rational-legal economic system, based on which Chinese firms could "get onto the international track" as quickly as possible. Among the important strides is the construction of numerous laws and regulations directly tied to the building of a rational economy, such as the Joint Venture Law (1979), the Enterprise Bankruptcy Law (1986), the Company Law (1994), the Labor Law (1994), and the Securities Law (1998). At the beginning of this century, China's entry into the WTO will bring more intensive pressure in this ongoing institution-building process.

Third, influences from foreign investors and global trade partners are also evident in the organizational changes at the firm level that are affecting millions of Chinese citizens on a

daily basis. With China's increasing involvement with international organizations and Western investors, a process of
rationalization has been occurring in the workplace, where
Chinese companies are adopting a number of the rational bureaucratic systems that are most often found in Western organizations. China's accession to the WTO will likely accelerate
the rationalization of the country's economic system both at
the state level and within firms. While stable rational/legal
systems are adopted more often to attract foreign investors or
comply with the universal rules than they are for the good of
workers, they nevertheless have radical implications for the
structure of authority relations and, therefore, for the lives of
individual Chinese citizens.

CONCLUSIONS

It is no longer controversial to state that China will play a
pivotal role in the political and economic structure of the
world in the twenty-first century; the question that remains is
what that role will be. China's reform process has been an
inherently global one, and all indications are that China's
growth will continue to integrate the country into the global
economy. The reforms of the last two-and-a-half decades have
radically transformed China's economy and society. From the
agricultural policies that transformed rural China and the
transformation of the state sector to the institutional changes
that have transformed social life in China, the changes have
been radical and deep.

This is not a story about the ways that markets lead to
liberal policies. Rather, it is about the ways in which reform-
minded elites have engineered a gradual reform process,
slowly liberalizing economic, political, and social realms. In
this book, I have emphasized four key points about the
economic reforms in China. First, changes in China are

much more radical than is often understood by outside observers.

Second, the enacting of China's reforms has fundamentally been a state-led process. For decades, we have been skeptical about the possibility of a successful transition to capitalism in which the state plays a key role. China's reforms not only show that states can be effective in this process, they suggest that state-led development may be far superior to letting the market work its magic. The reasons for this, I argue, are stability and experimentation. New economic and political systems take time to learn, and it is important for states to provide stability as societies make the transition between the two. These processes of change are driven by state-led initiatives that have gradually transformed the rules of society across the board. Experimentation has emphasized getting the institutions right rather than blindly assuming that one path of institutional change—rapid privatization—will necessarily lead to the successful development of a market economy. The state begins this process of gradual experimentation that is then codified in broad-based institutional changes (in the form of laws and policies). As the state gradually implements these new policies, Chinese citizens adapt to these new rules, and the social worlds that they live in are transformed as well.

Third, economic reform in China will lead to democratization, but not because of what some neoliberals argue is the fundamental connection between liberal economic and political systems. Rather, China will become a democracy because that is the agenda some of the key powerful leaders in China have had over the course of the economic reforms. They have used the economic reforms to bring this change about. They have not talked about it openly, because, since 1989, they have lived in the shadow of Zhao Ziyang's fate. But both Zhao

Ziyang and Zhu Rongji were clearly pushing radical reform agendas; and now Hu Jintao is following in the footsteps of his predecessors. Markets do not, in and of themselves, breed liberalism; liberal-minded leaders do. This process of change in China has been a fundamentally global one. Chinese leaders have leveraged the process of global integration to transform China from within. China's role in the global economy will continue to grow and transform, and that role will also continue to transform China from within.

Finally, it is important to note the extent to which China's rise signals a shift in the balance of power not only among nations but also in terms of models of capitalism and global corporations. The sub-prime credit crisis of 2007–08 (and subsequent write-downs, near bankruptcies, and bailouts) of storied American banks like Merrill Lynch, Citigroup, and Bear Sterns was yet another example of the fact that the self-regulating notion of a market discipline is a flawed concept. As we learned with the Savings and Loan Crisis of the late 1980s and the accounting scandals of the early 2000s, minimally-regulated market actors will push the boundaries of ethical (and sensible) behavior as far as they can, especially when they believe that, as global corporations, they often act beyond the reach of the law (and when they believe that the US government will bail them out). These scandals have left a serious black-eye on the face of American capitalism, and they have had a significant impact on the American and Chinese consumer alike. However, it is also interesting to note that in the decade that brought us the accounting and sub-prime credit, we have also seen Chinese hybrid state-owned companies emerge as forces in the global economy. We have seen Lenovo's growth from a small-scale privately-owned high tech company to a global player in the PC industry that would eventually purchase IBM's laptop division; we would see Hiaer's growth to a global brand that would build a $40 million science park in North Carolina and eventually make a bid to buy Maytag; we would see CNOOC's bid for Unocal. And in the last year alone, we have seen Chinese MNCs emerge as the largest IPO in history (Chinese International Monetary Bank) and (briefly) as the largest company in the world in terms of market capitalization (PetroChina, valued at over $1 trillion). The performance of these companies has been impressive. But this is not just a story of Chinese economic growth and a few large state-owned corporations; it is also a story of superior economic management and the fact that model of state ownership was not quite as clear-cut as we believed it to be in the 1980s and 1990s. Since the 1980s, it has widely been assumed that the problem with SOEs was that they could never be efficient. The Chinese process of change has proved this story incomplete; in fact, it is very possible to get the incentives aligned so that state officials can actually run corporations that are much more efficient than the classic state-owned firms of command economies around the world.

However, the issues also extend beyond efficiency to the question of the stakeholders that corporations serve. In the US system, multi-national corporations often operate beyond the reach of the US law and they rarely serve any national interests beyond the narrowly-defined interests of their shareholders. But China's hybrid-form corporations are a different breed. They are increasingly efficient in ways that other MNCs are, but they are also directed toward a much broader set of stakeholders. They are also constrained in a way that might just be healthy from an economic perspective. In the decade that has given us the economic debacles of Enron and Bear Sterns, it seems increasingly difficult to make the case that the unfettered capitalist model is truly superior. As China's influence grows over the course of this century, it will be interesting to see just how powerful and prominent Chinese corporations become.

The year 2007–08 has been a humbling stretch for the Beijing regime. In the 12 months that were supposed to be a yearlong celebration leading up to the coming out party of the Beijing Olympics, that celebration has been overshadowed by other, darker events. We have seen scandalous recalls of poorly-manufactured toys and poisonous dog food; the world has focused a significant amount of attention on Beijing's handling of Tibet; we have seen poorly-made schools tragically crumble in the earthquake of May 2008. Nevertheless, despite these problems, the fundamentals are strong and the economic (and political) future is bright for the world's largest nation.

The Chinese economy and Chinese firms will increasingly be central players in the global economic system. As the Chinese economy continues to expand and grow, it will reshape global politics and also our core assumptions about how firms work within the global political economy.

ONE

1. *Pocket world in Figures* (2008).
2. A country's GDP represents all of the income the country generates within its borders. GDP is generally used as a measure of national wealth. The countries with the top GDP in the world are, in order, the United States, Japan, and Germany. One problem with the GDP statistic is that it does not account for the cost of goods in a given country. For example, if a bushel of rice costs half as much in China as in the United States, then a unit of currency is twice as valuable there. As a solution to this problem, GDP statistics will, when appropriate, be adjusted for purchasing power parity (PPP), a statistic that adjusts for cost-of-living differences by replacing exchange rates with relative measures of local purchasing power. In terms of PPP, China is second only to the United States. PPP was introduced into the international accounting system by the International Monetary Fund in 1993.
3. In the mid-1990s, world grain exports totaled about 250 million tons per year. China currently produces and consumes about 330 million tons of grain per year. However, if trends of declining productivity in grain yields within China follow trends from the 1990s, China's grain production will fall to about 270 million tons by 2030; this despite a continuously growing population that is projected to reach 1.5 billion people by 2017. For further discussion, see Brown 1995.
4. *Time Asia*, October 18, 2004.
5. Gordon Chang (2001).
6. Sachs and Woo (1997, 5). See also Sachs (1992, 1993, 1995b); Woo et al. (1993); and Woo (1999). To be fair to Sachs, he

has significantly changed his tune about the importance of understanding institutions, social inequality, and even culture. However, in the years that he was among the most influential economists in the world, shaping processes of economic reform in developing nations, he saw little beyond a deep-seated trust in the magic of the market.

7. Also implicit in Sachs and Woo's (1994a, 1997) argument is the a priori assumption that private ownership will always outperform state ownership. This is a stance that is reflected in the privatization school in general. See especially Woo (1999) and Sachs (1992, 1993, 1995b).

8. Essentialism is the notion that a group of people are defined by a few key traits or some sort of essence.

9. The Dun and Bradstreet experiences discussed here are based upon personal interviews with Dun and Bradstreet executives who were knowledgeable about the company's China venture.

10. "Manager" [jingli] is the term that is used for upper-level executives in industrial organizations that have made the transition to being companies [gongsi] through adoption of the 1994 Company Law (Guthrie 1999). For industrial organizations that have not made this transition—they are still referred to as factories [gongchang]—the top positions are referred to as factory director [changzhang] and vice director [fu changzhang]. In both organizational types, I spoke with the top- or second-ranked individual in the organization. For the sake of simplicity, I refer to these positions as managerial or executive positions throughout the book.

TWO

1. For discussion of the structure of Chinese society under Mao, see, for example, Schurmann 1968; Parish and Whyte 1978; Whyte and Parish 1984; and Walder 1986a. For discussion of the process of economic reforms in China, see, for example, Field 1984; Wong 1991; Field 1992; Wong 1992; Rawski 1994; Naughton 1995; and Walder 1995a.

2. Unless otherwise noted, the historical details in this section draw upon Hsu 1999 and Spence 1999.

3. Today, there are actually four municipalities that hold provincial-level administrative status—Chongqing being the recent addition to the group of Beijing, Shanghai, and Tianjin.

4. Bian 1994, 9. See also Walder 1992a and 1995a and Guthrie

1999. Walder 1992a and Bian 1994a refer to this administrative structure as the "budgetary rank" of a given work unit, placing emphasis on the variable access to resources that organizations had in this system. I use the more general term nested hierarchy to emphasize the fact that this administrative hierarchy had many purposes of governmental control over work units, with budgetary control being only one of these areas.

5. Note that these last two issues were not problems in their own right in the era of the planned economy. In the prereform era, the Chinese socioeconomic system—the so-called iron rice bowl—was a redistributive system, so factories were never meant to cover their own costs in terms of the social welfare of their employees. Revenues flowed up the hierarchy and were redistributed by the government to cover the costs of the factories under their jurisdictions. The social welfare burden for factories in the command economy would become a major challenge in the reform era, as budget constraints were gradually hardened from factories.

6. There was an additional critical moment in this narrative, which played a central role in Mao's decision to "deepen" the revolution. In the spring of 1956, Mao spoke of the need to help relationships between party members and non-party members. Mao was encouraging people to speak out about their experiences in, and grievances with, the party. He called this the movement of letting "one hundred flowers bloom"; in other words, he was calling for all of the differing opinions within the party to be put on the table. Mao spent a good deal of political capital to make this movement happen—overcoming resistance from Liu Xiaoqi and many others in the party—and by April 1957, intellectuals were encouraged to speak out against such abuses and vices of the party as bureaucratism, sectarianism, and subjectivism. The criticism became much stronger than Mao anticipated it would, quickly spreading beyond the party-defined agenda of the "reform" to more difficult issues of democracy, totalitarianism, human rights, and freedom. In response to this, Mao launched his "anti-rightist campaign," turning on intellectuals as if his plan all along had been to root out the intellectuals who did not support the party. By the end of 1957, over 300,000 intellectuals had been branded "rightists" and "enemies of the party."

7. Although the economic architects of the planned economy did not acknowledge "unemployment" as a problem, they did

acknowledge a growing category of individuals who were "waiting for employment" in the job assignment system.

8. A number of scholars have used the term quiet revolution to describe China's reforms. See, for example, Goodman and Hooper 1994; Walder 1995c; and Guthrie 2003.

9. Sachs 1995a; Sachs and Woo 1997.

10. For discussion of the "attenuation of property rights" and the local control over enterprises, see Walder 1994a and Walder 1995a.

11. The "One-China" policy actually dates back to the Shanghai Communiqué, which was signed by both Mao Zedong and U.S. president Richard M. Nixon on February 28, 1972. As the communiqué stated,

> The Taiwan question is the crucial question obstructing the normalization of relations between China and the United States; the Government of the PRC is the sole legal government of China; Taiwan is a province of China which has long been returned to the motherland; the liberation of Taiwan is China's internal affair in which no other country has the right to interfere; and all U.S. forces and military installations must be withdrawn from Taiwan. The Chinese Government firmly opposes any activities which aim at the creation of "one China, one Taiwan," "One China, two governments," "an independent Taiwan" or advocate that "the status of Taiwan remains to be determined."
>
> As a result of this agreement, any country wanting to form diplomatic relations with China had to end its formal diplomatic relations with Taiwan.

12. As a result of the Carter-Deng Normalization Agreement, in April 1979 the U.S. Congress passed the Taiwan Relations Act, which reflected the worries of pro-Taiwan forces by reaffirming the U.S. commitment to Taiwan and especially by underlining that the United States intended to provide Taiwan with arms of a defensive character and pledged to resist any coercion that would jeopardize the security or the social or economic system of the people of Taiwan.

13. Debora Spar, "China (A): The Great Awakening." Harvard Business School Case 9-794-019.

14. See Wong 1991; see also Oi 1992; Wong 1992; Walder 1995a; and Guthrie 1999.

15. This was first discussed at a working conference of the Central Committee in April 1979; it was officially adopted on November 26, 1981.

16. Naughton (1995) puts forth a broad analysis of the institutions that defined China's command economy, the new institutions that emerged in the market reforms, and the process of transition between the systems. Naughton's explanation of this process is one of the most comprehensive and insightful accounts published to date. He limits his study to the industrial economy because, as industry is so closely tied to state investment and saving—and therefore to governmental fiscal policy—reforming the industrial economy becomes the central task of economic transitions from planned to market-based systems. Naughton's work is also important because of what it says about the economic reform debate. Observing the early years of transforming command economies in Europe, China's reform experience and, more recently, the aggressive reform programs in Czechoslovakia and Russia have given researchers the rare opportunity to comparatively assess various strategies of economic reform. The central debate that has emerged over the utility of different reform strategies pits the gradualist, incremental approach to reforms against an approach that emphasizes rapid privatization—the so-called big bang or shock therapy models of economic reform. Advocates of the former argue that there are clear benefits to a gradual approach to economic reforms, while proponents of shock therapy argue that rapid and complete destruction of the command system is the only possible approach to creating a market-based system. Naughton takes a strong and convincing position in this debate, arguing that the China case shows that gradual reform is not only feasible but also preferable to the radical transformation of shock therapy.

17. While many accounts focus on the performance of the non-state sector, Naughton's focus is on the fact that this sector was an essential link to the creation of a competitive marketplace, which changed the behavior of firms in the state and non-state sectors alike.

18. *Statistical Yearbook of China* (National Statistical Bureau of China 1999). See also the discussions in Oi and Walder 1999.

19. For example, according to Li's (1997) study of state enterprises

in the 1980s, those enterprises supervised by local governments were more likely to reduce workers' wages based on "poor performance" than those supervised by the central state. Li's study also indicates the enterprise's hardening budget constraints in local governments' supervision of state enterprises.

20. In many ways, firms at this level of the industrial hierarchy are proving to be much more successful in reform than those at other levels of the urban industrial economy. For example, previous research suggests that firms under municipal companies have not only adopted the most extensive changes in intra-organizational structure but have also been the most productive in Shanghai's urban industrial economy (Guthrie 1999, 2001).

21. For a discussion of the 1984 Reform Declaration, see Naughton 1995, 248; for a discussion of the "price reformers" and "enterprise reformers" see Naughton 1995, 188–196; for a discussion of a lack of reform by the end of 1984, see Naughton 1995, 136.

22. As a document from the State Council put it in 1983, "The current system of employment in China, under which the majority are permanent workers, in practice operates as a kind of unconditional system of life tenure" (People's Republic of China 1983; for a full translation, see Josephs 1989, Appendix A). The Great Leap Forward (1958–60) actually provides a caveat to this system, as approximately sixteen million workers were laid off and sent down to the countryside during that campaign. This is the only period, however, where layoffs were not accompanied by reassignment (Walder 1986a).

23. The main reason for the difference is that the Japanese law on foreign investment, which dates to 1950, was extremely restrictive.

24. The term rational-legal refers to Max Weber's notion of rational-legal authority, one of the three ideal types of authority that characterize modern states. According to Weber, rational-legal authority is characterized by bureaucracy and a reliance on the rule of law.

25. Officially, revenue extraction was replaced by taxation in the Decision of the Standing Committee of the National People's Congress on Authorizing the State Council to Reform the System of Industrial and Commercial Taxes and Issue Relevant Draft Tax Regulations for Trial Application, adopted September 18, 1984, at the Seventh Meeting of the Standing Committee of the Sixth National People's Congress and later codified in the

State-Owned Enterprise Second Phase Profits to Taxes Reform of 1985 (*Statistical Yearbook of China* 1994, 226); for other discussions, see Institutional Economic Yearbook of Shanghai 1994. The first of these documents states that the Standing Committee and State Council recommend "introducing the practice according to which state enterprises pay taxes instead of turning over their profit to the state and in the course reforming the system of industrial and commercial taxes" (People's Republic of China 1984a). However, in practice, revenue extraction (and management and oversight fees) lasted for many more years, declining gradually over time. See Naughton 1995 for a further discussion of tax reform.

26. See "The Practical Applications and Experimental Methods of 'The Separation of Taxes and Profits, Fees After Taxes, and Residuals After Taxes' for State-Owned Enterprises," pp. 64–66 in The Shanghai Institutional Economic Yearbook, 1989–1993 (1994).

27. For other estimates of the number of cases brought before court, see *New York Times*, April 27, 1998. For discussion of the percentage rise in suits against the government, see Pei 1995 and 1997.

THREE

1. This chapter was coauthored with Junmin Wang.
2. See, for example, Calhoun 2002.
3. The notion of a "world of total institutions" is an allusion to Erving Goffman's work on the ways that certain societies create institutional environments that engulf the individuals who reside within them.
4. Some scholars, like Vivienne Shue (1988), have argued that the "honeycomb"-like village structure that emerged in Mao's China actually protected individuals from "the reach of the state." However, her point of comparison is the era of economic reform, where, she argues, the state is actually more able to penetrate down to the level of individuals. Regardless, it is unquestionably true that the state was a greater force of social control in Mao's era than it was in the era prior to the Communist Revolution.
5. When individuals were sent to the countryside for "reeducation," it meant essentially that they needed to engage in manual labor in the agricultural or industrial sectors (usually

the former) in order to better understand the class issues confronted by the Communist Revolution.

6. Information on population-growth trends in the People's Republic of China is drawn largely from Spence 1999.

7. The Great Leap Forward was a major project of social reorganization in order to "deepen" the revolution. In 1957–58 this meant setting up the people's communes; by the end of 1958, 740,000 cooperatives had been merged into 26,000 communes; these comprised 120 million rural households—99 percent of the rural population. One of the central problems with production was that grain was not being produced at a high-enough rate. Grain was a necessary part of industrial growth, because it was the primary product China could export to the Soviet Union. In 1957, the Chinese Communist Party began organizing people into huge workforces for irrigation, construction projects, and the like. The year 1958 also saw the creation of over one million backyard steel furnaces. The result was a huge famine from 1959 to 1962 in which twenty million people died of starvation.

8. See, for example, Wolff et al. 1995 and Wong 2004.

9. "China's Missing Girls," *Shanghai Star*, October 24, 2002.

10. This information comes from the Xinhua News Agency. Note that these figures are officially reported figures and likely underrepresent the problem.

11. If non-party members are elected in village-level elections to leadership positions in the village, they are required to join the party.

12. Other members of the Politburo Standing Committee of the Chinese Communist Party occupy such leadership positions: Huang Ju is vice premier of the State Council of China; Jia Qinglin is chairman of the People's Political Consultative Conference; Li Changchun has no formal position but is known to many as "propaganda chief"; Luo Gan is a state councilor and secretary of the Political and Legislative Affairs Committee; Wu Guanzheng is secretary of the Central Commission for Discipline Inspection; and Zeng Qinghong is vice president of the People's Republic of China.

13. "Grassroots Democracy is Flourishing in China," *China Daily*, October 18, 2002.

14. Where Oberschall (1996) presents the party-state and work units as distinct institutions, the situation was actually a little more complicated than this, as the exercise of political control

from the party-state operated largely through the dependence that was created through the work-unit system; see Walder 1986a.

15. A large volume of literature exists on this phenomenon. Typical studies in this approach include, for example, Ho and Tsou 1969; Solomon 1971; Hsu 1999; Rozman 1981; Fairbanks 1983; Pye 1988; Pye 1992; and Chen and Deng 1995.
16. See the results from Transparency International's 2003 index.
17. For further discussion, see Gold et al. 2002.

FOUR

1. For further discussion, see Yang 1990 and 1991 and Vogel 1989.
2. This lack of control was viewed by conservatives as partially responsible for the Tiananmen Square uprising.
3. Primary goods refers to food and live animals chiefly used for food; beverages and tobacco; nonedible raw materials; mineral fuels, lubricants, and related materials; and animal and vegetable oils, fats, and wax. Manufactured goods refers to chemicals and related products; light and textile industrial products; rubber products; minerals and metallurgical products; machinery and transport equipment; miscellaneous products; and products not otherwise classified.
4. In the case of Taiwan, this trend gained momentum after 1989, when many countries of the Organization for Economic Cooperation and Development pulled out of China in response to the Tiananmen Square massacre; foreign investment dropped from US$2 billion in the fourth quarter of 1988 to $900 million in the first quarter of 1990. In order to win back foreign capital, China appealed to Chinese investors from Hong Kong, Macao, and Taiwan by offering favorable investment conditions. Among these were several industrial zones in Fujian Province, the ancestral birthplace of many Taiwanese citizens, which were designated for Taiwanese investors. As a direct result, Taiwanese investment in China increased by 75 percent in 1990 (Hsing 1998).
5. *BusinessWeek*, October 13, 2003.
6. Under GNP, the earnings of multinational corporations were counted according to where a multinational corporation was owned and where the profits were eventually returned. Under GDP, the profits are attributed to where the site of production is

located, regardless of where the organization is owned or incorporated.

7. James Flanigan, *Los Angeles Times*, April 17, 2005.

8. See Guthrie 1998b, 1999, 2002b. Although labor contracts officially afforded SOEs the opportunity to end lifetime employment, the practice continued for many years, though it has been declining steadily since these formal changes in 1986.

9. As with all reforms adopted over the course of China's transition, these formal laws and regulations that governed enterprise behavior were first experimented with in many venues over significant periods of time before becoming officially codified in formal laws and regulations.

10. See *The Decision on Several Issues for Establishing a Socialist Market Economy System*, passed in the Third Plenary Session of the Fourteenth National Congress of the Chinese Communist Party in 1993.

11. For further discussion, see Wong 2002.

12. For example, a city government divided the land for one foreign project into several small lots and granted land-use permission individually, in order to satisfy the standard of the smaller size of land that this level of government had the authority to grant (see Hsing 1998). Similar strategies have been used more widely for foreign investment arrangements in regions throughout southern China.

13. In the simplest terms, classical definitions of business organizations would posit that they are (1) comprised of relationships between owners and workers and (2) established for the purpose of pursuing profits in exchange for the provision of goods and/or services (see Sparling 1906). For example, Noble (1927, 232) defines business organizations as an "association expressed in a variety of relationships—joint owners, joint operators, agent and principal, trustee and beneficiary, employer and employee. The history of efforts of these individuals or groups of individuals within the business unit to accomplish that purpose for which the business unit was formed, namely, the making of profit, is recorded in the accounts of the enterprise." Howard (1917, 107) places the concept squarely in the realm of property rights, positing the right that owners have as residual claimants on revenues generated by the services: business organizations are "cooperative arrangements of men for the purpose of acquiring ... property rights (quantitatively measured by the unit of value, the dollar) by producing some product or service exchangeable

for some form of property, usually a right to money, which may be distributed as income to individuals." According to these terms, only private enterprises and some foreign-funded enterprises in China would fall under the category of business organizations.

14. The data here comes from the *Statistical Yearbook of China, 2006*. The figure includes "all the state-owned and non-state-owned industrial enterprises."

15. There are obvious and famous exceptions here; state-owned enterprises like Baoshan Steel were still closely monitored and supported by the state (Steinfeld 1998). However, while these organizations are often viewed as the markers of what is occurring in the Chinese reform process, this view is mistaken. While important to the economy, these largest state-owned organizations are not representative of the economy as a whole. Thus, while many scholars view these organizations as measures of the progress of China's reforms, they are more accurately the exceptions that prove the rule.

16. It is important to note the interdependence of these sectors here: as state-owned enterprises were placed on the dual-track system, private firms were allowed to emerge in the economy, becoming a force that essentially forced the state sector to compete (Naughton 1995). Similarly, the foreign sector has been a key factor in the teaching of management practices (Guthrie 1999) as well as in the transfer of technology.

17. Here again, we are speaking of joint-venture partnerships as opposed to other types of foreign investment.

18. Details of this venture are taken from Smith 2001.

19. Most of the large joint-venture deals come in at just under US$30 million, as this is the level at which approvals need not go beyond the municipal government. A joint-venture deal the size of Time Warner and Legend's must be approved directly by the State Council.

20. The Third Annual Meeting of the Advisory Council of International Business Leaders was held on May 9–10, 2001, in Beijing.

21. Arbitration clauses are particular cases in which the government gives away control over joint-ventures. If a joint-venture contract specifies nothing about how a dispute will be resolved, disputes that arise will be handled by the Chinese courts. This is the best-case scenario for the Chinese government in terms of sovereignty, because the courts, at this point, are still an arm

of the authoritarian government. However, if a joint-venture agreement specifies that disputes will be settled through arbitration, there are two possible venues for this. The first is the Chinese International Economic Trade and Arbitration Commission (CIETAC), an institution of arbitration in Beijing (with branches in Shanghai and Shenzhen). The significant fact about CIETAC, in terms of arbitration, is that one-third of the arbitrators who sit on any case are from other countries. Thus, once cases go to CIETAC, the Chinese government no longer has control over their outcome. A second possibility is that a joint-venture agreement can specify third-country arbitration, in which the dispute will be settled in the arbitration institution of some specified third country. The Chinese government has even less control—if any at all—over the outcome of these cases (Guthrie 1999, Chap. 7).

22. This is actually the way that many factories in the late 1970s were started or, in some cases, expanded in size. As a way of dealing with the excess population that resulted from the return to urban areas of the Red Guard youth who were sent to the countryside in the *xiangxia* campaign, the government created jobs in the urban industrial economy by expanding the work-forces of urban collectives. Urban collectives tend to be smaller organizations under the jurisdiction of state administrative offices called municipal and district administrative companies [*xingzheng gongsi*].

23. The Shanghai Kang Hua Meat and Foods Company is not the company's real name; I have used a pseudonym.

24. Although this was before the Company Law (1994) was passed, experimentation with the new regulations that would later be codified in the Company Law was occurring as early as 1990. Thus, this factory became one of the early experiments in the transition from "enterprises" [*qiye*] to "companies" [*gongsi*].

25. Although the Patent Law (People's Republic of China 1984b), which was put into effect on April 1, 1985, may have been relevant for this dispute, the more pertinent question is which Chinese body (e.g., the Chinese courts or the Chinese International Economic Trade and Arbitration Commission— CIETAC) was hearing this dispute and to what extent that body chose to seriously consider DuPont's claims. In the DuPont case, the joint-venture contact presumably did not specify CIETAC arbitration, as disputes over contracts that do not specify

arbitration (CIETAC or third-country) go automatically to the courts, which was the case with DuPont's dispute.

26. With respect to the former, there are other types of contractual relations between foreign and Chinese firms that are not commitments over time. For example, the piece-rate production agreements that prevail in the garment and shoe industries tend to be per project and are renegotiated and shopped in a competitive production market in each round of production. Thus, the commitment of a company like Liz Claiborne or the Gap to an individual factory is marginal, as they are always shopping for cheaper production prices. This is fundamentally different from a licensing agreement or a joint venture, as these commitments are long-term agreements.

27. The Shanghai Number 10 Electronics Tube Factory is not the company's real name; I have used a pseudonym.

28. The comparison here is not between state/collective on the one hand and foreign firms on the other; rather, it is between those state- and collectively-owned firms that have received some kind of foreign involvement through joint-venture deals, licensing agreements, and other types of "cooperative" agreements, and those who have not. Note also that a common misconception with the "collective" sector is that these organizations are somehow hybrid or mixed-property-rights organizations. Collectively owned organizations are fundamentally state organizations; the variation is in the level of government control over property rights and the period of the founding of such organizations (Walder 1995e; Guthrie 1999).

29. For econometric analyses of these effects, see Guthrie 2005.

30. In a few places, such as Xinjiang and Tibet, foreign-funded firms consistently perform worse across economic indicators like productivity (the same holds true for ratios of profits to cost and output to assets). However, for those economic indicators listed in Table 4.1, no fewer than twenty-eight (out of thirty-one) administrative areas show better performance among foreign-funded firms than state-owned firms that have no such relationships with foreign corporations.

31. For econometric analyses, see Guthrie (2005).

FIVE

1. This chapter was coauthored with Junmin Wang.
2. The details of these men's lives are taken from Roberts 1999.

3. Beijing and Tsinghua Universities (widely regarded as the top two universities in China) received an additional 1.8 billion yuan, spread over three years (1999–2001), while Nanjing and Fudan (widely regarded as the third, and fourth, best universities, respectively) received an additional 1.2 billion yuan.
4. United Nations Development Programme, 2001.
5. See Figure 2.1 for an example of the nested hierarchy of state administration.
6. For a sense of scale, note that this population of migrant laborers is equal to the entire population of Northern Europe or about one-third of the total U.S. population.

SIX

1. The facts of this case are presented in Lo and Tian 2005.
2. See, for example, Sik 1994; Boisot and Child 1996; Shao 1998; Lu 2000; and Sik 2000. This is not to say there are not proponents of the view that a rational-legal system is gradually emerging. For example, Pei 1994, Naughton 1995, and Guthrie 1999 have all taken the view that the emergence of a rational-legal economy in China is significant and real. However, the overwhelming tenor of scholarship on China's transition is that despite the success of the reforms, corporatism, corruption, crony-capitalism, and a still-authoritarian government are all impeding the development of a rational-legal economy in China.
3. For further discussion, see Guthrie 1999, esp. Chapters 3, 7, and 9.
4. As Walder (1986a, 11) puts it, "The discretion of supervisors, relatively unrestrained by enforceable regulations and contracts, [was] quite broad . . . [supervisors had] considerable ability to influence the promotions, raises, and, more importantly, the degree to which a worker and his or her family may enjoy the many nonwage benefits and advantages potentially supplied by the enterprise."
5. As a document from the State Council put it in 1983, "The current system of employment in China, under which the majority are permanent workers, in practice operates as a kind of unconditional system of life tenure" (People's Republic of China 1983); See also Guthrie 1998a and Josephs 1989 for further discussion.
6. The Great Leap Forward (1958–60) provided a caveat to this

system, as approximately 16 million workers were laid off and sent down to the countryside during that campaign. This is the only period, however, where layoffs were not accompanied by reassignment (Walder 1986a). For further discussion of "waiting for employment," see Gold 1989a.

7. See People's Republic of China 1986a and 1986b. See also Zhongguo tongji nianjian (*Statistical Yearbook of China* 1994, 131); and Josephs 1989. These documents explicitly define three types of contracts: the fixed limited-term contract [*guding qixian laodong hetong*], the nonfixed limited-term contract [*wuguding qixian laodong hetong*], and the per-project work limited-term contract [*yixiang gongzuo wei qixian laodong hetong*]. My interviews with managers indicate that, of these three, the fixed limited-term contract is the most stable in that it guarantees employment at an organization for the duration of the time period defined in the contract. It is also the type of contract that workers in industrial factories are signing. The nonfixed limited-term contract and the per-project work limited-term contract are typically used in more project-oriented sectors, such as construction. Accordingly, I focus here on the fixed limited-term contract.

8. See Naughton 1995, 210–212.

9. While the official Provisional Regulations document (see People's Republic of China 1986a and 1986b) was promulgated in 1986, local governments began experimenting with contracts as early as 1983, by order of the Trial Implementation Notice of the State Council promulgated that year; see People's Republic of China 1983. Typically, this is the way broad institutional changes are set in motion in China: an institutional change begins with a policy idea that emerges as a "notice" from the State Council and is then experimented with in different localities and different sectors of the economy. When the kinks have been worked out to some degree, the institutional change is legitimized through an official law, rule, regulation, or decree from the State Council.

10. As with most other indicators, there is significant variation across the administrative regions of China: Shanghai, for example, has a considerably higher proportion of its laborers on labor contracts (49.9 percent). The less-developed areas of Tibet and Anhui Province are among the lowest, with 10.5 percent and 12.5 percent of the labor force on contracts, respectively. However, it is also clear that the implementation of the labor contract is not only a function of industrial development, as

Tianjin—one of the major industrial municipalities in China—is also among the lowest, with 13.8 percent of the labor force on contracts.

11. It is important to note here that, with respect to the findings in Guthrie 1999, I am not talking about comparing Chinese factories to joint-venture factories; rather, that study compares Chinese firms that have joint-venture relationships to those that do not. Thus, I am not comparing Chinese firms to foreign firms (a comparison that, arguably, would not make much sense) but rather Chinese firms that have foreign partnerships to those that do not.

12. *Statistical Yearbook of China* 2002.

13. Some officials and managers hold the view that these legal frameworks have a direct impact on the use of outside arbitration. As one government official explained,

> We believe that the Labor Law will have a huge impact on the labor arbitration situation. We think this is already beginning to happen. Over the last few years there has been a steady increase of applications to the Labor Arbitration Commission. But this year we expect a huge increase because of the Labor Law. Because of the Labor Law, everyone will start to know what kind of personal power they have. The Labor Law is changing peoples' understanding of their rights. . . . We are hoping that the combination of the Labor Law and the Labor Arbitration Commission will force all types of organizations to focus on the laws more and more. Now that we are developing a market economy, changes are happening so quickly, and it's very important that everyone is protected by the laws.
>
> (Personal interview, Shanghai, 1995, originally reported in Guthrie 1999)

14. Individuals can also apply to serve in this group, but few do, because it is not a paid position. Of the people that do apply as volunteers, most are lawyers working at universities who want to get some experience with the legal changes that are happening in China. According to officials, there are really not enough individuals working in this capacity, and, as a result, many cases are simply heard by the presiding governmental official.

15. The representation of workers in dispute resolution and more

generally overseeing the implementation of the Labor Law have become the primary functions of labor unions in China. As of 1999, labor unions had set up more than 140,000 agencies to oversee the implementation of the Labor Law in local workplaces.

16. Although there is a separate section for disputes relating to benefits and pay in the LAC, individuals generally rely on labor unions to solve such problems.

17. Relying on internal documents, public sources, and personal interviews with former prisoners, Seymour and Anderson put together a comprehensive comparative study of the *laogai* in three provinces in Northwest China—Gansu, Qinghai, and Xinjiang—the heart of the *laogai* system. The comparison of the labor reform system in these provinces allows the authors to explore variations across geographic boundaries, and the differences across the cases reveal a fact that is well known to China scholars but often lost in the political rhetoric over the Chinese government and its policies: despite the Chinese government's interest in having a unified set of policies, the reality is one of a decentralized and fragmented system, with often divergent structures and outcomes. The comparative framework allows for variation in levels of economic development and ethnic composition, as well as a comparison of one case that is often viewed as representative of the Chinese system (that of Gansu) with two that are often viewed as unique within this system.

18. For discussions of the "quiet revolution" within China, see Walder 1995c; Goodman and Hooper 1994; and Guthrie 2003.

19. For discussion of the adoption of these systems in U.S. workplaces, see Dobbin et al. 1993 and Sutton et al. 1994. These scholars have shown that U.S. firms responded to federal mandates that were not directly aimed at labor reform by rationalizing labor processes, which has parallels in U.S. labor history as well. For example, U.S. firms rapidly adopted rational labor processes in the late 1960s and early 1970s in response to the civil rights legislation of the 1960s.

SEVEN

1. For discussions of the "quiet revolution" within China, see Walder 1995c; Goodman and Hooper 1994; and Guthrie 2003.

2. I refer to this movement throughout my discussion as the 1989 Chinese movement, rather than the 1989 student movement,

as it is commonly called, because the widespread participation of "ordinary citizens" (Strand 1990) is part of what distinguishes this movement from its predecessors (Guthrie 1995; Walder 1989a).

3. Extensive discussions of this movement can be found in Calhoun 1989; Walder 1989b; Shen 1990; Calhoun 1991; Perry and Wasserstrom 1991; Esherick and Wasserstrom 1992; Perry and Wasserstrom 1991; Calhoun 1995; Guthrie 1995; Deng 1997; and Zhao 1997.

4. This description of events is taken primarily from Shen Tong's *Almost a Revolution* (1990), which, along with Craig Calhoun's *Neither Gods Nor Emperors* (1995), is the best firsthand account of the movement available.

5. Though not central to my discussion here, workers were actually an important part of this movement, and declining party power operated in workplaces and universities in similar ways. Walder and Gong 1991 and Calhoun 1995 all examine the importance of workers in the movement.

6. Here again, we come back to fundamental institutional changes of the reform era: the loosening of the household passport laws in 1983 (and the fact that political dossiers do not follow individuals around the way they did when the Labor Bureau was allocating jobs) changed the extent to which students could leave their pasts behind. Under the old system, individuals could not simply pick up and move to a new city or province. In China today, there are no such restrictions on social mobility.

7. *New York Times*, May 13, 2000.

8. This was the case with Motorola in 1996. Up until that time, Motorola had only a wholly owned foreign enterprise in China and a licensing agreement with a variety of factories, including the Hangzhou Telecommunications Factory, to produce their handsets. Motorola made a great deal of money through this arrangement, which allowed them to produce and sell phones without transferring any technology in the process. Then, in 1995, they began negotiating a joint venture with the Hangzhou Telecommunications Factory. In a personal interview with one of the insiders on this deal, I inquired as to what had led to the change of heart. The American manager said, "Let's just say that the [Chinese] government decided it was time for us to share the wealth. And if we were going to keep doing what we are doing in China, we were going to have to set up a joint venture deal with someone."

9. With China's recent entry into the World Trade Organization, changes in the state's control of this sector are imminent, as the agreement China and the United States reached in the negotiations over China's entry mandates that foreign firms will be able to own minority stakes in the telecommunications industry.

10. It is very likely that the strife between the former chief executive officer, Wang Zhidong, and the board of directors is most likely the result of the complex business structure that was required in establishing Sina.com's initial public offering of stock, which was a result of Beijing's prohibitions against foreign ownership in this sector. When Sina.com went public, the company had to give up its control over the Internet within China. Sina.com, which is an Internet portal company in China, actually can only provide "technical assistance" to the Chinese-based Sina Internet Information Service Company, Ltd., which has an Internet content provider license, of which Wang also owns a majority stake. Thus, we have an American listed company, with an American board of directors, that is purportedly an Internet content provider but does not have an Internet content license in China and has to rely solely on a Chinese-based company for access to the Internet.

11. *China Daily*, June 26, 2001.

12. Industry experts predicted that China would reach an online population of about twenty million by 2002, roughly equal to that of Germany and France (see, e.g., "State of the Internet in China," *Chinaonline*, July 21, 2000). More recently, predictions have suggested that the number would be closer to 30 million by 2002 (see Smith 2001).

13. As was discussed in Chapter 3, decollectivization reversed the main economic policy through which farmers in China have been organized since the 1950s. Namely, in 1952, the new government of the People's Republic of China began organizing Chinese farmers into cooperative units of anywhere from thirty to three hundred households (communes), where production was monitored and controlled by the government (Spence 1999).

14. This change is not so different from the "dual track" system that industrial work units were placed on in the 1980s and 1990s, as they were gradually weaned off the planned economy (Naughton 1995). The important difference here is that, inasmuch as the market and economic autonomy teach citizens

about the fundamental changes occurring in China's economic and political system, Chinese citizens were exposed to this autonomy at the household level, while only managers of industrial work units were exposed to this change in the transformation of the industrial work unit in urban areas.

15. It is important to note that while the changes occurring in urban China are much more conspicuous and therefore much clearer throughout the world, only about 25 percent of the Chinese population resides in urban China. The other 75 percent resides in the township and village areas of rural China.

16. See, for example, Pearson 1994; Unger and Chan 1995 and 1996; Foster 2002; and Kang 2002.

17. The Chinese Academy of Social Sciences recently released a report on social stratification of contemporary China in 2004 that suggested China's "middle class" accounted for 19 percent of the country's 1.3 billion population by 2003. According to the academy's standard in their report, families with assets valued from 150,000 yuan (US$18,137) to 300,000 yuan (US$36,275) can be classified as middle class.

EIGHT

1. Cox Report (United States Congress 2001).

2. Newman 2005.

3. I use 2001 as the comparison point here, because this was before the rapidly escalating expenditures of the recent Iraq War kicked in.

4. China was one of the twenty-three original signatory nations of the General Agreement on Tariffs and Trade (GATT) in 1948. After the Communist Revolution, two things happened. First, the nationalist government of Taiwan announced that it, not the Beijing Regime, would be the participant in the GATT. Second, the People's Republic of China became extremely isolationist in the decades following the founding of the People's Republic of China, so there was little follow-up to the Taiwan announcement until 1986.

5. Adopted by Congress in 1974, the Jackson-Vanick Amendment was established to limit trade with the Soviet Union in response to its poor record in the area of human rights, particularly in the area of emigration. It became more general policy and was applied to countries like China to address the question of whether the country deserved "most favored nation" trade status.

6. President Bill Clinton, quoted in Drake et al. 2000.
7. Hong Kong and Macau accounted for more than 60 percent of China's total outward foreign direct investment from 1979 until the mid-1990s. North America accounted for 15 percent during this time period.
8. "China's Real Weapon?" *Asia Times*, April 9, 2005. See also Williams 2004.

References

Bian, Yanjie. 1994a. *Work and Inequality in Urban China*. Albany: State University of New York Press.

——— . 1994b. "Guanxi and the Allocation of Urban Jobs in China." *China Quarterly* 140: 971–999.

——— . 1997. "Bringing Strong Ties Back In: Indirect Ties, Network Bridges, and Job Searches in China." *American Sociological Review* 62: 366–385.

Bian, Yanjie, and S. Ang. 1997. "Guanxi Networks and Job Mobility in China and Singapore." *Social Forces* 75(3): 981–1005.

Bian, Yanjie, and John R. Logan. 1996. "Market Transition and the Persistence of Power: The Changing Stratification System in Urban China." *American Sociological Review* 61: 739–758.

Bian, Yanjie, John Logan, and X. Shu. 2000. "Wage and Job Inequalities in the Working Career of Men and Women in Tianjin." In *Re-Drawing Boundaries: Work, Household, and Gender in China*, ed. Barbara Entwisle and Gail Henderson. Berkeley and Los Angeles: University of California Press.

Blanchard, Oliver, Maxin Boycho, Marek Dabrowski, Rudiger Dorubusch, Richard Layard, and Andrei Shleifer. 1993. *Post Communist Reform: Pain and Progress*. Cambridge, MA: MIT Press.

Boisot, Max, and John Child. 1996. "From Fiefs to Clans and Network Capitalism: Explaining China's Emerging Economic Order." *Administrative Science Quarterly* 41: 600–628.

——— . 1999. "Organizations as Adaptive Systems in Complex Environments: The Case of China." *Organization Science* 10(3): 237–252.

Borton, James. 2002. "Motorola University scores high grades in China." *Asia Times Online* (June 4).

Brinton, Mary C., Yean-Ju Lee, and William L. Parish. 1995. "Married Women's Employment in Rapidly Industrializing Societies: Examples from East Asia." *American Journal of Sociology* 100: 1099–1130.

Brown, Lester. 1995. *Who Will Feed China?* New York: W. W. Norton.

Burawoy, Michael. 1985. *Politics of Production: Factory Regimes under Capitalism and Socialism*. London: Verso.

Burawoy, Michael, and Pavel Krutov. 1992. "The Soviet Transition from Socialism to Capitalism: Worker Control and Economic Bargaining in the Wood Industry." *American Sociological Review* 57: 16–38.

Burawoy, Michael, and János Lukacs. 1985. "Mythologies of Work: A Comparison of Firms in State Socialism and Advanced Capitalism." *American Sociological Review* 50: 723–737.

Busenitz, Lowell, and Jay B. Barney. 1997. "Differences between Entrepreneurs and Managers in Large Organizations: Biases and Heuristics in Strategic Decision-Making." *Journal of Business Venturing* 12: 9–30.

Cai, Kevin G. 1999. "Outward Foreign Direct Investment: A Novel Dimension of China's Integration into the Regional and Global Economy." *China Quarterly* 160: 856–80.

Calhoun, Craig. 1989. "Protest in Beijing: The Conditions and Importance of the Chinese Student Movement of 1989." *Partisan Review* 4: 563–80.

———. 1991. "The Problem of Identity in Collective Action." In *Macro-Micro Linkages in Sociology*, edited by J. Huber, 51–75. Beverly Hills, CA: Sage.

———. 1995. *Neither Gods Nor Emperors: Students and the Struggle for Democracy in China*. Berkeley and Los Angeles: University of California Press.

———, ed. 2002. *Dictionary of the Social Sciences*. New York: Oxford University Press.

Chai, Joseph C. H. 1992. "Consumption and Living Standards in China." *China Quarterly* 131: 721–749.

Chan, Kam Wing, and Li Zhang. 1999. "The Hukou System and Rural-Urban Migration in China: Processes and Changes." *China Quarterly* 160: 818–855.

Chang, Gordon. 2001. *The Coming Collapse of China*. New York: Random House.

Chang, Jesse T. H., and Charles J. Conroy. 1987. "Trademark Law in the People's Republic of China." In *Foreign Trade, Investment, and the Law in the People's Republic of China*, edited by Michael J. Moser, 427–452. New York: Oxford University Press.

Chen, Jie, and Peng Deng. 1995. *China Since the Cultural Revolution: From Totalitarianism to Authoritarianism*. Westport, CT: Praeger.

Chen, Kuan, Wang Hongchang, Zheng Yuxin, Gary H. Jefferson, and Thomas G. Rawski. 1988. "Productivity Change in Chinese Industry: 1953–1985." *Journal of Comparative Economics* 12: 570–591.

Cheng, Lucie, and Arthur Rosett. 1991. "Contract with a Chinese Face: Socially Embedded Factors in the Transformation from Hierarchy to Market, 1978–1989." *Journal of Chinese Law* 5: 143–244.

Child, J. 2001. "Learning through Strategic Alliances." In *Handbook of Organizational Learning and Knowledge*, edited by M. Dierkes, A. B. Antal, J. Child and I. Nonaka, 657–680. Oxford: Oxford University Press.

China International Economic and Trade Arbitration Commission. 1994. *Arbitration Rules*. Beijing: People's Republic of China.

China Online. 2000. "China to become Asia-Pacific Region's Second-Largest IT Market, Study Says." *China Online*, June 22, www.chinaonline.com.

Chinese Directory of Organizations and Institutions Publishing Committee. 1993. Zhongguo qi shi ye ming lu quan shu [Chinese Directory of Organizations and Institutions]. Beijing: People's Republic of China.

Christiansen, Flemming. 1992. "Market Transition in China: The Case of the Jiangsu Labor Market, 1978–1990." *Modern China* 18: 72–93.

Clarke, Donald C. 1991. "Dispute Resolution in China." *Journal of Chinese Law* 5: 245–296.

Cohen, Wesley M., and Daniel A. Levinthal. 1990. "Absorptive Capacity: A New Perspective on Learning and Innovation." *Administrative Science Quarterly* 35(1): 128–152.

Cooper, Caroline. 2000. "Look at India, It's Where China Wants to Be." *China Online*, June 22, www.chinaonline.com.

Cui, Ning. 2001. "Technology a Growth Engine to Economy." *China Daily*, June 18.

Davis, Deborah, and Steven Harrell. 1993. "Introduction: The Impact of Post-Mao Reforms on Family Life." In *Chinese Families in the Post-Mao Era*, edited by Deborah Davis and Steven Harrell, 1–22. Berkeley and Los Angeles: University of California Press.

Dean, Earl Howard. 1917. "Economics and the Science of Business." *Journal of Political Economy* 25(1): 106–110.

Demsetz, Harold. 1967. "Toward a Theory of Property Rights." In *Ownership, Control, and the Firm: The Organization of Economic Activity*, Volume 1. Oxford: Blackwell.

Deng, Zhenglai. 1997. *Guojia yu shehui* [*The State and the Society*]. China: Sichuan People's Press.

Deng, Zhenglai, and Jing Yuejin. 1992. "Constructing China's Civil Society." *Chinese Social Sciences Quarterly* Sept.

Dickson, Bruce. 2003. *Red Capitalists in China: The Party, Private Entrepreneurs, and Prospects for Political Change*. New York: Cambridge University Press.

DiMaggio, Paul. 1988. "Interest and Agency in Institutional Theory." In *Institutional Patterns and Organizations: Culture and Environment*, edited by Lynne Zucker, 3–22. Cambridge, MA: Ballinger.

DiMaggio, Paul, and Walter Powell. 1983. "The Iron Cage Revisited: Institutional Isomorphism and Collective Rationality in Organizational Fields." *American Sociological Review* 48: 147–161.

Dobbin, Frank, and John Sutton. 1998. "The Strength of a Weak State: The Rights Revolution and the Rise of Human Resources Management Divisions." *American Journal of Sociology* 104: 441–476.

Dobbin, Frank, John R. Sutton, John W. Meyer, and W. Richard Scott. 1993. "Equal Opportunity Law and the Construction of Internal Labor Markets." *American Journal of Sociology* 99: 396–427.

Drake, William J., Shanthi Kalathil, and Taylor C. Boas. 2000. "Dictatorships in the Digital Age: Some Considerations on the Internet in China and Cuba." *Information Impacts*, October.

Edelman, Lauren B. 1990. "Legal Environments and Organizational Governance: The Expansion of Due Process in the American Workplace." *American Journal of Sociology* 95: 1401–1440.

———. 1992. "Legal Ambiguity and Symbolic Structures: Organizational Mediation of Civil Rights Law." *American Journal of Sociology* 97: 1531–1576.

Entwisle, Barbara, and Gail Henderson, eds. 2000. *Re-Drawing Boundaries: Work, Household, and Gender in China.* Berkeley and Los Angeles: University of California Press.

Entwisle, Barbara, Gail E. Henderson, G. E. Short, J. E. Bouma, and F. Y. Zhai. 1995. "Gender and Family Business in Rural China." *American Sociological Review* 60: 36–57.

Ericson, Richard E. 1991. "The Classical Soviet-Type Economy: Nature of the System and Implications for Reform." *Journal of Economic Perspectives* 5(4): 11–27.

Esherick, Joseph W., and Jeffery N. Wasserstrom. 1992. "Acting Out Democracy: Political Theater in Modern China." In *Popular Protest and Political Culture in Modern China: Learning from 1989*, edited by Elizabeth Perry and Jeffery Wasserstrom, 28–66. Boulder, CO: Westview.

Fabel, Oliver. 1990. *Insurance and Incentives in Labor Contracts: A Study in the Theory of Implicit Contracts.* Frankfurt: Anton Hain.

Fairbanks, John King. 1983. *The United States and China.* Cambridge, MA: Harvard University Press.

———. 1992. *China: A New History.* Cambridge, MA: Belknap Press of Harvard University Press.

Farh, Jiing-Lih, Anne Tsui, Katherine Xin, Bor-Shiuan Cheng. 1998. "The Influence of Relational Demography and Guanxi: The Chinese Case." *Organization Science* 9(4): 471–488.

Fei, Xiaotong. 1992. *From the Soil: the Foundations of Chinese Society.* Berkeley and Los Angeles: University of California Press.

———. 1946. "Peasantry and Gentry: An Interpretation of Chinese Social Structure and Its Change." *American Journal of Sociology* 52: 1–17.

Fewsmith, Joseph. 1999. "Elite Politics." In *The Paradox of China's Post-Mao Reforms*, edited by Merle Goldman and Roderick MacFarquhar, 47–75. Cambridge, MA: Harvard University Press.

Field, Robert M. 1984. "Changes in Chinese Industry Since 1978." *China Quarterly* 100: 742–761.

———. 1992. "China's Industrial Performance Since 1978." *China Quarterly* 131: 577–607.

Fields, Karl J. 1995. *Enterprise and State in Korea and Taiwan.* Ithaca, NY: Cornell University Press.

Fischer, Stanley. 1992. "Privatization in Eastern European Transformation." In *The Emergence of Market Economies in Eastern Europe*, edited by Christopher Clague and Gordon C. Rausser, 227–243. Cambridge, MA: Blackwell.

Fishman, Ted. 2004. "The Chinese Century." *New York Times Magazine*, July 4.

Fitzgerald, C. P. 1964. *The Birth of Communist China.* Harmondsworth, England: Penguin.

Fligstein, Neil. 1990. *The Transformation of Corporate Control.* Cambridge, MA: Harvard University Press.

———. 1996. "Markets as Politics: A Sociological View of Market Institutions." *American Sociological Review* 61: 656–673.

Fortes, Meyer. 1969. *Kinship and the Social Order.* Chicago: Aldine.

Foster, Kenneth W. 2002. "Embedded with State Agencies: Business Associations in Yantai." *China Journal* 47: 41–65.

Fruin, W. Mark, and Penelope Prime. 1999. "Competing Strategies of FDI and Technology Transfer to China: American and Japanese Firms." William Davidson Institute Working Paper Series no. 218. Ann Arbor: University of Michigan School of Business.

Fu, Jun. 2000. *Institutions and Investments: Foreign Direct Investment in China During an Era of Reform.* Ann Arbor, MI: University of Michigan Press.

Furubotn, Eirik, and Svetozar Pejovich, eds. 1974. *The Economics of Property Rights.* Cambridge, MA: Ballinger.

Gao, Sheldon. 2002. "China Stock Market in a Global Perspective." Research report. New York: Dow Jones.

Gates, Hill. 1993. "Cultural Support of Birth Limitation among Urban Capital-Owning Women." In *Chinese Families in the Post-Mao Era*, edited by Deborah Davis and Steven Harrell, 251–274. Berkeley and Los Angeles: University of California Press.

Gelatt, Timothy A. and Richard D. Pomp. 1987. "China's Tax System: An Overview and Transactional Analysis." In *Foreign Trade, Investment, and the Law in the People's Republic of China*, edited by Michael J. Moser, 42–89. New York: Oxford University Press.

Gerber, Theodore P. and Michael Hout. 1995. "Educational Stratification in Russia During the Soviet Period." *American Journal of Sociology* 101: 611–660.

Gerlach, Michael L. 1992. *Alliance Capitalism: The Social Organization of Japanese Business.* Berkeley and Los Angeles: University of California Press.

Gold, Thomas B. 1980. "Back to the City: The Return of Shanghai's Educated Youth." *China Quarterly* 84: 55–70.

———. 1985. "After Comradeship: Personal Relations in China Since the Cultural Revolution." *China Quarterly* 104: 657–675.

———. 1989a. "Guerilla Interviews among the Getihu." In *Popular Culture and Thought in the People's Republic*, edited by Perry Link, Richard Madsen, and Paul Pickowicz, 175–192. Boulder, CO: Westview.

———. 1989b. "Urban Private Business in China." *Studies in Comparative Communism* 22(2–3): 187–201.

———. 1990. "Urban Private Business and Social Change." In *Chinese Society on the Eve of Tiananmen: The Impact of Reform*, edited by Deborah Davis and Ezra F. Vogel, 157–178. Cambridge, MA: Harvard University Press.

———. 1991. "Urban Private Business and China's Reforms." In *Reform and Reaction in Post-Mao China: The Road to Tiananmen*, edited by Richard Baum, 84–103. New York: Routledge.

Gold, Thomas, Doug Guthrie, and David Wank, eds. 2002. *Social Connections in China: Institutions, Culture, and the Changing Nature of Guanxi*. New York: Cambridge University Press.

Gong, Ting. 1994. *The Politics of Corruption in Contemporary China: An Analysis of Policy Outcomes*. Westport, CT: Praeger.

Goodman, David. 1999. "The New Middle Class." In *The Paradox of China's Post-Mao Reforms*, edited by Merle Goldman and Roderick MacFarquhar. Cambridge, MA: Harvard University Press.

Goodman, David, and Beverley Hooper, eds. 1994. *China's Quiet Revolution*. Melbourne: Longman Cheshire.

Granick, David. 1990. *Chinese State Enterprises: A Regional Property Rights Analysis*. Chicago: University of Chicago Press.

Granovetter, Mark. 1985. "Economic Action and Social Structure: The Problem of Embeddedness." *American Journal of Sociology* 91: 481–510.

Groves, Theodore, Yongmiao Hong, John McMillan, and Barry Naughton. 1994. "Autonomy and Incentives in Chinese State Enterprises." *Quarterly Journal of Economics* 109(1): 193–209.

———. 1995. "China's Evolving Managerial Labor Market." *Journal of Political Economy* 103: 873–892.

Guo, Jiann-Jong. 1992. *Price Reform in China, 1979–86*. Basingstoke, England: St. Martin's.

Guthrie, Doug. 1995. "Political Theater and Student Organizations in the 1989 Chinese Movement: A Multivariate Analysis of Tiananmen." *Sociological Forum* 10: 419–454.

———. 1996. "Organizational Action and Institutional Reforms in China's Economic Transition: A Comparison of Two Industries." *Research in the Sociology of Organizations* 14: 181–222.

———. 1997. "Between Markets and Politics: Organizational Responses to Reform in China." *American Journal of Sociology* 102: 1258–1303.

———. 1998a. "Organizational Uncertainty and the End of Lifetime Employment in China." *Sociological Forum* 13(3): 457–494.

———. 1998b. "The Declining Significance of Guanxi in China's Economic Transition." *China Quarterly* 154: 254–282.

———. 1999. *Dragon in a Three-Piece Suit: The Emergence of Capitalism in China.* Princeton, NJ: Princeton University Press.

———. 2001. "The Emergence of Market Practices in China's Economic Transition: Price Setting in Shanghai's Industrial Firms." In *Managing Organizational Change in Transition Economies*, edited by Daniel Denison. Mahwah, NJ: Lawrence Erlbaum.

———. 2002a. "Information Asymmetries and the Problem of Perception: The Significance of Structural Position in Assessing the Importance of Guanxi in China." In *Social Connections in China: Institutions, Culture, and the Changing Nature of Guanxi*, edited by Thomas Gold, Doug Guthrie, and David Wank. New York: Cambridge University Press.

———. 2002b. "The Transformation of Labor Relations in China's Emerging Market Economy." *Research in Social Stratification and Mobility* 19: 137–168.

———. 2002c. "Entrepreneurial Action in the State Sector: The Economic Decisions of Chinese Managers." In *The New Entrepreneurs of Europe and Asia: Patterns of Business Development in Russia, Eastern Europe and China*, edited by Vicki Bonnell and Thomas Gold, 159–190. Boulder, CO: M. E. Sharpe.

———. 2003. "The Quiet Revolution: The Emergence of Capitalism in China." *Harvard International Review* 25(2): 48–53.

———. 2004. "Information Technology, Sovereignty, and Democratization in China." In *Digital Formations: Cooperation and Conflict in a Connected World*, edited by Robert Latham and Saskia Sassen, Princeton, NJ: Princeton University Press.

———. 2005. "Organizational Learning and Productivity: State Structure and Foreign Investment in the Rise of the Chinese Corporation." *Management and Organization Review* 1(2): 165–195.

Guthrie, Doug and Junmin Wang. 2007. "Business Organizations in China." In *Handbook of Asian Business*, edited by Henry Yeung, 99–121. London: Edward Elgar Publishing.

Guthrie, Doug, Zhixing Xiao, and Junmin Wang. 2007. "Aligning the Interests of Multiple Principals: Ownership Concentration and Profitability in China's Publicly Traded Companies." Stern School of Business, Department of Economics, Working Paper Series.

Hamilton, Gary G. 1991. *Business Networks and Economic Development in East and Southeast Asia.* Centre for East Asian Studies, Hong Kong: University of Hong Kong Press.

———. 1996. "The Theoretical Significance of Asian Business Networks." In

Asian Business Networks, edited by Gary Hamilton, 283–298. Berlin: Walter de Gruyter.

Hamilton, Gary, and Robert Feenstra. 1994. "Varieties of Hierarchies and Markets: An Introduction." Paper presented at the annual meeting of the American Sociological Association, August 5–9, Los Angeles.

Hamilton, Gary, and Nicole Woolsey Biggart. 1988. "Market, Culture, and Authority: A Comparative Analysis of Management and Organization in the Far East." *American Journal of Sociology* 94: S52–S94.

Hannum, Emily, and Yu Xie. 1994. "Trends in Educational and Gender and Inequality." *Research in Social Stratification and Mobility* 13: 73–98.

Harner, Stephen. 2000. "Shanghai's New Five-Year Plan: The Pearl Starts to Shine." *China Online*, December 18, www.chinaonline.com.

Hertz, Ellen. 1998. *The Trading Crowd: An Ethnography of the Shanghai Stock Market*. New York: Cambridge University Press.

Hessler, Peter. 1999. "Tibet through Chinese Eyes." *Atlantic Monthly*, February.

Hill, David, and Krishna Sen. 2000. "The Internet in Indonesia's New Democracy." *Democratization*, Spring.

Ho, Ping-ti, and Tang Tsou, eds. 1969. *China in Crisis*. Chicago: University of Chicago Press.

Hoff, Karla, and Joseph E. Stiglitz. 1990. "Introduction: Imperfect Information and Rural Credit Markets—Puzzles and Policy Perspectives." *World Bank Economic Review* 4(3): 235–250.

Hohfeld, Wesley. 1913. "Some Fundamental Legal Conceptions as Applied to Judicial Reasoning." *Yale Law Journal* 23(1): 16–59.

Holt, Thomas Ford. 1969. *Dictionary of Modern Sociology*. Lanham, MD: Littlefield Adams.

Honig, Emily, and Gail Hershatter. 1988. *Personal Voices*. Stanford, CA: Stanford University Press.

Howard, Earl Dean. 1917. "Economics and the Science of Business." *The Journal of Political Economy* 25 (1 Jan., 1917): 106–110.

Hsing, You-tien. 1998. *Making Capitalism in China: The Taiwan Connection*. New York: Oxford University Press.

Hsu, Immanuel C. Y. 1999. *The Rise of Modern China*. New York: Oxford University Press.

Huang, Ruicai and Xiaowen Cong. 1994. *Xiandai qiye caichan guanli* [*Managing Property in the Modern Enterprise*]. Jinan: Jinan University Press.

Huang, Laiji, and Zhou Jingen, eds. 1994. *Gongsifa huiyi yu zujian gongsifa jingyan* [*Answers to Questions Regarding the Company Law and the Experience of Constructing the Company Law*]. Beijing: Shijie tuanti chuban gongsi.

Huang, Yasheng. 1990. "Web of Interests and Patterns of Behaviour of Chinese Local Economic Bureaucracies and Enterprises During Reform." *China Quarterly* 123: 431–458.

———. 1995a. "Administrative Monitoring in China." *China Quarterly* 143: 828–843.

———. 1995b. "Why China will not Collapse." *Foreign Policy* 99: 54–68.

———. 2003. *Selling China: Foreign Direct Investment during the Reform Era.* New York: Cambridge University Press.

Hui, C., and G. Graen. 1997. "Guanxi and Professional Leadership in Contemporary Sino-American Joint Ventures in Mainland China." *Leadership Quarterly* 8(4): 451–465.

Jakobson, Linda. 1998. *A Million Truths: A Decade in China.* New York: M. Evans Publishing.

Jefferson, Gary H., and Wenyi Xu. 1991. "The Impact of Reform on Socialist Enterprises in Transition: Structure, Conduct, and Performance in Chinese Industry." *Journal of Comparative Economics* 15: 45–64.

Johnson, Chalmers. 1987. "Political Institutions and Economic Performance: The Government-Business Relationship in Japan, South Korea, and Taiwan." In *The Political Economy of the New Asian Industrialism,* edited by Frederic C. Deyo, 136–164. Ithaca, NY: Cornell University Press.

Josephs, Hilary K. 1989. *Labor Law in China: Choice and Responsibility.* Sevenoaks, England: Butterworth Legal Publishers.

Kamm, John. 1989. "Reforming Foreign Trade." In *One Step Ahead in China: Guangdong under Reform,* 338–92. Cambridge, MA: Harvard University Press.

Kang, Xiaoguang. 2002. "A Study of China's Political Stability in the 1990s." *Twenty-First Century* 72: 33.

Keister, Lisa A. 2000. *Chinese Business Groups: The Structure and Impact of Interfirm Relations during Economic Development.* New York: Cambridge University Press.

———. 2002. "Guanxi in Business Groups: Social Ties and the Formation of Economic Relations." In *Social Connections in China: Institutions, Culture, and the Changing Nature of Guanxi,* edited by Thomas Gold, Doug Guthrie, and David Wank. New York: Cambridge University Press.

Kennedy, Michael D., and Pauline Gianoplus. 1994. "Entrepreneurs and Expertise: A Cultural Encounter in the Making of Post-Communist Capitalism in Poland." *East European Politics and Societies* 8(1): 58–93.

King, Ambrose Y. C. 1985. "The Individual and Group in Confucianism: A Relational Perspective." In *Individualism and Holism: Studies in Confucian and Taoist Values,* edited by Donald J. Munro, 57–70. Ann Arbor: Center for Chinese Studies, University of Michigan.

Kipnis, Andrew. 1997. *Producing Guanxi: Sentiment, Self, and Subculture in a North China Village.* Durham, NC: Duke University Press.

Kirby, William C. 1995. "China Unincorporated: Company Law and Business Enterprise in Twentieth-Century China." *Journal of Asian Studies* 54: 43–63.

Kornai, János. 1980. *The Shortage Economy.* Amsterdam: North-Holland.

———. 1990. *The Road to a Free Economy*. New York: W. W. Norton.

Kristof, Nicholas, and Sheryl WuDunn. 2001. *Thunder from the East*. New York: Vintage.

Krug, Barbara. 1994. Review of *Price Reform in China, 1979–86*, by Jiann-Jong Guo, *China Quarterly* 138: 528–530.

Kwong, Julia. 1997. *The Political Economy of Corruption in China*. Armonk, NY: M.E. Sharpe.

Lardy, Nicholas R. 1984. "Consumption and Living Standards in China, 1978–83." *China Quarterly* 100: 849–865.

———. 1992. *Foreign Trade and Economic Reform in China, 1978–1990*. New York: Cambridge University Press.

———. 1994. *China in the World Economy: issues, Recommendations, Results.* Washington, DC: Peterson Institute.

———. 1995. "The Role of Foreign Trade and Investment in China's Economic Transformation." *China Quarterly* 144: 1065–1082.

———. 1996. "The Role of Foreign Trade and Investment in China's Economic Transition." In *China's Transitional Economy*, edited by Andrew Walder. New York: Oxford University Press.

———. 2002. *Integrating China into Global Economy*. Washington DC: Brookings Institution Press.

Lee, Ching-Kwan. 1995. "Engendering the Worlds of Labor: Women Workers, Labor Markets, and Production Politics in the South China Economic Miracle." *American Sociological Review* 60: 378–397.

Lee, Hong Yung. 1991. *From Revolutionary Cadres to Party Technocrats in Socialist China*. Berkeley: University of California Press.

Levitt, Barbara, and James G. March. 1988. "Organizational Learning." *Annual Review of Sociology* 14: 319–340.

Li, Cetao. 1993. *Gufen zhi lilun yu qiye gai zhi zao zuo* [*The System and Theory of Stocks and Enterprise Reform*]. Shanghai: Fudan University Press.

Li, Lianjiang and Kevin O'Brien. 1999. "The Struggle Over Village Elections." In *The Paradox of China's Post-Mao Reforms*, edited by Merle Goldman and Roderick MacFarquhar, 129–144. Cambridge, MA: Harvard University Press.

Li, Linda Chelan. 1997. "Provincial Discretion and National Power: Investment Policy in Guangdong and Shanghai, 1978–93." *China Quarterly* 152: 778–804.

Li, Peilin, and Zhang Yi. 2000. "Consumption Stratification in China: An Important Tool in Stirring up Economy." *Zhongguoshehuikexi* (*Chinese Social Science*). *Development and Society* 29(2, December): 55–72.

Li, Yushan. 1992. *Shehui zhuyi guojia jingji: gaige yu fazhan gongcheng* [*Socialism and National Development: Reform and Development*]. Dalian, China: Ligong University Press.

Lieberthal, Kenneth. 1995. *Governing China: From Revolution through Reform*. New York: W. W. Norton.

Lin, Nan, 1995. "Local Market Socialism: Local Corporatism in Action in Rural China." *Theory and Society* 24: 301–354.

Lin, Nan, and Bian Yanjie. 1991. "Getting Ahead in Urban China." *American Journal of Sociology* 97: 657–688.

Liu, Pak-Wai, Xin Meng, and Junsen Zhang. 2000. "Sectoral Gender Wage Differentials and Discrimination in the Transitional Chinese Economy." *Journal of Population Economics* 13: 331–352.

Lo, Vai Io, and Xiaowen Tian. 2005. *Law and Investment in China: The Legal and Business Environments after China's WTO Accession*. London: RoutledgeCurzon.

Lovett, Steve, Lee Simmons, and Raja Kali. 1999. "Guanxi versus the Market: Ethics and Efficiency." *Journal of International Business Studies* 30(2): 231–247.

Lu, Xiaobo, 2000. *Cadres and Corruption: The Organizational Involution of the Chinese Communist Party*. Stanford, CA: Stanford University Press.

Lu, Xiaobo, and Elizabeth Perry, eds. 1997. *Danwei: The Changing Chinese Workplace in Historical and Comparative Perspective*. Armonk, New York: M. E. Sharpe.

Lubman, Stanley. 1986. *China's Economy Looks Toward the Year 2000, Vol. 1: The Four Modernizations*. Joint Economic Committee. Washington, DC: Government Printing Office.

——— . 1987. "Technology Transfer in China: Policies, Law, and Practice." In *Foreign Trade, Investment, and the Law in the People's Republic of China*, edited by Michael J. Moser, 170–198. New York: Oxford University Press.

——— . 1995. "Introduction: The Future of Chinese Law." *China Quarterly* 141: 1–21.

Lubman, Stanley B., and Gregory C. Wajnowski. 1993. "International Commercial Dispute Resolution in China: A Practical Assessment." *American Review of International Arbitration* 4: 107–178.

Luffman, George A., and Richard Reed. 1984. *The Strategy and Performance of British Industry, 1970–80*. New York: St. Martin's.

Luo, Xiaopeng. 1990. "Ownership and Status Stratification." In *China's Rural Industry: Structure, Development, and Reform*, edited by William A. Byrd and Lin Qingsong, 134–171. New York: Oxford University Press.

Luo, Yadong. 1997. "Partner Selection and Venturing Success: The Case of Joint Venturing Firms in the People's Republic of China." *Organization Science* 8(6): 648–662.

——— . 1998. "Timing of Investment and International Expansion Performance in China." *Journal of International Business* 29(2): 391–407.

——— . 2001a. "Toward a Cooperative View of MNC-Host Government Relations: Building Blocks and Performance Implication." *Journal of International Business Studies* 32(3): 401–419.

——— . 2001b. "Antecedents and Consequences of Personal Attachment in Cross-Cultural Cooperative Ventures." *Administrative Science Quarterly* 46(2): 177–201.

Luo, Yadong, and Mike Peng. 1999. "Learning to Compete in a Transition Economy: Experience, Environment, and Performance." *Journal of International Business Studies* 30(2): 269–295.

Luo, Yadong, Oded Shenkar, and Mee-Kau Nyaw. 2001. "A Dual Perspective on Control and Performance in International Joint Ventures: Lessons from a Developing Economy." *Journal of International Business* 32(1): 41–58.

March, James. 1981. "Footnotes to Organizational Change." *Administrative Science Quarterly* 26(2): 563–577.

——— . 1991. "Explorations and Exploitation in Organizational Learning." *Organization Science* 2(1): 71–87.

Matthews, R., and Victor Nee. 2000. "Gender Inequality and Economic Growth in Rural China." *Social Science Research* 29: 2–32.

McKinnon, Rónald. 1992. "Taxation, Money, and Credit in a Liberalizing Socialist Economy." In *The Emergence of Market Economies in Eastern Europe*, edited by Christopher Clague and Gordon C. Rausser, 109–127. Cambridge, MA: Blackwell.

Meyer, John W., and Brian Rowan. 1977. "Institutionalized Organizations: Formal Structure as Myth and Ceremony." *American Journal of Sociology* 83: 340–363.

Meyer, Marshall. 2005. "Is China for Sale?" *Management and Organization Review* 1(2): 303–307.

Min, Anchee. 2000. *Becoming Madame Mao*. New York: Houghton Mifflin.

Mizruchi, Mark, and Lisa Fein. 1999. "The Social Construction of Organizational Knowledge: A Study of the Uses of Coercive, Mimetic, and Normative Isomorphism." *Administrative Science Quarterly* 44: 653–683.

Moser, Michael J. 1987. "Foreign Investment in China: The Legal Framework." In *Trade, Investment, and the Law in the People's Republic of China*, edited by Michael J. Moser, 90–169. New York: Oxford University Press.

Mote, Frederick. 1989. *Intellectual Foundations of China*. New York: Alfred A. Knopf.

Mueller, D. 1997. "First-Mover Advantages and Path Dependence." *International Journal of Industrial Organization* 15(6): 827–850.

Murphy, Michael. 1993. "Competition under the Laws Governing Soviet Producer Cooperatives during Peristroika." In *Capitalist Goals, Socialist Past: The Rise of the Private Sector in Command Economies*, edited by Perry L. Patterson, 147–167. Boulder, CO: Westview.

Murrell, Peter. 1990. *The Nature of Socialist Economies: Lessons from Eastern Europe Foreign Trade*. Princeton, NJ: Princeton University Press.

——— . 1992. "Evolution in Economics and in the Economic Reform of the

Centrally Planned Economies." In *The Emergence of Market Economies in Eastern Europe*, edited by Christopher Clague and Gordon C. Rausser, 35–53. Cambridge, MA: Blackwell.

National Statistical Bureau of China. 1994. 1996. 1999. 2000. 2002. 2003. 2006. *Statistical Yearbook of China*. Beijing: National Statistical Bureau of China Press.

Naughton, Barry. 1992. "Hierarchy and the Bargaining Economy: Government and Enterprise in the Reform Process." In *Bureaucracy, Politics, and Decision Making in Post-Mao China*, edited by Kenneth G. Lieberthal and David M. Lampton, 245–279. Canberra: Contemporary China Center, Australian National University.

——. 1993. "Deng Xiaoping: The Economist." *China Quarterly* 135: 491–512.

——. 1994. "What is Distinctive about China's Economic Transition? State Enterprise Reform and Overall System Transformation." *Journal of Comparative Economics* 18: 470–490.

——. 1995. *Growing Out of the Plan: Chinese Economic Reform 1978–1993*. New York: Cambridge University Press.

——. 2007. *The Chinese Economy: Transitions and Growth*. Cambridge, MA: MIT Press.

Nee, Victor. 1985. "Peasant Household Individualism." In *Chinese Rural Development: The Great Transformation*, edited by William Parish, 164–190. Armonk, NY: M. E. Sharpe.

——. 1989a. "A Theory of Market Transition: From Redistribution to Markets in State Socialism." *American Sociological Review* 54: 663–681.

——. 1989b. "Peasant Entrepreneurship and the Politics of Regulation." In *Remaking the Economic Institutions of Socialism: China and Eastern Europe*, edited by Victor Nee and David Stark, 169–207. Stanford, CA: Stanford University Press.

——. 1991. "Social Inequalities in Reforming State Socialism: Between Redistribution and Markets in China." *American Sociological Review* 56: 267–282.

——. 1992. "Organizational Dynamics of Market Transition: Hybrid Forms, Property Rights, and Mixed Economy in China." *Administrative Science Quarterly* 37: 1–27.

——. 1996. "The Emergence of a Market Society: Changing Mechanisms of Stratification in China." *American Journal of Sociology* 101: 908–949.

Nee, Victor, and Yang Cao. 1999. "Path Dependent Societal Transformation: Stratification in Mixed Economies." *Theory and Society* 28: 799–834.

Nee, Victor, and Rebecca Matthews. 1996. "Market Transition and Societal Transformation in Reforming State Socialism." *Annual Review of Sociology* 22: 401–435.

Newman, Richard. 2005. "The Rise of a New Power." *U.S. News and World Report*, June 20.

Noble, Howard S. 1927. "The Relation of Business Organization to Accounting." *Accounting Review* 2(3): 232–236.

Nolan, Peter. 2004. *Transforming China: Globalization, Transition and Development.* London: Anthem Press.

North, Douglass C. 1990. *Institutions, Institutional Change and Economic Performance.* New York: Cambridge University Press.

O'Brien, Kevin. 1990. "Is China's National People's Congress a 'Conservative' Legislature?" *Asian Survey* 30(8): 782–94.

Oberschall, Anthony. 1996. "The Great Transition: China, Hungary, and Sociology Exit Socialism into the Market." *American Journal of Sociology* 101: 1028–1041.

Ogden, Suzanne, ed. 2004. *Global Studies: China.* New York: Dushkin/McGraw-Hill.

Ohe, Takeru, Shuji Honjo, and Ian MacMillan. 1990. "Japanese Entrepreneurs and Corporate Managers: A Comparison." *Journal of Business Venturing* 5: 163–176.

Oi, Jean C., 1989. *State and Peasant in Contemporary China: The Political Economy of Village and Government.* Berkeley and Los Angeles: University of California Press.

——. 1992. "Fiscal Reform and the Economic Foundations of Local State Corporatism." *World Politics* 45: 99–126.

——. 1995. "The Role of the Local State in China's Transitional Economy." *China Quarterly* 144: 1132–1149.

Oi, Jean C., and Andrew Walder, eds. 1999. *Property Rights and Economic Reform in China.* Stanford, CA: Stanford University Press.

Orrù, Marco, Nicole Woolsey Biggart, and Gary G. Hamilton. 1991. "Organizational Isomorphism in East Asia." In *The New Institutionalism in Organizational Analysis*, edited by Walter W. Powell and Paul DiMaggio, 361–389. Chicago: University of Chicago Press.

Palmer, Michael. "The Re-Emergence of Family Law in Post-Mao China: Marriage, Divorce, and Reproduction." *China Quarterly* 141: 110–134.

Parish, William L., and Ethan Michelson. 1996. "Politics and Markets: Dual Transformations." *American Journal of Sociology* 4: 1042–1059.

Parish, William, and Martin King Whyte. 1978. *Village Life in Contemporary China.* Chicago: University of Chicago Press.

Parris, Kristen. 1999. "The Rise of Private Business Interests." In *The Paradox of China's Post-Mao Reforms*, edited by Merle Goldman and Roderick MacFarquhar, 262–282. Cambridge, MA: Harvard University Press.

Pearson, Margaret. 1994. "The Janus Face of Business Associations in China: Socialist Corporatism in Foreign Enterprises." *Austrian Journal of Chinese Affairs* 31: 25-46.

——. 1997. *China's New Business Elite: The Political Consequences of Economic Reform.* Berkeley and Los Angeles: University of California Press.

Pei, Minxin. 1994. *From Reform to Revolution: The Demise of Communism in China and the Soviet Union.* Cambridge, MA: Harvard University Press.

———. 1995. "Creeping Democratization in China." *Journal of Democracy* 6(4): 65–79.

———. 1997. "Citizens v. Mandarins: Administrative Litigation in China." *China Quarterly* 152: 832–862.

———. 1998. "Is China Democratizing?" *Foreign Affairs* 68–82.

Peng, Mike, and Peggy Sue Heath. 1996. "The Growth of the Firm in Planned Economies in Transition: Institutions, Organizations, and Strategic Choice." *The Academy of Management Review* 21(2): 492–528.

Peng, Mike, and Anne Ilinitch. 1998. "Export Intermediary Firms: A Note on Export Development Research." *Journal of International Business Studies* 29(3): 609–620.

Peng, Mike, and Yadong Luo. 2000. "Managerial Ties and Firm Performance in a Transitional Economy: The Nature of a Micro-Macro Link." *Academy of Management Review* 43(3): 486–501.

Peng, Mike, and Anne York. 2001. "Behind Intermediary Performance in Export Trade: Transactions, Agents, and Resources." *Journal of International Business Studies* 32(2): 327–346.

Peng, Yusheng. 1992. "Wage Determination in Rural and Urban China: A Comparison of Public and Private Industrial Sectors." *American Sociological Review* 57: 198–213.

People's Republic of China [*Zhonghua renmin gongheguo*] (PRC). 1979. *Law of the People's Republic of China on Chinese-Equity Joint Ventures.* Adopted on July 1, 1979, at the Second Session of the Fifth National People's Congress.

———. 1981. *Economic Contract Law of the People's Republic of China.* Adopted on December 13, 1981, at the Fourth Session of the Fifth National People's Congress.

———. 1983. *Laodong renshi bu guanyu jiji shixing laodong hetong zhide tongzhi* [*Notice of the Ministry of Labor and Personnel on Active Trial Implementation of the Contract Employment System*]. Sixth State Council Gazette, 213.

———. 1984a. "Decision of the Standing Committee of the National People's Congress on Authorizing the State Council to Reform the System of Industrial and Commercial Taxes and Issue Relevant Draft Tax Regulations for Trial Application." Adopted on September 18, 1984 at the Seventh Meeting of the Standing Committee of the Sixth National People's Congress.

———. 1984b. *Patent Law of the People's Republic of China.* Adopted at the 4th Session of the Standing Committee of the Sixth National People's Congress on March 12, 1984.

———. 1986a. *Guoying qiye shixing laodong hetong zhanxing guiding* [*Provisional Regulations on the Implementation of the Contract Employment System in State Enterprises*].

Promulgated by the State Council on July 12, 1986; effective October 1, 1986.

———. 1986b. *Guoying qiye citui weiji zhigong zanxing guiding* [Provisional Regulations on the Dismissal of Workers and Staff for Work Violations in State Enterprises]. Promulgated by the State Council on July 12, 1986; effective October 1, 1986.

———. 1986c. *Guoying qiye zhaoyong gongren zhanxing guiding* [Provisional Regulations on the Hiring of Workers in State Enterprises]. Promulgated by the State Council on July 12, 1986, effective October 1, 1986.

———. 1988. *Law of the People's Republic of China on Chinese-Foreign Contractual Joint Ventures.* Adopted at the First Session of the Seventh National People's Congress and promulgated by Order No. 4 of the President of the People's Republic of China on April 13, 1988.

———. 1993. *The Company Law of the People's Republic of China.* Adopted at the Fifth Meeting of the Standing Committee of the Eighth National People's Congress on December 12, 1993; effective July 1, 1994.

———. 1994. *The Labor Law of the People's Republic of China.* Adopted at the Eighth Meeting of the Standing Committee of the National People's Congress on July 5, 1994; effective January 1, 1995.

———. 1995. *The National Compensation Law of the People's Republic of China.* Adopted at the Seventh Meeting of the Standing Committee of the Eighth National People's Congress on May 5, 1994; effective January 1, 1995.

———. 1999. *Securities Law of the People's Republic of China.* Adopted at the 6th Meeting of the Standing Committee of the 9th National People's Congress on December 29, 1998.

———. 2001. *The Tentative Measures for Decreasing State Shareholding.* National People's Congress.

Perry, Elizabeth, and Jeffery Wasserstrom. 1991. *Popular Protest and Political Culture in Modern China: Learning from 1989.* Boulder, CO: Westview.

Pocket World in Figures 2004. 2005. 2008. London: Profile.

Polanyi, Karl. 1957. *The Great Transformation: The Political and Economic Origins of Our Time.* Boston: Beacon.

Potter, Pitman B. 1994. "Riding the Tiger: Legitimacy and Legal Culture in Post-Mao China." *China Quarterly* 138: 325–358.

———. 1988. *The Mandarin and the Cadre.* Ann Arbor: University of Michigan Center for Chinese Studies.

Pye, Lucian. 1992. *The Spirit of Chinese Politics.* Cambridge, MA: MIT Press.

———. 1995. "Factions and the Politics of Guanxi: Paradoxes in Chinese Administrative and Political Behaviour." *China Journal* 34: 35–53.

Rawski, Thomas G. 1994. "Progress without Privatization: The Reform of China's State Industries." In *Changing Political Economies: Privatization in Post-Communist and Reforming Communist States,* edited by Vedat Milor, 27–52. Boulder, CO: Lynn Reinner.

——— . 1995. "Implications of China's Reform Experience." *China Quarterly* 144: 1150–1173.

——— . 1999. "Reforming China's Economy: What Have We Learned?" *The China Journal* 41: 139–156.

Redding, Gordon S. 1990. *The Spirit of Chinese Capitalism*. Berlin: Walter de Gruyter.

Reynolds, Bruce L., ed. 1987. *Reform in China: Challenges and Choices*. Armonk, NY: M. E. Sharpe.

Riedel, James, Jing Jin and Jian Guo. 2007. *How China Grows: Investment, Finance and Reform*. Princeton, NJ: Princeton University Press.

Roberts, Dexter. 1999. "A Tale of Two Families: How China's Transformation to a Market Economy is Having Jarringly Different Effects on Ordinary Citizens." *BusinessWeek* 3635: 48–53.

Róna-Tas, Ákos. 1994. "The First Shall Be Last? Entrepreneurship and Communist Cadres in the Transition from Socialism." *American Journal of Sociology* 100: 40–69.

Rosenthal, Elisabeth. 1998. "A Day in Court, and Justice, Sometimes, for the Chinese." *New York Times*, April 27, A1.

Rozman, Gilbert, ed. 1981. *The Modernization of China*, New York: Free Press.

Ruttan, V. 1997. "Induced Innovation, Evolutionary Theory and Path Dependence: Sources of Technical Change." *Economic Journal* 107(444): 1520–1529.

Sachs, Jeffrey D. 1992. "Privatization in Russia: Some Lessons from Eastern Europe." *American Economic Review* 80: 43–48.

——— . 1993. *Poland's Jump to the Market Economy*. Cambridge: MIT Press.

——— . 1995a. "Consolidating Capitalism." *Foreign Policy* 98: 50–64.

——— . 1995b. Reforms in Eastern Europe and the Former Soviet Union in Light of the East Asian Experience. *Journal of the Japanese and International Economies* 9: 454–485.

Sachs, Jeffrey D., and Wing Thye Woo. 1994a. "Experiences in the Transition to a Market Economy." *Journal of Comparative Economics* 18(3): 271–275.

——— . 1994b. "Structural Factors in the Economic Reforms of China, Eastern Europe, and the Former Soviet Union." *Economic Policy* 9(18): 101–131.

——— . 1997. "Understanding China's Economic Performance." Working Paper #5935, National Bureau of Economic Research, Inc. Working Paper Series.

Santoro, Michael. 1999. *Profits and Principles*. Ithaca, NY: Cornell University Press.

Schumpeter, Joseph A. 1934. *The Theory of Economic Development*. Cambridge, MA: Harvard University Press.

——— . 1949. "Economic Theory and Entrepreneurial History." In *Essays on*

Entrepreneurs, Innovation, Business Cycles, and the Evolution of Capitalism, edited by Richard Clemence. Wokingham, England: Addison-Wesley.

Schurmann, Franz. 1968. *Ideology and Organization in Communist China*. 2nd edn. Berkeley and Los Angeles: University of California Press.

Segal, Adam. 2003. *Digital Dragon: High-Technology Enterprises in China*. Ithaca, NY: Cornell University Press.

Seymour, James D., and Richard Anderson. 1998. *New Ghosts, Old Ghosts: Prisons and Labor Reform Camps in China*. New York: M. E. Sharpe.

Shanghai Academy of Social Sciences. 1986. *Shanghai shehui kexue yuan lunwen xuen* [*Shanghai Academy of Social Sciences Papers*]. Shanghai: Shanghai Academy of Social Sciences Press.

——. 1988. *Shanghai shehui kexue yuan lunwen xuen* [*Shanghai Academy of Social Sciences Papers*]. Shanghai: Shanghai Academy of Social Sciences Press.

——. 1990. *Shanghai shehui kexue yuan lunwen xuen* [*Shanghai Academy of Social Sciences Papers*]. Shanghai: Shanghai Academy of Social Sciences Press.

——. 1992. *Shanghai shehui kexue yuan lunwen xuen* [*Shanghai Academy of Social Sciences Papers*]. Shanghai: Shanghai Academy of Social Sciences Press.

——. 1994a. *Shanghai shehui kexue yuan lunwen xuen* [*Shanghai Academy of Social Sciences Papers*]. Shanghai: Shanghai Academy of Social Sciences Press.

——. 1994b. *Shanghai jingji nianjian 1994* [*Economic Yearbook of Shanghai 1994*]. Shanghai: Shanghai Economic Yearbook Department.

——. 1994c. *Xiangzhen qiye yunxing jizhi yanjiu* [*The Institutional Structure of TVEs*]. Shanghai: Shanghai Academy of Social Sciences Press.

——. 1994d. *Chengshi jinbu, qiye fazhan he zhongguo xiandaihua* [*Urban Progress, Business Development, and China's Modernization*]. Shanghai: Shanghai Academy of Social Sciences Press.

——. 1995. *Shanghai kaifang shiwu nian* [*Fifteen Years of Economic Development in Shanghai*]. Shanghai: Shanghai Academy of Social Sciences Press.

Shanghai Foreign Investment Commission. 1995. *Guide to Foreign Investment in China*. Shanghai: Shanghai Foreign Investment Commission.

Shanghai Municipal Statistical Bureau. 1990. *Shanghai tongji nianjian 1990* [*Statistical Yearbook of Shanghai 1990*]. Shanghai: Chinese Statistics Publishing House of the Shanghai Municipal Statistical Bureau.

——. 1991. *Shanghai tongji nianjian 1991* [*Statistical Yearbook of Shanghai 1991*]. Shanghai: Chinese Statistics Publishing House of the Shanghai Municipal Statistical Bureau.

——. 1993. *Shanghai tongji nianjian 1993* [*Statistical Yearbook of Shanghai 1993*]. Shanghai: Chinese Statistics Publishing House of the Shanghai Municipal Statistical Bureau.

——. 1994. *Shanghai tongji nianjian 1994* [*Statistical Yearbook of Shanghai 1994*]. Shanghai: Chinese Statistics Publishing House of the Shanghai Municipal Statistical Bureau.

Shanghai Reform Collections Office. 1994. *Shanghai jingji tizhi gaige 1989– 1993* [*Shanghai Economic Institutional Reform Yearbook 1989–1993*]. Shanghai: Shanghai Reform Collections office.

Shanghai Stock Exchange (SSEa). 2005. *Shanghai Stock Exchange Factbook, 2004*. Shanghai, China.

Shao, Chongzhu, ed. 1998. *Zhong gong fan tan da an zhong an* [*Big Cases and Serious Cases in the Chinese Communists' Fight against Corruption*]. Hong Kong: Xiafeier.

Shen, Tong. 1990. *Almost a Revolution*. Boston, MA: Houghton Mifflin.

Shenzhen Stock Exchange (SSEb). 2005. *Shenzhen Stock Exchange Factbook, 2004*. Shenzhen, China.

Shi, Tianjin. 1997. *Political Participation in Beijing*. Cambridge: Harvard University Press.

Shi, Yizheng. 1998. *Chinese Firms and Technology in the Reform Era*. London: Routledge.

Shue, Vivienne. 1988. *The Reach of the State: Sketches of the Chinese Body Politic*. Stanford, CA: Stanford University Press.

Sik, Endre. 1994. "Network Capital in Capitalist, Communist, and Post-Communist Societies." *International Contributions to Labor Studies* 4: 73–70.

——. 2000. "The Bad, the Worse and the Worst: Guesstimating the Level of Corruption." Paper presented to the Princeton University–CEU Joint Conference on Corruption, Budapest, April.

Singer, Joseph. 1982. "The Legal Rights Debate in Analytical Jurisprudence from Bentham to Hohfeld." *Wisconsin Law Review*: 980–1059.

——. 1988. "The Reliance Interest in Property." *Stanford Law Review* 40(3): 611–751.

Siu, Helen. 1989. "Socialist Peddlers and Princes in a Chinese Market Town." *American Ethnologist* 16(2): 196–212.

Smith, Adam. 1789. *An Inquiry into the Nature and Causes of the Wealth of Nations*. Reprint, New York: Random House, 1994.

Smith, Craig. 2001. "AOL Joins Chinese Venture, Gaining a Crucial Foothold: A Deal to Develop Services for the Internet." *New York Times*, June 12.

Solinger, Dorothy. 1999a. "Chinese Floating Population." In *The Paradox of China's Post-Mao Reforms*, edited by Merle Goldman and Roderick MacFarquhar. Cambridge, MA: Harvard University Press.

——. 1999b. *Contesting Citizenship in Urban China: Peasant Migrants, the State, and the Logic of the Market*. Berkeley and Los Angeles: University of California Press.

Solomon, Richard. 1971. *Mao's Revolution and Chinese Political Culture*. Berkeley and Los Angeles: University of California Press.

Solomon, Richard H. 1999. *Chinese Negotiating Behavior: Pursuing Interests through "Old Friends."* Washington, DC: United States Institute of Peace Press.

Sorensen, Aage B. 1994. "Firms, Wages, and Incentives." In *Handbook of*

Economic Sociology, edited by Neil J. Smelser and Richard Swedberg, 504–528. Princeton, NJ: Princeton University Press.

Spar, Debora. 1993. "China (A): The Great Awakening." Harvard Business School Case 9–794–019.

Sparling, Samuel E. 1906. Introduction to Business Organization. New York: Macmillan.

Spence, Jonathan. 1999. The Search for Modern China. New York: W.W. Norton.

Stark, David. 1992. "Path Dependence and Privatization Strategies in Eastern Europe." Eastern European Politics and Societies 6: 17–54.

——— . 1996. "Recombinant Property in East European Capitalism." American Journal of Sociology 101: 993–1027.

Stark, David, and Victor Nee. 1989. Remaking the Economic Institutions of Socialism. Stanford, CA: Stanford University Press.

State Statistical Bureau (SSB). 1994. Zhongguo tongji nianjian, 1994 [Statistical Yearbook of China, 1994]. Beijing: Statistical Publishing House of China.

State Statistical Bureau's City Social Survey Team. 1990. Zhongguo chengshi tongji nianjian [Statistical Yearbook of Chinese Cities 1990]. Beijing: Chinese Statistical Publishing House.

Steinfeld, Edward. 1998. Forging Industrial Reform in China: The Fate of State-Owned Industry. New York: Cambridge University Press.

Stiglitz, Joseph E. 1992. "The Design of Financial Systems for the Newly Emerging Democracies of Eastern Europe." In The Emergence of Market Economies in Eastern Europe, edited by Christopher Clague and Gordon C. Rausser, 161–184. Cambridge, MA: Blackwell.

Stiglitz, Joseph E., and A. Weiss. 1981. "Credit Rationing in Markets with Imperfect Information." American Economic Review 71(3): 393–410.

Strand, David. (1990), "Protest in Beijing: Civil Society and Public Sphere in China," Problems of Communism 34: 1–19.

Su, Si-jin. 1994. "Hybrid Organizational Forms in South China: 'One Firm, Two Systems.'" In The Economic Transformation of South China: Reform and Development in the Post-Mao Era, edited by Thomas P. Lyons and Victor Nee, 199–213. Ithaca, NY: Cornell University East Asia Program.

Sutton, John R., Frank Dobbin, John W. Meyer, and W. Richard Scott. 1994. "The Legalization of the Workplace." American Journal of Sociology 99: 944–971.

Szelényi, Iván. 1978. "Social Inequalities in State Socialist Redistributive Economies." International Journal of Comparative Sociology 19: 63–87.

——— . 1983. Urban Inequalities under State Socialism. Oxford: Oxford University Press.

——— . 1988. Socialist Entrepreneurs: Embourgeoisement in Rural Hungary. Madison: University of Wisconsin Press.

——— . 1989. "Eastern Europe in Transition." In Remaking the Economic

Institutions of Socialism: China and Eastern Europe, edited by Victor Nee and David Stark, 208–232. Stanford, CA: Stanford University Press.

Taizhou Property Rights Reform Leadership Group. 1994. *Chanquan Gaige* [*Property Rights Reform*]. Taizhou, China: Taizhou Economic Reforms Commission.

Tanner, Murray Scot. 1994. "The Erosion of Communist Party Control over Lawmaking in China." *China Quarterly* 138: 381–403.

——. 1995. "How a Bill Becomes a Law in China: Stages and Processes in Lawmaking." *China Quarterly* 141: 39–64.

——. 1999. "The National People's Congress." In *The Paradox of China's Post-Mao Reforms*, edited by Goldman and MacFarquhar. Cambridge, MA: Harvard University Press.

Torbert, Preston M. 1987. "Contract Law in the People's Republic of China." In *Foreign Trade, Investment, and the Law in the People's Republic of China*, edited by Michael J. Moser, 321–342. New York: Oxford University Press.

——. 1994. "Broadening the Scope of Investment." *China Business Review* 21(3): 48–55.

Tsang, Mun C. 1996. "The Financial Reform of Basic Education in China." *Economics of Education Review* 15(4): 429.

——. 2000. "Education and National Development in China since 1949: Oscillating Policies and Enduring Dilemmas." *China Review*.

Tsui, Anne S., and Jing-lih Larry Farh. 1997. "Where Guanxi Matters: Relational Demography and Guanxi in the Chinese Context." *Work and Occupations* 24(1): 56–79.

Unger, Jonathan. 1996. "Bridges: Private Business, the Chinese Government, and the Rise of New Associations." *China Quarterly* 147: 795–819.

Unger, Jonathan, and Anita Chan. 1995. "China, Corporatism, and the East Asian Model." *Australian Journal of Chinese Affairs* 33: 29–53.

——. 1996. "Corporatism in China: A Developmental State in an East Asian Context." In *China after Socialism: In the Footsteps of Eastern Europe or East Asia*, edited by Jonathan Unger. Armonk, NY: M. E. Sharpe.

United Nations Development Programme (UNDP). (2001) *United Nations Development Programme*. New York: United Nations.

United States Congress. 2001. *The Report of the Select Committee on U.S. National Security and Military/Commercial Concerns with the People's Republic of China*. United States Congress, Christopher Cox. Washington, DC.

Vogel, Ezra. 1989. *One Step Ahead in China*. Cambridge, MA: Harvard University Press.

Wakeman, Frederic, Jr. 1975. *The Fall of Imperial China*. New York: Free Press.

Walder, Andrew. 1986a. *Communist Neo-Traditionalism: Work and Authority in Chinese Industry*. Berkeley and Los Angeles: University of California Press.

——. 1986b. "The Informal Dimension of Enterprise Financial Reforms."

In *China's Economy Looks Toward the Year 2000, Vol. 1: The Four Modernizations*, edited by Joint Economic Committee, 630–645. Washington, DC: Government Printing Office.

———. 1989a. "Factory and Manager in an Era of Reform." *China Quarterly* 118: 242–264.

———. 1989b. "The Political Sociology of the Beijing Upheaval of 1989." *Problems of Communism* 38: 30–40.

———. 1991. "Workers, Managers, and the State: The Reform Era and the Political Crisis of 1989." *China Quarterly* 127: 467–492.

———. 1992a. "Property Rights and Stratification in Socialist Redistributive Economies." *American Sociological Review* 57: 524–539.

———. 1992b. "Local Bargaining Relationships and Urban Industrial Finance." In *Bureaucracy, Politics, and Decision-Making in Post-Mao China*, edited by Kenneth G. Lieberthal and David M. Lampton, 308–333. Berkeley and Los Angeles: University of California Press.

———. 1994a. "Corporate Organization and Local Government Property Rights in China." In *Changing Political Economies: Privatization in Post-Communist and Reforming Communist States*, edited by Vedat Milor, 53–66. Boulder, CO: Lynn Reinner.

———. 1994b. "The Decline of Communist Power: Elements of a Theory of Institutional Change." *Theory and Society* 23: 297–323.

———. 1995a. "Local Governments as Industrial Firms: An Organizational Analysis of China's Transitional Economy." *American Journal of Sociology* 101: 263–301.

———. 1995b. "Career Mobility and the Communist Political Order." *American Sociological Review* 60: 309–328.

———. 1995c. "The Quiet Revolution from Within: Economic Reform as a Source of Political Decline." In *The Waning of the Communist State*, edited by Andrew Walder, 1–24. Berkeley and Los Angeles: University of California Press.

———. 1995d. "China's Transition Economy: Interpreting Its Significance." *China Quarterly* 144: 963–979.

Walder, Andrew, ed. 1995e. *The Waning of the Communist State: Economic Origins of Political Decline in China and Hungary*. Berkeley and Los Angeles: University of California Press.

———. 1996. "Markets and Inequality in Transitional Economies: Toward Testable Theories." *American Journal of Sociology* 4: 1060–1073.

———. 2004. "The Party Elite and China's Trajectory of Change." *China: An International Journal* 2(2): 189–209.

Walder, Andrew, and Xiaoxia Gong. 1991. "Workers in the Tiananmen Protests: The Politics of the Beijing Workers' Autonomous Federation." *Australian Journal of Chinese Affairs* 29: 1–29.

Walder, Andrew, Zhou Lu, Peter M. Blau, Danching Ruan, and Zhang Yuchun. 1989. "The 1986 Survey of Work and Social Life in Tianjin, China: Aims, Methods, and Documentation." *Working Paper Series*. Cambridge, MA: Harvard University Department of Sociology, Center for Research on Politics and Social Organization.

Wang, Shaoguang. 1995. "The Rise of the Regions: Fiscal Reform and the Decline of Central State Capacity in China." In *The Waning of the Communist State: Economic Origins of Political Decline in China and Hungary*, edited by Andrew Walder. Berkeley and Los Angeles: University of California Press.

Wang, Shaoguang, and Hu Angang. 2001. *The Chinese Economy in Crisis: State Capacity and Tax Reform*. Armonk, NY: M. E. Sharpe.

Wang, Wallace Wen-Yeu. 1992. "Reforming State Enterprises in China: The Case for Redefining Enterprise Operating Rights." *Journal of Chinese Law* 6: 89–136.

Wank, David. 1995a. "Civil Society in Communist China? Private Business and Political Alliance, 1989." In *Civil Society: Theory, History, Comparison*, edited by John A. Hall, 56–73. Cambridge: Polity Press.

———. 1995b. "Bureaucratic Patronage and Private Business: Changing Networks of Power in Urban China." In *The Waning of the Communist State: Economic Origins of Political Decline in China and Hungary*, edited by Andrew Walder, 153–183. Berkeley and Los Angeles: University of California Press.

———. 1996. "The Institutional Process of Market Clientelism: Guanxi and Private Business in a South China City." *China Quarterly* 147: 820–838.

———. 1999. *Commodifying Communism: Business, Trust, and Politics in a Chinese City*. New York: Cambridge University Press.

———. 2002. "Business-State Clientelism in China: Decline or Evolution?" In *Social Connections in China: Institutions, Culture, and the Changing Nature of Guanxi*, edited by Thomas Gold, Doug Guthrie, and David Wank. New York: Cambridge University Press.

Weber, Max. 1968. *The Religion of China: Confucianism and Taoism*, transl. and ed. by Hans H. Gerth. New York: Free Press.

———. 1976. *The Protestant Ethic and the Spirit of Capitalism*, transl. by Talcott Parsons with an introduction by Anthony Giddens. New York: Charles Scribner's Sons.

Westney, D. Eleanor. 1987. *The Transfer of Western Organizational Patterns to Meiji Japan*. Cambridge, MA: Harvard University Press.

White, Gordon. 1996. "The Dynamics of Civil Society in Post-Mao China." In *The Individual and the State in China*, edited by Brian Hook. Oxford: Clarendon Press.

White, Gordon, Jude A. Howell and Shang Xiaoyuan. 1996. In *Search of Civil*

Society: Market Reform and Social Change in Contemporary China. Oxford: Clarendon Press.

White, Harrison C. 1981. "Where do Markets Come From?" *American Journal of Sociology* 87: 517–547.

Whitley, R., J. Henderson, L. Czaben, and G. Langgel. 1996. "Trust and Contractual Relations in an Emerging Capitalist Economy: The Changing Trading Relationships of Ten Large Hungarian Enterprises." *Organization Studies* 17(3): 397–420.

Whitley, Richard. 1990. "East Asian Enterprise Structures and the Comparative Analysis of Business Organizations." *Organization Studies* 8: 125–147.

———. 1992a. *Business Systems in East Asia: Firms, Markets, and Societies.* London: Sage.

Whitley, Richard, ed. 1992b. *European Business Systems: Firms and Markets in Their National Context.* London: Sage.

———. 1992. "Urban China: A Civil Society in the making?" In *State and Society in China: The Consequences of Reform,* edited by Arthur Lewis Rosenbaum. Boulder, CO: Westview.

Whyte, Martin K. 1993. "Deng Xiaoping: The Social Reformer." *China Quarterly* 135: 513–533.

Whyte, Martin K., and William L. Parish. 1984. *Urban Life in Contemporary China.* Chicago: University of Chicago Press.

Wiemer, Calla. 1992. "Price Reform and Structural Change: Distributional Impediments to Allocative Gains." *Modern China* 18: 171–196.

Wijnberger, Sweder van. 1992. "Intertemperol Speculation, Shortages and the Political Economy of Price Reform." *Economic Journal* 102: 1396–1406.

Williams, Ian. 2004. "China-U.S.: Double Bubbles in Danger of Colliding." *Asia Times,* January 23.

Wilson, Scott. 1997. "The Cash Nexus and Social Networks: Mutual Aid and Gifts in Contemporary Shanghai Villages." *China Journal* 37: 91–112.

Wolf, Alexander, David Fleming, and Jeff Lilley. 1995. "The China Syndrome: Chinese Athletes are Increasingly Subject to the Ills and Temptations that Afflict Sports in the West." *Sports Illustrated,* October 16.

Wong, Christine. 1991. "Central-Local Relations in an Era of Fiscal Decline: The Paradox of Fiscal Decentralization in Post-Mao China." *China Quarterly* 128: 691–715.

———. 1992. "Fiscal Reform and Local Industrialization: The Problematic Sequencing of Reform in Post-Mao China." *Modern China* 18: 197–227.

———. 1997. *Financing Local Government in the People's Republic of China.* New York: Oxford University Press.

———. 2002. "China's Provincial Public Expenditure Review." Paper presented at the World Bank Workshop on Decentralization and Intergovernmental Fiscal Reform, Washington DC, May 13–15, 2002.

Wong, Christine, Christopher Heady, and Wing Thye Woo. 1995. *Fiscal Management and Economic Reform in the People's Republic of China*. Oxford: Oxford University Press.

Wong, Desmond. 2004. "It's High Noon in China: Do You Know Where Your Customers and Competitors Are?" Global Automotive Center, Ernst and Young, LLP. SCORE Retrieval File No. QQ419, CSG No. 0309-0463870.

Wong, John, and William T. Liu. 1999. *The Mystery of China's Falun Gong: Its Rise and Its Sociological Implications*. Singapore: World Scientific Publishing and Singapore University Press.

Wong, Kar-Yiu. 1992. "Inflation, Corruption, and Income Distribution: The Recent Price Reform in China." *Journal of Macroeconomics* 14: 105–123.

Woo, Wing Thye. 1999. "The Real Reasons for China's Growth." *The China Journal* 41: 115–137.

Woo, Wing Thye, Wen Hai, Yibiao Jin, and Gang Fan. 1993. "How Successful Has Chinese Enterprise Reform Been? Pitfalls in Opposite Biases and Focus." *Journal of Comparative Economics* 18: 410–437.

World Bank. 1997. *China 2020: Sharing Rising Incomes: Disparities in China*. Washington, DC: World Bank.

World in Figures 1999. New York: John Wiley and Sons.

Xie, Yu, and Emily Hannum. 1996. "Regional Variation in Earnings Inequality in Reform-Era Urban China." *American Journal of Sociology* 101: 950–992.

Xin, K., and J. Pearce. 1996. "Guanxi: Connections as Substitutes for Formal Institutional Support." *Academy of Management Journal* 39(6): 1641–1658.

Yan, Yunxiang. 1996. *The Flow of Gifts: Reciprocity and Social Networks in a Chinese Village*. Palo Alto, CA: Stanford University Press.

Yang, C. K. 1959. *Chinese Communist Society: The Family and the Village*, Cambridge, MA: MIT Press.

Yang, Dali. 1990. "Patterns of China's Regional Development Strategy." *China Quarterly* 230–257.

——. 1991. "China Adjusts to the World Economy: The Political Economy of China's Coastal Development Strategy," *Public Affairs* 42–64.

Yang, Mayfair. 2002. "The Resilience of Guanxi and Its New Deployments." *China Quarterly* 170: 459–476.

Yang, Mayfair Mei-hui. 1989. "Between State and Society: The Construction of Corporateness in a Chinese Socialist Factory." *Australian Journal of Chinese Affairs* 22: 31–60.

——. 1994. *Gifts, Favors, and Banquets: The Art of Social Relationships in China*. Ithaca, NY: Cornell University Press.

Yeh, K. C. 1992. "Macroeconomic Issues in China in the 1990s." *China Quarterly* 131: 501–544.

Yeung, Henry Wai-Chung. 1997. "Business Networks and Transnational Corporations: A Study of Hong Kong Firms in the ASEAN Region." *Economic Geography* 73(1): 1–25.

Yeung, I., and R. Tung. 1996. "Achieving Business Success in Confucian Societies: The Importance of Guanxi (Connections)." *Organizational Dynamics* 25(2): 54–65.

Zhang Wenxiang, and Zhen Fazhi. 1991. *Zengqing qiye huoli: baijai zhengming ji* [*Building Enterprise Participation: Letting One Hundred Flowers Bloom*]. Shanghai: Shanghai Academy of Social Sciences Press.

Zhao, Dingxin. 1997. "Decline of Political Control in Chinese Universities and the Rise of the 1989 Chinese Student Movement." *Sociological Perspectives* 40: 159–182.

Zhou, Xueguang, 1993a. "Unorganized Interests and Collective Action in Communist China." *American Sociological Review* 58 (1):54–73.

——— . 1993b. "The Dynamics of Organizational Rules." *American Journal of Sociology* 98: 1134–1166.

Zhou, Xueguang, Nancy Brandon Tuma, and Phyllis Moen. 1997. "Institutional Change and Job-Shift Patterns in Urban China, 1949 to 1994." *American Sociological Review* 62: 339–365.

Zhu, Enjoyce. 2001. "China's Silicon Valley Ready to Take Off." *Beijing Business*, June.

Zhu, F. D., X. M. Wang, D. J. Bennett, and K. G. Vaidya. 1995. "Technology Transfer under China's Economic Reforms: Business Environment and Success Factors." *Technology Management* 2(1): 2–17.

Index

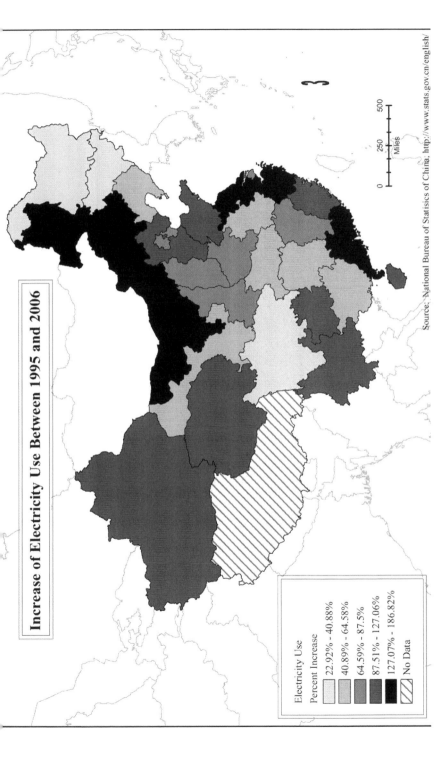

Increase of Electricity Use Between 1995 and 2006

Electricity Use
Percent Increase

22.92% – 40.88%
40.89% – 64.58%
64.59% – 87.5%
87.51% – 127.06%
127.07% – 186.82%
No Data

Source: National Bureau of Statisics of China; http://www.stats.gov.cn/english/

0   250   500
Miles

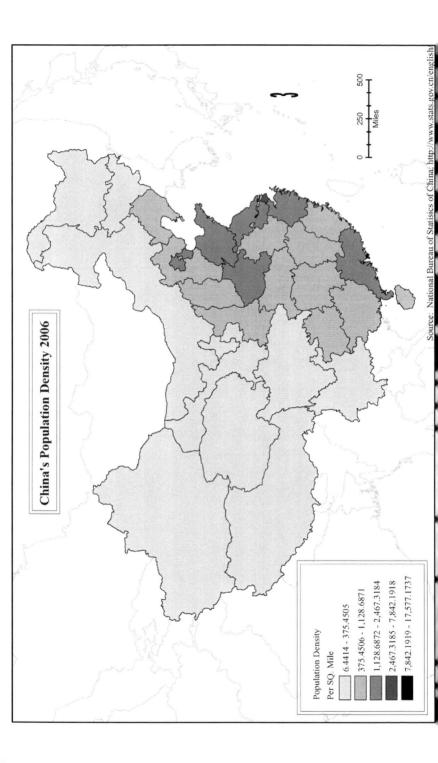

China's Population Density 2006

Population Density
Per SQ. Mile

	6.4414 - 375.4505
	375.4506 - 1,128.6871
	1,128.6872 - 2,467.3184
	2,467.3185 - 7,842.1918
	7,842.1919 - 17,577.1737

0   250   500
Miles

Source: National Bureau of Statisics of China; http://www.stats.gov.cn/cn/english

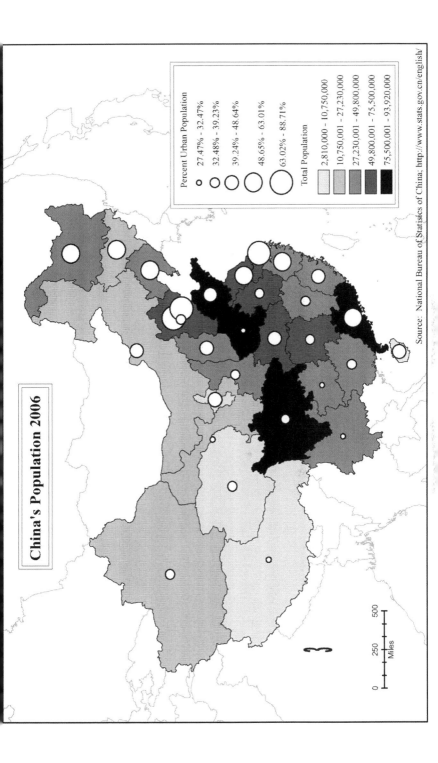

China's Population 2006

Percent Urban Population

27.47% – 32.47%
32.48% – 39.23%
39.24% – 48.64%
48.65% – 63.01%
63.02% – 88.71%

Total Population

2,810,000 – 10,750,000
10,750,001 – 27,230,000
27,230,001 – 49,800,000
49,800,001 – 75,500,000
75,500,001 – 93,920,000

0   250   500
Miles

Source: National Bureau of Statistics of China; http://www.stats.gov.cn/english/